Georgia's Last Frontier

THE DEVELOPMENT OF CARROLL COUNTY

Painted by Harding.   Eng. by A.B. Durand.

CHARLES CARROLL OF CARROLLTON.

Georgia's Last Frontier

THE DEVELOPMENT OF CARROLL COUNTY

James C. Bonner

UNIVERSITY OF GEORGIA PRESS, ATHENS

Library of Congress Catalog Card Number: 77–156040
Standard Book Number: 8203–0303–8

The University of Georgia Press, Athens 30601

Printed in the United States of America
by The TJM Corporation
Baton Rouge, Louisiana 70821

In Memoriam

PAGE BONNER CRAGHEAD (*1938–1968*)

AND

WILLIAM ALLEN BONNER II (*1948–1957*)

who walked these hills so gently
for so short a time

Contents

List of Illustrations

List of Illustrations

Preface

THIS study was conceived to include the entire area of the original county of Carroll, an area represented on the Georgia map by an inverted triangle whose base line begins near Sandtown on the Chattahoochee River several miles west of Atlanta and runs in a slightly north-western direction to the Alabama line. The two sides of this triangle are the Georgia-Alabama boundary on the west and the Chattahoochee River on the east, which form a vertex at West Point in the lower part of modern Troup County.

The region possesses certain natural features which distinguish it from the Georgia Piedmont of which it is a longitudinal part. The Appalachian highlands run in a southwesterly direction across the eastern part of the United States to find here its most southern limits in Georgia. Between this range of dying mountains and the Chattahoochee River is a region of uneven surface whose altitude varies from 700 to 1,300 feet. It possesses a few residual summits bold enough to be designated as mountains in local tradition. The area is interspersed with glades, small valleys, and sloping hillsides. This somewhat rugged topography early encouraged a type of subsistence agriculture and single-family enterprise in contrast to the plantation region to the east where there was a greater reliance upon slave labor. Economic diversity was further encouraged by the presence of minerals and by natural waterfalls on numerous streams, which contributed to the development of small-scale industry.

Historically, the region is among Georgia's youngest. For a brief period the county's northern and western boundaries divided its white settlements respectively from the Cherokee and Creek Indians. During the decade following its original settlement in 1827, Carroll County was Georgia's most exposed frontier and its last white outpost against the dwindling perimeter of the Indian's eastern territorial limits. In all chapters concerned with the frontier days, the entire region composing Old Carroll is considered. As the narrative progresses its scope is narrowed to the smaller, modern county, which embraces part of the northern and all of the central portion of its original area.

An effort has been made to make this story more than one of local interest exclusively. I have attempted to present the story within the broad framework of state and regional history and to include a full spectrum of social, political, and economic aspects. Because the region made the transition from a frontier to a mature society within a single century, no effort has been made to include a comprehensive treatment of developments after 1930.

In 1893 the historian Frederick Jackson Turner suggested that the detailed study of a local community from its frontier origins would provide a key to the interpretation of the whole American story and reveal its peculiar characteristics. Others later have urged such studies as an aid to understanding the stages of all historical development. Such a microcosm brings to the surface certain primitive stratifications, thus revealing to the historian what the exposed side of a cliff does to the geologist. As an enterprise in historical scholarship, therefore, this study has been a highly rewarding experience.

Yet the writing of local history can be a bruising affair, particularly when it may concern people who are remembered by the author's contemporaries. Sir Walter Raleigh in his preface to *History of the World* recognized this hazard when he wrote: "Whosoever in writing a modern history shall follow truth too near the heels, it may haply strike out his teeth." Despite this wise admonition from the seventeenth century, truth is the principal virtue which any history needs to possess. In its pursuit the author eschews all assistance either from the imagination of fiction writers or from the memories of older men. On the other hand, he would be remiss if he did not take full cognizance of the views and memories of men who are still living, if only to test and collate these findings with written records. Working in this way, I have attempted to resolve many contradictions in the story of this community. Those which may yet remain will not do significant violence to the general substance of the narrative.

My obligations to others are acknowledged with gratitude and humility. I am particularly grateful to Lynn W. Holmes for his encouragement and help in making possible the publication of this book. The transcription and alphabetizing of thousands of names and their corresponding data from the manuscript records of the decennial census of 1850 to 1880 inclusive was done by Janice Baker and Peggy Allain Williams, history students at Georgia College. Miss Baker also made the original typescript. Kay Dance was helpful in the preparation of maps and illustrations. This aid was made possible by a grant from the Committee on Faculty Research at this college. Carolyn Herne Rotter has typed the study in its final form, including hundreds of cursive and barely decipherable interpolations which she rendered with skill and accuracy. Page Bonner Craghead has read the manuscript and suggested many improvements. I owe a special debt of gratitude to Radford Hamrick who is a native of Carroll County and an avid collector of historical materials. He has been more than generous in giving me access to his personal store of local materials, collected over a lifetime. Particularly valuable have been his old files of the *Carroll County Times*. His cooperation and that of others throughout the state who possess archival materials has made my work much easier than it would have been otherwise.

James C. Bonner
Georgia College
at Milledgeville

I

The Earliest Inhabitants

THE Indians who lived in western Georgia in the general vicinity of what later became Carroll County belonged to two linguistic stocks. The Cherokees spoke the Iroquoian tongue, and the Creeks who lived south of them spoke Muscogean. An Indian trail running from Buzzard Roost on the Chattahoochee River, near the present site of Sandtown, northwest to a point near Dugdown Mountain in Haralson County was the approximate boundary between the Creeks and the Cherokees in the western part of the state. This trail later became the original northern boundary of Carroll County.[1] Southward from this line to the southern tip of Florida, the Muscogean tongue was spoken. The name "Creek" was given by the English to the Georgia Muscogeans because of the numerous small streams on which they dwelt; the name "Seminole," a Muscogean word meaning "wanderer," was applied to the Florida Indians. The Cherokees were mountain Indians whose basic tongue was spoken throughout the Appalachian mountain chain from the headwaters of the Little Tallapoosa River in Carroll County all the way to Canada. The Cherokees were therefore the southernmost Iroquoian Indians and their language had been modified somewhat by the addition of many Muscogean elements. Their northern kinsmen included the Tuscaroras, the Oneidas, the Senecas, Onondagas, Cayugas, and the Mohawks.

These Cherokees were among the more remarkable Indians in

North America. A few years before the organization of Carroll County, in the early part of the nineteenth century, the Cherokees organized themselves into a single "nation." They wrote a constitution fashioned somewhat after that of the United States and began to move rapidly toward civilization and to adopt a few rudiments of sedentary life. Their capital at New Echota was about eighty miles north of the modern city of Carrollton. One of the most remarkable achievements of any American Indian was accomplished by the Cherokee Sequoyah. In the early 1800s he produced for his people the only written Indian language ever created. The Cherokee syllabary—sometimes incorrectly called an alphabet—contained seventy symbols, each representing a common syllable used in the Cherokee language. The Cherokees had at New Echota a newspaper called the *Cherokee Phoenix* and a printing press which produced broadsides in both English and in the Cherokee dialect.

The Creeks who lived to the south were less progressive than their mountain-dwelling neighbors. The first white European to observe them was Hernando de Soto who, in 1540, led an expedition of a thousand men into the heart of the Creek country. He found them scantily clad during the summer, when only adults wore any clothing at all. This consisted only of a loin cloth which covered the middle portion of the body. In winter they donned blankets of dressed skins, and moccasins and leggins made of leather. They were fond of ornaments such as feathers, bracelets, and armlets, and they painted their bodies yellow, red, blue, and black. Their houses were of pine poles interlaced with vines, twigs, or canes; they were roofed with bark, pine straw, and sometimes animal skins. In winter the Creeks lived in huts plastered with clay to keep out the cold wind. Their food consisted of corn, wild fruits, nuts, game, and fish. Their tools and weapons at this time were fashioned from wood and stone.[2]

Two centuries later, at the approximate time of Georgia's founding, the Spanish governor of Florida described them as "lazy and poor, naturally evil, talkative, variable and undependable."[3] He had learned to distrust their offers of friendship apparently because their leaders had mastered the duplicity of the white man's diplomacy. By hard necessity it was their policy to pretend friendship to the British, French, and Spanish, all of whom by now had them surrounded by settlements on all sides except on the northwest, and here they were faced by the unfriendly Cherokees.

At this time the Creeks, like their Cherokee neighbors, had already begun to adopt many elements of the white man's civilization. Both

2

groups had long been in close contact with English settlers to the east and more particularly with Scotch traders with whom many of their women had intermarried. In addition to these transient merchants, other white men had drifted into the Indian country, taken up abodes among the natives, and lapsed into a life of primitive irresponsibility. Known as "Indian countrymen" (a term sometime later used interchangeably with "squaw-men"), they appeared to be somewhat numerous in western Georgia and Alabama. Among these inhabitants of the Indian country apparently was Kerney Young, whose gravestone indicates that he died in 1811.[4] He lies buried on the north side of the old McIntosh road two miles west of Roopville (now Route 5). Young was thirty-six years old at the time of his death. At the bottom of a cover stone over his grave is the enigmatic line: "H. Fitzsimmons, Cherokee Gov.," which suggests that the marker was placed there by the direction of the Cherokee Nation. Whether he was an Indian countryman or a Cherokee of mixed blood is unknown.

By 1825 there was a numerous progeny of mixed bloods among the Indians of western Georgia. Many of these bore Scotch surnames, indicating the ubiquitousness of the Scotch traders who sired them. Among the more famous mixed bloods were the Cherokees John Ross, Joseph Vann, and Joe Guess (Sequoyah); and the Creeks William McIntosh, Sam and Ben Hawkins, Paddy Carr (the son of an Irishman Patrick Carr), and numerous figures of lesser fame.

John Ross, who was only one-eighth Indian, became the principal chief of the Cherokee Nation in 1828. He once lived at the head of the Coosa River within the future limits of Rome, where he owned a fine house and combined the roles of planter, merchant, and Indian statesman. Nearby was the house of Chief Major Ridge, part of which was still standing in 1965. Joseph Vann at Spring Place lived in a two-story brick house which has been preserved for more than a century and a half, perhaps the most elegant house ever built by an Indian east of the Mississippi. Vann held eight hundred acres of cultivated valley land on which there were forty-two slave cabins. In addition to barns, cribs, smokehouses, and blacksmith shops, his establishment included a grist mill and sawmill, a still, and a merchandizing post. He possessed large orchards of apple and peach trees.[5]

Only a little less famous than these Cherokee leaders were the Creeks William McIntosh and Sam Hawkins, both of whom lived at this time in what later became Carroll County. McIntosh, whom the Creeks called Tustunugee Hutkee (White Warrior), was chief of the Cowetas, one of the leading subtribal groups within the Creek Nation.

He was in many respects the most remarkable character who has ever lived in this part of Georgia. His principal residence was on the west bank of the Chattahoochee near the future site of Whitesburg. Known as Lockchau Talofau (Acorn Bluff), his large plantation consisted of a vast acreage of river bottomland cultivated by Negro slaves and supporting a sizable settlement.[6] McIntosh's house was a large two-story structure of hewn logs. An inventory made of his estate in 1825 shows that he owned seventy-two slaves, 1,522 head of cattle, and quantities of hogs, sheep, and horses. His larder and trading house contained 530 venison hams, large quantities of pork, salt, sugar, corn, flour, and coffee. His household equipment consisted of many items which ranged from primitive simplicity to costly luxury. These suggest that their owner's transition from an Indian barbarian to a civilized European was not yet complete. Of the appurtenances of civilization were plows, hoes, blacksmith's and carpenter's tools, spinning wheels, and looms; a beaver hat and silver spurs, a frock coat, pantaloons, vest coats, and shirts; mirrors, razors, and feather beds; cassimere shawls, silk handkerchiefs, and gold earrings. There were also a few books by English authors and "a portrait of likeness." Indicating that the older Indian culture had not yet disappeared was the presence of homespun clothing, moccasins, wooden spoons and "dirt pots," calico frocks and turkey-red shawls, silver pendants and breast plates.[7]

McIntosh's slaves bore appellations which represent a mixture of classical, biblical, and English names, with a rare suggestion of Indian words. They were Tartar, Hector, and Cyrus; Samson, Glory, Abram, and Judah; Bob, Nancy, Sambo, and Katey; Offer, Suffer, Gepter [Jeptha?], and Molinta. The McIntosh family was said to have lost $40,000 in property when Lockchau Talofau was destroyed on May 1, 1825. This included $20,000 in cash and bonds which were either stolen or burned. In addition to his agricultural interests, McIntosh operated a trading house, two taverns, and a ferry at the Chattahoochee River near his home.[8]

The Indians of western Georgia in the 1820s not only were beginning to adopt the dress and manners of their white neighbors, but many were speaking broken English. A few of their children had been taught to read and write in English. Their agricultural activities consisted largely of the primitive cultivation of corn, tobacco, and beans, but they also grew melons, grapes, and orchard fruits. They kept cattle, hogs, and poultry.[9] A small field of cotton was not uncommon, and their women often were adept at spinning and weaving. A few had learned to be tidy and diligent in their house-keeping.

Like their agriculture, their dress was also slowly coming to conform to that of white Americans, although the general air of Indian apparel was oriental.[10] A turban, a robe of fringed and gaudily figured calico, scarlet leggings, beaded belts, garters, and a pouch were the usual male habiliments. The manner in which the more advanced Georgia Indians dressed at this time is preserved in a vivid description which John Howard Payne, the author of "Home Sweet Home," gave of Sequoyah. He wrote:

> We were all in the cock-loft of Mr. [John] Ross' story and a half house where the light and wind entered thousands of chinks. Guess [the English name of Sequoyah was George Guess or Guest] sat in one corner of the fireplace and I at the other end. Guess had a turban of roses and poises [sic] upon a white background girding his venerable grey hair—a long dark-blue robe bordered around the lower edge and the cuffs, with black; a blue and white minutely checked calico tunic under it, held by an Indian beaded belt, which sustained a large wooden handled knife in a rough leathern sheaf; the tunic open at the breast and its collar apart, with a twisted handkerchief flung around his neck and gathered within the bosom of the tunic. He wore plain buckskin leggings and one a deeper chocolate hue than the other. His moccasions were unornamented buckskin. He had a long dusky white bag of sumac with him and a long Indian pipe, and smoked incessantly. . . . Over all this was a whitish-brown overcoat with huge bone buttons of which some remained. The fragments of the coat draped about him on every side in fantastic shapes.[11]

More significant than their manner of dress was the intricate web of Indian-white ancestry identified with many of these celebrated Indians of western Georgia. Chief McIntosh, for example, could perhaps lay claim to as high a degree of wilderness aristocracy as the Indian country ever produced. His paternal grandfather was John McIntosh, a Scotsman who had come to Georgia with Oglethorpe. Receiving a Crown grant on the Tombigbee River in what is now Alabama, this royally descended adventurer soon became a colonial official. He came to possess a well-stocked plantation deep in the Creek back country. One of his six children was Captain William McIntosh who, like his father before him, remained a Tory and fought with the British during the Revolution, when he commanded a contingent of Creek warriors allied with the British.[12] During this period he formed a liaison with a Creek woman of unmixed blood. According to tradition her name was Senoyah (Senoia) and she

5

once lived at a village by that name in what became Coweta County. In addition to William she bore at least two other sons. One of these, Hogey, was a full-blooded Indian. The other, known by the whites as Rolly and by the Indians as Artus Micco, was a half-breed. All three of these boys apparently had different fathers. In addition to these, Chief McIntosh had another half-brother, William R. McIntosh, who was a full white man and in 1817 a member of the Georgia legislature. Chief McIntosh also possessed several half-sisters, some of Indian blood and others of pure white descent. One of the former achieved notice in a public record when she became the wife of a white man named George Stinson.[13] McIntosh's white father was an uncle of George M. Troup, governor of Georgia in the 1820s.

The free and easy virtue for which Creek maidens were notorious was abruptly ended by their marriage, for adultery was severely punished by tribal law and custom. The traditional Creek marriage ceremony included such prosaic customs as the suitors building a house and bringing in meat from the hunt. He might also appear in the field to help the young woman in planting a crop of corn. It is safe to assume that nearly all marriages between white men and Indian women were "corn patch weddings" of this type, and that wedded life was frequently cut short by impatient and transient males.[14]

The traditional tribal marriages on the Creek side of his house provided Chief McIntosh with an imposing set of Indian relations. His mother's membership in the famous Wind clan brought him certain inherited privileges not generally enjoyed by members of other clans. Two of his mother's brothers were Indians of considerable standing and influence. One of these was a half-breed named Howard who was chief of Chehehaw town on the Flint River, and the other, Tomoc Micco, was a subordinate chief known as a lawmender who lived on the Chattahoochee. In the Creek nation a lawmender was a combination of sheriff and prosecuting attorney.[15] Chief Howard of Chehehaw town, together with a number of his warriors friendly to the whites, were mistakenly murdered in 1814 by a contingent of the Georgia Militia under Captain Obed Wright while on their march from Milledgeville to join Andrew Jackson in the Seminole War in Florida. At McIntosh's insistence, Jackson ordered Captain Wright arrested and tried. This incident touched off a bitter controversy between Governor William Rabun and General Jackson in which the former challenged Jackson's jurisdiction in the case. Rabun was successful in his championship of states' rights over national military authority, for Obed Wright went unpunished. He lived to become the owner for a brief period in 1844 of the land near Carrollton on which the main campus of West Georgia College later stood. At a sheriff's sale on December 26, 1844, this land passed into the hands of Thomas Bonner for $306.90.[16]

McIntosh's genealogy is further complicated by the intricate web of his own polygamous marriages, a practice common to the more affluent Indians of this period. He possessed three wives who bore him numerous children, eleven of whose names are known. The oldest of these wives was a Creek woman known as Susanna Roe, and the youngest was a Cherokee girl named Peggie. In the year 1825, Susanna and Peggie lived at the principal McIntosh residence at Lockchau Talofau on the Chattahoochee. About fifty miles west, on the Tallapoosa, McIntosh maintained another plantation and a house occupied by Eliza, his third wife. This place was said to have been part of the farm later owned by George A. Davis near Tallapoosa. Eliza was the white-blooded daughter of Stephen Hawkins whose brother Sam Hawkins had taken to wife the oldest daughter of McIntosh by his Creek wife. This daughter whose name was Jane, together with her brother, Chilly, had been sent to school in Milledgeville in 1819, where both learned to speak and to write "fairly good English." Before her marriage to Hawkins, Jane had been the wife of William Mitchell, whose family home was Mt. Nebo near Milledgeville and whose father, David B. Mitchell, was a Creek agent and a former governor of Georgia.[17] In 1825 Jane and Sam Hawkins lived on the Little Tallapoosa River 24 miles west of Lockchau Talofau. It was here that she witnessed the execution of her husband by the same party of Upper Creeks who earlier in the day had taken vengeance on her father.

Jane's diverse connubial career did not end with the death of her husband, Sam Hawkins. She later married Paddy Carr, a famous interpreter who in time became the owner of valuable race horses and one of the wealthiest men of the Creek aristocracy. Being the oldest of Paddy Carr's three wives, Jane was separated from him after a brief interlude and went to Arkansas with an early migration of Lower Creeks.[18]

Somewhat suggestive of intricate matrimonial bargaining, the Hawkins-McIntosh relationship was further strengthened by a marriage between Sam's brother, Ben Hawkins, and Rebecca, the second daughter of William and Susanna McIntosh. Some years later Ben Hawkins became associated with Sam Houston in some of his wild adventures, and in one instance he was involved in the illicit slave traffic at Columbus. This ambitious rascal finally met a death in Texas no less violent than that of his brother in 1825 on the banks of the Little Tallapoosa. After this his widow Rebecca married a Texan named Spire Haggerty. Also after Chief McIntosh's death his widow Susanna, the mother of Jane and Rebecca, became the wife of her husband's brother, Rolly. This illiterate half-breed became the head chief of the Lower Creeks in Arkansas (later Oklahoma) in which capacity he remained until a few years before his death in 1863.[19]

In addition to Jane and Rebecca, Susanna bore McIntosh three other children. They were Delilah, and Hetty, daughters, and Daniel Newnan, whom the Indians called Unee, the youngest of his three sons. Unee was named for his father's close friend Daniel Newnan (for whom the city of Newnan was also named), who was at one time the adjutant general of Georgia. Unee was born at Lockchau Talofau in 1822 and removed to Arkansas in 1830 in one of the earliest Creek migrations. Educated later at Smith Institute in Kentucky, he became a leader in the educational and religious life of his people.[20]

McIntosh's progeny by his Cherokee wife Peggie is somewhat obscure, although she is known to have borne him three children. One of these was Lewis (Interfleckey), who died at Lockchau Talofau at the age of fifteen. The youngest of these probably was Croesy who, after her father's assassination, was thrown upon the charity of white settlers living on the east side of the Chattahoochee. Later she was adopted by Richmond Bridges, who built for her a cabin on his plantation near Senoia where she was employed in spinning and weaving. Having only limited social contacts, she married a mulatto slave belonging to Richmond Bridges. She and her son Chilly, who had served in the Confederate Army, died of smallpox at Senoia during the Civil War.[21] Thus the strange peregrinations of the McIntosh children led the oldest daughter to a marriage with the son of an ex-governor of Georgia and the youngest to a lonely death in a pesthouse as the wife of a Negro slave.

McIntosh's oldest son, Chilly, was only a little less illustrious than the youngest, Unee. Born of Eliza in 1800 and educated at the Milledgeville Academy, he became the official clerk of the Creek nation. Although both of his parents were half-white, his physical features bore no indications of Caucasian stock other than the light color of his skin. Removing to Arkansas shortly after his father's death, Chilly finally settled on choice lands near the site of Tulsa and became in-

8

creasingly wealthy. Later in life he combined the role of Baptist minister with that of a political functionary. His death occurred in 1875 soon after he served as peacemaker between the Kiowas and the Comanches.[22]

The McIntosh family and their numerous kinsmen and tribal associates in Georgia belonged to a schismatic group known as the Lower Creeks. Their antagonists, the Upper Creeks, lived farther west, in Alabama, and were somewhat more primitive than the Georgia Indians. The latter had lived for two centuries in close proximity to the white Europeans. Racial, cultural, economic, and religious differences were therefore highly apparent in this schism. The Upper Creeks of Alabama were less receptive to the white man's civilization and they did not take readily to his church missions, dress, and mode of agricultural life. More particularly they resented the white man's encroachment upon their lands for it deprived them of an extensive wilderness necessary to maintain a primitive hunting culture. On the other hand, the Lower Creeks had learned that land was the most important negotiable commodity which could be converted into cash. Money was essential for acquiring the accoutrements of the white man's civilization to which many of them now had become accustomed.[23]

This schism among the Creeks was noticeable as early as the American Revolution, when the Upper Creeks had shown less loyalty to the English. It broke out in great violence in 1813 when the two groups became arrayed against each other in the Creek civil war. The precursor of this internecine conflict was a weird demonstration of primitive racism under the leadership of Tecumseh and Seekaboo, who had come to the Upper Creek villages a few months earlier. These primitive philosophers renounced the white man's civilization and sought a return to the traditions of their ancestors.[24] Though Tecumseh was a Shawnee, his mother was a Creek, yet he spoke in the northern dialect which was later translated by an interpreter. As late as 1860 Tecumseh's speech was quoted in the *Carrollton Advocate* by one who was present at this meeting a half-century earlier. This discourse was described as having many aspects of a camp meeting revival. "I have heard many orators," wrote the observer at this time, "but I never saw one with the vocal powers of Tecumseh, or the same command of muscles in his face. Had I been deaf, the play of countenance would have told me what he said." The speech was quoted as follows:

9

Accursed be the race that has seized on our country and made women of our warriors. Our fathers from their graves reproach us as slaves and cowards. I hear them now on the wailing winds. . . . The Muscogee was once a mighty people. The Georgians trembled at our war-whoop . . . and now your very blood is white, your tomahawks have no edge, and your bows and arrows are buried with your fathers. Oh Muscogee! brethren of my mother, brush from your eyelids the sleep of slavery. . . . The spirits of the mighty dead complain. The tears drop from weeping skies. Let the white race perish. They seize your land. They corrupt your women. They trample on the ashes of your dead! Back them again into the great water whose accursed waves brought them to our shores! Burn their dwellings! Destroy their stock! Slay their wives and children! The red man owns the country and the pale face must never enjoy it!

War! War forever! War upon the living! War upon the dead! Dig their corpses from the grave. Our country must give no rest to a white man's hands.[25]

The effect of such remarks as these on the untutored Creeks of the back country is not difficult to imagine. "More than once," wrote the white man who heard the address, "I saw the [hand of a warrior] clutched spontaneously to the handle of his knife." A short time following this demonstration of violent fanaticism, a veritable holy war of burning and murdering was begun. It was inadvisedly directed against Fort Mims in the lower part of Alabama, where a number of Creek half-breeds and their families had taken refuge. After the indiscriminate massacre of the inhabitants of this fort, on August 30, 1813, the Creek civil war became a war against the United States. This was a conflict which many white men welcomed, for the defeat of the Upper Creeks would provide some excuse for despoiling them of their lands.

General Andrew Jackson was sent to Alabama where he administered a severe defeat to the Upper Creeks at the Battle of Horseshoe Bend, some fifty miles southwest of the future site of Bowdon. In this battle and in a subsequent campaign against the Seminoles of Florida (whence many of the Upper Creek survivors of Horseshoe Bend had fled), McIntosh and a number of his tribal associates led a large contingent of friendly Lower Creeks. The Florida campaign completely broke the resistance of the hostile Indians, destroyed most of their remaining leaders, and paved the way for subsequent land cessions that ended forever the Creek foothold on their tribal lands in western Georgia.[26] These events also were the opening phases of the Indian reservation system west of the Mississippi. This system, conceived by Thomas Jefferson early in the nineteenth century, had not yet been fully crystallized.

At the treaty made in 1814 at Fort Jackson (at the future site of Montgomery) the Creeks were forced to cede a wide L-shaped corridor from Tennessee southward across western Alabama and thence eastward across southern Georgia almost to the St. Marys River. In this cession the Creeks lost 20 million acres of land and were left isolated from all other tribes except the unfriendly Cherokees on the north. It is significant to note that no responsible chief of the Upper Creeks signed this treaty. Of those who did so, most were from the lower towns and included many mixed bloods such as McIntosh, Timpochee Barnard, John Carr, and Alexander Grayson (Grierson). Indeed, McIntosh signed it in four places, once as "Major of the Cowetas" (his rank was later raised to that of brigadier general), and again as proxy for his uncle Chehehaw Tustunugee, and for two other chiefs who were probably his relatives.[27]

McIntosh again played a leading role in signing subsequent treaties of cession, particularly that at Indian Springs in 1821, which ceded the land between the Ocmulgee and the Flint rivers, and the more famous treaty made at the same place in 1825. Although it proved to be abortive, the latter treaty ceded all remaining Creek lands within the chartered limits of Georgia.

It was the Indian Springs treaty of 1825 in which the land now composing Carroll County was directly involved. In addition to ceding all land between the Flint and Chattahoochee rivers, the cession included a triangular area on the west side of the Chattahoochee, the western boundary of which began at "the first principal falls on the Chattahoochee" near the modern city of Columbus and running northwest into Alabama to the Tallapoosa River near the present site of Alexander City. From thence the line ran north to the Coosa River near Gadsden. It included much of the land on the Coosa and Tallapoosa rivers occupied by the Upper Creeks.[28] These lands were to be exchanged for an equal acreage in Arkansas and the Indians were to be compensated for improvements on their ceded lands. For the latter purpose the United States government was to pay them $4 million. They were given until September, 1826, to vacate their old hunting grounds.

This treaty is most significant for the conditions under which it was made. It had been preceded a few months previously by a council at Broken Arrow near Coweta Falls near the future site of Columbus.

At this council a full representation from the Creek Nation had informed the United States commissioners of their firm refusal to dispose of additional land under any conditions. Big Warrior, now the recognized leader of the Upper Creek faction and a personal enemy of McIntosh, declared that he "would not take a house-full of money" for his interest in the land. At this meeting McIntosh was deprived of his title as Speaker for the Creek Nation and threats were made upon his life by his Upper Creek enemies. Because of his influence among the lower towns, however, he was permitted to remain as chief of the Cowetas.[29]

McIntosh left Broken Arrow and went to Lockchau Talofau, where he began to organize his followers among the Lower Creeks for the drama which was now approaching its climax. He assembled forty more-or-less influential Creeks from the lower towns. Approximately half of these were mixed bloods, and a few were his own relatives. A great majority of them were not chiefs at all and some could neither be ranked as head men nor even as warriors. Securing from this somewhat nondescript and unrepresentative group of Creeks a power-of-attorney to continue treaty negotiations, McIntosh and a small party set out on horseback to visit President John Quincy Adams in Washington.[30] On arriving at Milledgeville, McIntosh was told by his cousin, Governor George M. Troup, that Duncan G. Campbell had already preceded him to the nation's capital and would return shortly with authorization to negotiate a federal treaty. Campbell, together with James Meriwether, another Georgian, returned a few days later armed with commissions from Secretary of War John C. Calhoun to negotiate with the McIntosh group at Indian Springs, but "subject to the approval of the Creek nation." [31]

These United States commissioners subsequently met with the McIntosh party at Indian Springs. In the surreptitious proceedings prior to the signing of the agreement, there is every indication of bribery and corruption in which McIntosh was one of the principal beneficiaries. The treaty itself was signed by only fifty-one Creeks representing only eight of the fifty-six towns in the nation. Of the total, fourteen are known to have been mixed bloods, although the actual figure probably would be considerably higher. Only McIntosh was a ranking chief of the nation but, since his dismissal at Broken Arrow, he was only a chief of fifth rank. Five were underling chiefs, all of whom were Cowetas. Twenty-six belonged to the category known as law-menders, and seventeen were Indians of no official standing whatever. The treaty was engrossed as having been signed "by all the principal chiefs present." The commissioners later admitted that "a competent fund . . . to defray the costs of the treaty" had been placed in their hands.[32]

One article of the treaty later became the object of considerable controversy. This article, which many claimed was never interpreted to the Indians, provided for the payment of $200,000 of the purchase money by the commissioners at the time the treaty was negotiated. When it was read in English in a low voice which only McIntosh and a few of his close adherents could understand, one observer noted a pained look of incredulity on the face of John Crowell, the Creek Indian Agent who was an avowed enemy of McIntosh and opposed to Indian removal. It was the opinion of General Edmund P. Gaines, later sent by the United States government to investigate the conditions under which the treaty was negotiated, that the entire procedure "was the design of a few desperate half-breeds and white men" to obtain by fraud this sum of money.[33]

The final article of the treaty also was controversial, and there is little doubt that it represented part of the payment to McIntosh for his exertions in behalf of the treaty's culmination. This article was a grant of title from McIntosh to the United States of two large reservations which he held as gifts from the government under the treaty of 1821. McIntosh now was to receive the sum of $25,000 for this land. One of the reservations was a 1,000-acre plot around Indian Springs on which McIntosh had built a tavern in which the conference was being held, and the other a tract of 640 acres on the west bank of the Ocmulgee at Macon. Thus the vast Indian reservation system later used in Oklahoma Territory and elsewhere west of the Mississippi was an extension of a system used in Georgia in this period.

It is significant to note that the final article of the treaty was not presented until February 14, the day that the meeting adjourned, at which time the article was added. Only McIntosh and eight other Creeks signed this supplementary clause. Among the eight Creek signers was William Miller, Josiah Gray, Alexander Lasley, and William Canard (Kennard), all of whom were mixed bloods.[34]

Conspicuous by their absence from the Indian Springs session were all the surviving leaders of the Upper Creeks. They did send one Opoethala Yoholo and an entourage of seven warriors to the meeting as observers. These not only refused to sign but warned the others of a Creek law recently enacted by the Upper Creeks at Pole Cat Springs which decreed death "by ropes and guns" to anyone who should sell land without the full consent of the nation.[35]

Soon after the meeting adjourned, Chilly McIntosh, who had ventured no farther to his home at Broken Arrow than the Flint River, learned that his father and six others had been appointed to die. He sent a runner at once to Lockchau Talofau to warn his father to leave home immediately.[36]

McIntosh remained at his home apparently secure in his assurances from Governor Troup that he would be protected. Troup, although McIntosh's cousin, had never formed an intimate family relationship with him. He had become governor by legislative appointment in 1823 and now he faced an election to be held in 1825 which, for the first time in the history of the state, would determine by popular vote the state's chief executive. He was anxious to appear before the electorate as a successful executive who had secured from the Creek Indians all their lands within the chartered limits of the state. This consisted of more than 5 million acres of prime cotton land which, according to a system of land distribution inaugurated in 1803, would be given by lottery to more than 20,000 Georgians in 202½-acre lots.

While waiting at Lockchau Talofau, McIntosh received a number of communications from Troup concerning the latter's plan for an immediate survey of these lands. On April 10, McIntosh agreed to permit the survey at any time the Georgia legislature thought proper. Subsequently Troup called the legislature into extra session. On June 9, this body authorized a survey and a land lottery, these being preliminary steps in organizing the territory into new counties. News of these events aroused intense interest among land-hungry and speculative Georgians, and a "sooner movement" was the inevitable result. White men crossed over the boundary line in large numbers seeking to spot and to acquire some kind of prior claim to such Indian improvements as cleared fields, substantial houses, and mill sites. In order to bring this situation under control, Troup made McIntosh the registrar of such claims, and his house at Lockchau Talofau became the claims office.[37]

It was Troup's haste to have the territory surveyed, dictated largely by political considerations, which resulted both in bringing the governor into violent conflict with federal authorities and in strengthening the hands of the Upper Creeks in their determination to take vengeance on McIntosh. On three different occasions since the opening of the Creek civil war in 1813, a surveyor's chain had been dragged across Creek lands, and each time the rattle of this chain had been a death-knell for their hopes. It was a final and irrevocable act confirming the white man's possession.

Near the end of April an execution party of nearly 200 Upper Creeks was dispatched from Okfuskee and Tuckabatchee in Alabama under the command of Menawa, one of the few surviving leaders of the Creek and Seminole wars. They reached the vicinity of McIntosh's house at Lockchau Talofau on the afternoon of April 30 and concealed themselves in the woods. They watched McIntosh ride with his sons to pen up some cattle, and later they observed him riding with his son-in-law Sam Hawkins to a road fork where both parted and McIntosh returned to his house. The two had planned to leave early on the following morning for Arkansas, where they were to view lands which the government had promised to exchange for the Georgia cession.

About three o'clock on that morning, which was Sunday, May 1, 1825, the hostile Indians who had surrounded McIntosh's house quietly set fire to a nearby outbuilding, illuminating the yard and preventing McIntosh's escape in the darkness. Since the place was also used as a tavern, an unusually large number of white men were lodged there. Heavy rains and a swollen river had delayed their return to the white settlements. These white guests and the female members of McIntosh's family were permitted to leave the dwelling, which then was also fired with lightwood. Near the main house was a small building for the accommodation of extra guests in which Chilly McIntosh, a half-breed named Mooty Kennard, and a white peddler were sleeping. Chilly and Kennard leaped through a window and escaped into the woods. Later assisted by the former's sister, they succeeded in crossing the treacherous rapids of the river in a small boat.

McIntosh and Etome Tustunugee appeared momentarily in the doorway of the house, where Etome was shot dead and McIntosh was wounded. McIntosh retreated upstairs, where he fired at his executioners from a window. Finally he was forced by the flames to abandon the house. His body was pierced by several bullets as he descended the stairs. He fell to the floor and was dragged by the feet some distance from the burning building. He raised himself on the elbow and gave his enemies a last defiant look. At that instant the long knife of an Okfuskee warrior plunged into his heart.[38]

A full evaluation of McIntosh's character does not fall within the scope of this narrative, but it is well to remember what Gibbon said of the great Byzantine general, Belisarius. "His imperfections flowed from the contagion of the times; his virtues were his own."

Sam Hawkins, residing on the Little Tallapoosa River, was seized and executed later on the same day and his body thrown into the stream. The Okfuskees plundered Lockchau Talofau and feasted on provisions taken from the smokehouse. They took valuable objects from the commissary, drove off livestock, and seized horses. McIntosh's family fled to the white settlements on the east side of the river from whence they sent urgent requests to Governor Troup for aid.[39] However, the Georgia governor was now engrossed with more important problems of state, and he did not respond. Twenty years later McIntosh's widow, Peggie, made a statement to the Cherokee Indian agent in Oklahoma in which she described the plight of her family at this time: "My home is burned, myself and children run—my children—no bread . . . with one blanket I cover my three children and myself. The Government say Go! The Indians kill him. Between two fires my husband dies. I wander. Government does not feed me. No house, no bread, nothing . . . I suffer like some stray Indian dog!" [40]

In the meantime Chilly McIntosh hastened to Washington demanding vengeance upon the murderers of his father and seeking the money promised under the terms of the Indian Springs treaty. President John Quincy Adams, growing steadily more suspicious of the entire transaction, finally became convinced that Indian Springs had been the scene of bribery and corruption. He now withdrew the treaty and refused to act upon its provisions.[41]

A heated controversy followed between the President of the United States and the Governor of Georgia. Governor Troup declared in warlike tones his intention to go ahead with the surveys and to distribute the land by lottery to Georgia citizens. Realizing that an armed clash might result, Adams quietly assembled a new group of Creek representatives at Washington in January 1826 and presented them with a mild ultimatum. He informed them of an agreement in 1802 between Georgia and the federal government in which the latter agreed to remove all Indians from the chartered limits of Georgia in exchange for the trans-Chattahoochee territory then held by the state. By using a form of persuasion only a little less hypocritical than that used by federal commissioners at Indian Springs in the previous year, he obtained the coveted cession.[42]

The western boundary of the 1826 cession, however, instead of lying west of what became the Alabama line, was actually some distance east of it. This boundary, known as Bright's Line, began at a bend on the Chattahoochee River just below the future site of Franklin and ran northwest to a point on the Creek-Cherokee boundary near the future site of Felton in Haralson County. This line, which ran through what became Jonesville, just eight miles west of Carrollton, would have left in the state of Alabama the northwestern part of Troup County, the future communities of Glenn, Texas, and Rockalo in Heard County; Victory, Bowdon, and Barge in Carroll; and Tallapoosa in Haralson.[43]

Despite this restricted western boundary of the 1826 cession, Troup set the Georgia surveyors to work, with orders to include the controversial strip between Bright's Line and what later became the Georgia-Alabama boundary, thus including the future western areas of Troup, Heard, Carroll, and Haralson counties. The dividing line between Georgia and the Alabama territory had been roughly determined in the agreement of 1802. It was to begin "at the first big bend upstream from the mouth of Uchee Creek [below the future site of Columbus] on the Chattahoochee and then run in a direct line north to Nicajack on the Tennessee River." [44] Like most Indian villages, Nicajack apparently had been moved westward since 1802. Also there were many bends in the river near Uchee Creek. Hence a dispute arose as to the exact point on the river at which to begin the boundary. The Chattahoochee River's most westward position is at Miller's Bend or the lower edge of what became the town of West Point. This is where Troup insisted that the line should begin. The United States and Alabama claimed that it should begin at a point much farther up the river and east of the latitude at Miller's Bend. Edward Lloyd Thomas ran the line for Georgia in 1826 which began at the mouth of Uchee Creek and ran all the way to Nicajack just east of the present northwest corner of Georgia. Alabama protested this line and Thomas then ran another line from Nicajack to Miller's Bend, a distance of 145 miles and fifty-eight chains. However, this line was not accepted by Alabama until 1840.[45]

The running of the district lines was begun in late 1826 under an act of the legislature of the previous year. In the meantime disgruntled Upper Creeks became emboldened by the stand which the United States had taken against Georgia's contentions and began also to intimidate the state's surveyors found running their lines in the disputed area. On January 22, James A. Rogers and his party, consisting of chainbearers William Smith and Jacob Burton, axeman and marker George Reid, and flagman George Bevan, were surveying the line between lots 167 and 180 near Indian Creek in the Ninth District. They were accosted by a group of Indians who took their compass and instruments and forced them out of the area. Rogers did not return to his work until February 6.[46] In the meantime he wrote to Governor Troup: "[They] threatened me very severely if I should be caught over Bright's line again surveying. I have come on to McIntosh's old place and have stopped my hands until I hear from you . . . provisions is scarce and my hands uneasy to go home. As to the number of men it will take to guard me, I am unable to say. . . . There are three settlements of Indians in my district, that have in them about 10 men; and in two miles on the Alabama side . . . there is forty to fifty warriors . . . who are to be placed on the treaty line as spies. . . ." [47]

Wiley Williams, the surveyor of the Eleventh District, on the same day reported that "eight or ten lusty fellows" rode into his camp and ordered him to stop his work on the west side of the 1826 treaty line. He also asked the governor to send enough men to protect the whole frontier line to Miller's Bend. "There is about one-fourth of my district that lies west of Bright's line," he wrote to Troup, "and I yesterday completed my meridian lines through it. I shall today commence my traverse lines; but after mature reflection I cannot feel myself safe in crossing Bright's line. . . ." [48]

Within a few days of these events the War Department, under whose jurisdiction Indian affairs then lay, ordered the Georgia surveyors out of the disputed area west of Bright's Line under penalty of arrest and punishment. On February 17 Governor Troup retaliated by ordering the solicitors general of the state to liberate any surveyor arrested by federal officers and to bring to justice these offenders against the laws of Georgia. On the same day he ordered the mobilization of the Georgia militia "to repel any hostile invasion of the territory of the state." [49]

President Adams again retreated from his position and, on November 15, 1827, negotiated a final treaty with the Creeks which extinguished their claims to the controversial northwestern strip. Only the Indians themselves had succeeded temporarily in preventing a few surveyors from running their lines in this controversial region. It was in this manner that the Alabama line became established at its permanent location four or five miles west of Bowdon and Tallapoosa.[50]

The work of surveying the entire cession was completed early in 1827, before the final treaty was made ceding the northwestern strip. A surveyor with four helpers had been employed for each of the land districts. The average size of each district was 81 square miles and contained approximately 256 lots each of 202½ acres, the lots being forty-five chains square. All surveyor's lines ran east-west and north-south. Where the district boundry began or ended at a meandering stream or other line not on a true meridian, the lots created at these points were less than full size and hence were called fractional lots. Such lots occur along the Alabama line in the western part of the county and along the northern boundary which followed an Indian trial. The section and district lines were run first, the surveyors receiving $3.50 for each mile surveyed. The district surveyors who plotted the individual lots received three dollars per mile, out of which they paid all expenses. The law required surveyors to complete their work in ninety days, during which period an average of $850 was paid for the work of five men.

When they ran the boundaries of the lots, the surveyors blazed the smaller trees at a height of three or four feet. Young trees were used in order to distinguish these markings from those used to designate trails or other boundaries, for the marking of which larger trees were blazed. If the boundary of a lot passed to the left of a tree used for blazing, the cut was made on its right side; if to the right, it was made on the left side. Corners of lots were established by a stake, slab, a pile of stone, or a tree blazed on all four sides. These were called "monuments." [51] Cuts on a tree made by these surveyors never healed so completely that they could not be recognized by an expert. Since the outer shell formed annual rings over the cut, trees so marked could later be used to determine the date of the survey. Boundaries of the original survey made in 1827 are known to have been verified in this manner until well into the twentieth century.

The surveyors' field notes reveal much more than prosaic figures showing position and measurements. Often they indicated the location of an abandoned Indian village or a trail, and they sometimes took note of stray Indians lurking in the vicinity. Once a "comely Creek maiden" was observed by a surveyor who had an eye for a well-turned ankle. The surveyors had many adventures, such as falling into icy streams, being bitten by rattlesnakes, stung by yellow jackets, and afflicted with poison oak. They were frightened by bears and catamounts. Nearly all surveyors on the Alabama line were threatened by Indians at one time or another. At such a great distance from the white settlements, they frequently ran out of provisions. A

19

note of tragedy is found in the entries of the surveyor Edward Lloyd Thomas. While Thomas was running a line near Columbus, one of his sons, who had accompanied the expedition to help his father, caught pneumonia in the dampness of the cold January weather and died. His father had the sorrowful task of running the line near his son's grave in the wilderness, and his field notes contain a poetic comment on the primitive beauty of the burial site.[52]

As has already been noted, the northern boundary of the last Creek cession in Georgia became also the northern boundary of Carroll County. A map of the county's original limits is an inverted triangle whose vertex is at West Point. The base of this triangle in 1827 was a line from Buzzard Roost on the Chattahoochee westward along an old Indian trail to the Alabama line below the present northwest corner of Haralson County. In addition to modern Carroll, it included the southern part of Haralson and Douglas counties and that part of Heard and Troup which lies west of the Chattahoochee.

The line representing the original northern boundary first came into existence in 1821 as the boundary between the Creeks and the Cherokees. At this time eight representatives from each of the two Indian nations agreed on this line in a meeting at the home of William McIntosh at Lockchau Talofau. The entire length of the boundary at that time ran to the mouth of Will's Creek on the Coosa near the modern city of Gadsden, Alabama.[53] Later, in 1829, when the county and the state were in a bitter wrangle with the Cherokees over the boundary between the two, Georgians claimed that the line ran considerably north of this old Indian trail. The state again employed Edward Lloyd Thomas "to run the true line" between what was then the state and the Cherokee Nation. Thomas surveyed a line which began at Suwanee Old Town on the Chattahoochee, twenty miles north of Acworth, to a point on the Etowah River. The line then followed that stream to the Coosa at Rome. Despite his anti-Indian bias, President Andrew Jackson refused to accept the state's exaggerated claim and sent General John Coffee to Georgia to investigate the dispute. Coffee recommended a third line which split the difference between the two previous contentions. This line, which the President approved in 1830, began on the river north of Marietta (below the bridge on U. S. Highway 19) and ran in a westerly direction following the divide between the waters of the Chattahoochee on the south and those of the Etowah and Tallapoosa on the north. This line passed through Dallas and then struck the Alabama boundary at the old Indian path to Will's Creek.[54]

There were sixteen land districts in the original limits of the county. The total area was approximately 1,600 square miles, or twice that of Rhode Island. This land was distributed in a lottery held at Milledgeville in 1827. Persons entitled to one ticket in the drawing included bachelors who had reached their eighteenth year. They were required to be United States citizens with three years' residence in Georgia. Families of minor orphans, the child or children of a convict, as well as idiots, insane, deaf, dumb, or blind children also were entitled to a ticket. Families of one or two illegitimate children each were given one ticket, and families of three or more illegitimate children each were entitled to two. Veterans of the Revolution, widows and orphans of veterans killed in one of the wars, and certain other groups also were given special consideration. Fortunate drawers were required to pay a grant fee of eighteen dollars per lot of 202½ acres. An area of one square mile around McIntosh's home at Lockchau Talofau was withheld from the lottery, apparently because of the public ferry there which the state hoped to develop and operate. Known as the "McIntosh Reserve," this area was finally sold, in 1840, to Christopher Bowen. All fractional lots were also withheld from the lottery and later sold at public auction, as were lots found to have been drawn fraudulently.[55]

Lot number 128 in the Tenth District, on which the Carrollton public square later was situated, was surveyed on March 8, 1827, by Ulysses Lewis, whose field notes designated it as "2nd quality Oak and Hickory land." The lot was drawn by James Isaiah Durham of Fayette County. Lot number 126 in the same vicinity was the original property of the orphans of James Stephens of Clarke County. Lot number 99, on which West Georgia College stands, was drawn by Lawrence Richardson of Columbia County. Lot number 193 in the Sixth District, on which Villa Rica came to be located, was drawn by Lorenzo Hutcheson of Jones County. A lot adjacent to one of the finest water power sites in the county—on Snake Creek where the Bowenville factory later stood—was drawn by the illegitimate children of Sarah Hill of Washington County.[56]

It is evident from the earliest records that only a very small number of those who were successful in the drawing ever moved to Carroll to develop their land. Holders of successful lottery tickets generally sold their lots very cheaply, for land was a plentiful commodity in this period. Records of land sales show that prices frequently were below ten cents an acre. A rifle, a cow, or a dog were sometimes exchanged for an entire lot. An early innkeeper in Carrollton rejected a 202½-acre lot in payment for a night's lodging offered by one who arrived the previous day to view the land he had drawn. As late as 1831, a lot near Villa Rica exchanged hands for two bed quilts, and in the following year 17 acres just off what later became Carrollton's Maple Street sold for fifty dollars.[57] On the other hand, corn and food supplies were expensive. The former sold at four times the price it brought in the older communities. A bushel of meal was once exchanged for 25 acres of Carroll County land.

Although most of those who came to Carroll County arrived from the cotton-growing counties of Middle Georgia, their mode of living conformed closely to the pioneer pattern. Within three years after the lottery, Carroll had a population of 4,186 people, of whom only 487 were Negroes. Most of the slaveowners established farms in the eastern part of the county, particularly on the bottomlands along the Chattahoochee. The counties of Fayette, Coweta, Troup, Talbot, and Harris grew more rapidly than Carroll, although all were opened at the same time. Their settlers possessed a greater number of slaves, and they pursued the agricultural patterns of the plantation communities whence they had come. Absalom H. Chappell, who grew up in this area, later boasted that it "never knew a low, coarse, or rude state of society." [58] As will be apparent in a subsequent discussion, this could not be said of the region west of the Chattahoochee.

The frontier character of Carroll's early settlers is indicated not only in their socio-economic patterns but also by the census statistics. The latter shows that these settlers were considerably younger than the average resident of Georgia, there being among them 32 percent fewer people over forty years of age than in the state as a whole. Also there were 164 males to 100 females, and there were fewer deaf, blind, and insane among them than in the state as a whole. Their agricultural productions did not show a strong allegiance to cotton until a decade before the Civil War. It was not until 1850 that the county's population figures ceased to show disproportionate numbers of males and youths. The percentage of Negroes remained low throughout the antebellum period. This figure was approximately 10 percent of the total until 1860, when it rose to 15.6 percent.[59] Throughout this same period, the slave population of the state was in excess of 40 percent. These facts, combined with the fact that the county covered an exceedingly large area in its early history, help to explain the epithet, "Free State of Carroll," by which term it came to be known.

II

The First Decade of Settlement

THE act creating Carroll County was passed on December 11, 1826, at which time the counties of Muscogee, Lee, Troup, and Coweta (originally spelled "Cowetaw") also were formed. Named for Charles Carroll of Maryland, one of the signers of the Declaration of Independence then in his ninetieth year, Carroll became Georgia's sixty-sixth county and the twenty-seventh of Georgia's thirty-two original counties. The law provided that freeholders who lived in the area might meet on the first Monday in May, 1827, and elect county officials. On that date the election was held at the house of William O. Wagnon on "the McIntosh Reserve" where five justices of the inferior court, a county clerk, sheriff, tax collector, tax receiver, coroner, and surveyor were duly chosen.[1] Those named to these first county offices either served without pay or obtained their stipend entirely from fees. The office of county surveyor was in this period the most lucrative one.

The inferior court of that day exercised a jurisdiction somewhat analogous to a combination of the modern ordinary, the county commissioners, the justice of the peace, and the county or city court. In addition to its administrative functions, it possessed a jurisdiction extending to civil cases of all kinds and to any amount, except where land titles were concerned. The inferior court tried whites for petty larceny and similar offenses, but its jurisdiction over slaves included capital crimes. The five justices also officiated as a court of probate.

In addition to these justices, there were in each militia district two magistrates, or justices of the peace, who held monthly courts, taking cognizance of debts up to thirty dollars. The justices of the peace also tried slaves for noncapital crimes. In Georgia in 1827 there was a total of eight judicial circuits of the superior court whose judges, appointed by the legislature, held office for a term of three years. The superior court judge and the grand jury in the respective counties constituted a court of equity.[2]

The first Carroll Inferior Court was convened May 31, 1827, on lot 115 in the Fifth District at a site which the court promptly designated as the county seat. This lot had been purchased for $208 from Thomas W. Bolton, one of the members of the court.[3] Other business included the appointment of commissioners to lay out a road from this point to "one of the upper ferries on the Chattahoochee to provide the most direct way to Decatur." They also investigated the cutting of a road eastward to Hammond's ferry and southward to Philpot's ferry, both on the Chattahoochee. Later, in 1833, they designed and adopted an official seal for the county. This seal consisted of a spread eagle with the words "Carroll County, Georgia" written around the border.[4]

The county seat remained at "old Carrollton" on lot number 115 only briefly, during which time it was known simply as Carroll Court House. One superior court session was held there, at which Judge Walter T. Colquitt presided and three cases were tried with only two lawyers present. Tradition says that the judge's bench consisted of a pine log.[5] In March, 1829, the justices ordered the purchase from Jesse Tollison of lot number 193 in the Tenth District to be used as a new county site "if to be got at a fare [*sic*] price to be paid for out of the first moneys accrueing from the sale of the lots in the contemplated county site." [6] The site contemplated was 2.6 miles north of the future site of the public square of Carrollton and on the Temple road. Apparently this lot could not be purchased "at a fare price," for on November 14, 1829, the justices made another selection declaring lot number 128 in the Tenth District as the permanent county site. Henry Curtis gave his bond for title to the lot, the cost of which was $150. The original name given to the new county seat was Troupsville in honor of Governor George M. Troup, who had worked so aggressively to remove the Indians. However, the legislature which assembled at Milledgeville on December 22 was headed by Governor George R. Gilmer, who was not of the old Troup faction. This body incorporated the new county seat under the name of Carrollton, fixing the corporate limits "to extend over the entire lot." [7] The commissioners appointed for the town were Henry Curtis, Hiram Sharp, William Bryce, George Gibson, Jiles S. Boggess, "and their successors." After January 1, 1832, the freeholders of Carrollton chose by ballot the five town commissioners who held office one year.[8] These commissioners were given authority to pass regulations for the town and to collect all fines imposed. It was further stipulated that all superior and inferior courts and other public business would "hereafter be done in the village of Carrollton." At the same time two election districts were established, one at the house of John Griswold and one at the storehouse occupied by Roddy and Ninney, in the northern part of the county. The original act of 1827, designating Wagnon's house on the McIntosh Reserve as an election center, was now repealed.

Throughout the 1830s new election places were designated and older ones were discontinued. In 1831 a new election place was established in the Ninth District "at the place of holding justice courts," and another at the house of William Springer near the Chattahoochee River.[9] Slowly the place of holding elections merged with the location of justice courts and of local militia musters. As more people moved into the area, new militia districts were created. Each of these districts was to include approximately one hundred males of military age. In August, 1831, nine militia districts were created by a convention of militia officers assembled at Carrollton. These districts were known locally by numbers of one to nine and often were referred to by the name of the captain of the company they represented.[10] The "town district" of which the county courthouse was the center, embraced the west half of the Fifth (land) District and the east half of the Tenth. In time other districts became known locally by the name of the community around which they centered. In the meantime the militia districts were given official statewide designations. Thus the district centering at Carrollton became the 714th Georgia Militia District. The Seventh Militia District, embracing Villa Rica, became the 642nd.[11]

In 1833 all the militia companies in the counties of Carroll, Coweta, and Campbell were designated as the Second Brigade of the Ninth Division of the Georgia Militia.[12] Carroll's contingent became the Seventy-fourth, with Jiles Boggess as its colonel. The militia companies in the western half of the county formed the First Battalion, while those in the eastern half formed the Second Battalion. The creation of new militia districts as well as changes in the boundaries of existing units was the responsibility of the county militia officers. A convention of the officers of the Seventy-fourth Regiment held at Carrollton in June, 1835, recommended that a new militia district be created in the northeastern area of the county from parts of districts 642 and 649. The new district would "contain about sixty effective military men leaving 95 military men in the 642nd district and 73 men in the 649th district and Charles Hulsey a justice-of-the-peace and Neill Stone a justice of the 649th," they informed Governor Lumpkin.[13]

The early removal of the county site from the Fifth (land) District to the Tenth District required only a minimum of physical changes. Apparently the only substantial building ever constructed at old Carrollton was the jailhouse. The contract for this structure was let to Smith Bonner on June 28, 1828, at a low bid of $291. Specifications for the building required that the timber for the walls "be got out of oak sixteen feet long, twelve inches square, the cracks of the wall not to exceed ½ half inche." There was to be one round of these hewn logs on which the floor was laid, then nine rounds to the upper floor, and nine more rounds to the loft. The ends of the building were to be gabled and boarded with "drawn oak boards" one inch thick and "the shutters of the dungeon to be the strongest kind." The door was to be equipped with "the first rate patent padlocks." [14] Apparently the jail was still incomplete in July of the following year, for at that date the justices paid Crawford Wright eleven dollars "for conveying prisoner Dobbs 40 miles to the DeKalb jail." Finally, in May, 1830, the justices employed Calloway Burke to remove "the gaol from the old court house" to the new county site. It was taken down and reassembled on the west side of Rome street, two hundred feet from the public square.[15]

The construction of a second jail was begun in 1837 on a lot just west of the Square. This structure was completed in 1839. The upper floor, where criminals were kept, was designated as the dungeon; the lower floor, for misdemeanor inmates, was called "the debtor's room." [16] The outer walls of the new jail were 20 by 24 feet, made from logs hewn to a foot square. The dungeon had a double wall of logs, 1 foot square, upper and lower. There were triple doors, each made of 2-inch oak plank and lined with sheet iron. Jeremiah Cole, whose bid was $749, became the builder of the second jail. Each prisoner at this time was furnished with two blankets, one quilt, one "straw bead tick," and one pot.[17]

The inferior court on January 6, 1830, ordered the new town of

Carrollton surveyed and plotted "so far as to run out the public square, streets and front lots together with one range of back lots and necessary streets adjoining. . . ." Lawson Black was employed for this task, for which he was paid $29 on January 25. The sale of these lots was set for the first Tuesday in February, 1830. Thus "First Tuesday" for more than a century remained the day for Carroll farmers to assemble at the county seat to attend public sales, to trade horses, or to barter other commodities.[18]

There were sixteen prime town lots, each of which fronted 50 feet of the public square and ran back 100 feet. This left four rectangular lots which cornered on the Square and which were considerably larger than the others. These lots were bought at prices ranging from $5.00 to $160.00. Buyers were required to pay one-fourth of the purchase price at the time of sale and the remainder was to be paid in annual installments.[19]

The justices of the inferior court complained in 1837 that the town had been laid off in such a manner that it was impossible to know the location and numbers of unsold lots. A new survey of the unsold lots was then ordered. The 100-foot depth of the lots around the Square was reaffirmed and back of these there was to be a group of 1-acre lots separated from the former by a 20-foot alley. Next came a tier of 2-acre lots and another of 4 acres, each of these groups also being separated by a 20-foot alley. Back of all these was a perimeter of fractional lots of varying size and shape. Four years later, in 1841, the justices ordered that all unsold lots in the town be sold to the highest bidder, together with "seven head of sheep grazing on the commons."

The original boundaries of the town might be described as a 202½-acre square whose eastern boundary was the line of Dixie Street (which was also the line separating Land District Ten from Land District Five). The southern boundary was approximately the east-west line of Austin Avenue. The western boundary crossed Alabama Street at the lower edge of the city cemetery, and the northern boundary crossed Rome Street at the approximate line of Chandler Street.[20]

Carrollton's streets were not given official names until after the Civil War. However, the street running west from the Square was early known as the Alabama Road, that running north was Cedartown Road, and that running east was Newnan Road. What later became Dixie Street was early known as the Lower Ferry Road. The Jacksonville Road (to Jacksonville, Alabama) was later known as the Bremen Road; it turned west just across the Little Tallapoosa

River at the Kingsbury plantation. What later became Maple Street was early known as Bowdon Road, and turning south from this road at the modern St. Andrew Methodist Church was Franklin Road. What later became Longview Street was known as the Racepath, a name derived from its early use as a racetrack.[21]

The public square at Carrollton became the first center of commercial life in the county. A tavern was early constructed by Jiles Boggess facing the Square at the north side of Newnan Street. Another was later built on the west side, at the "Shaw Corner." The first courthouse was a simple structure which stood on the south side of Newnan Street, 100 feet from the Square. In 1830 the bid of $198 by John Routen was accepted for the construction of a new courthouse to be in the center of the Square. The specifications called for its completion by March, 1831. It was to be 20 feet square and 9 feet high "from floor to plates" and constructed "of good logs." It was further specified that it be floored with "inch planks one foot wide a good batten plank door Shelter the Cracks of the house to be lined with boards . . . all to be done in a neat stile agreeable to the grade of the building." This courthouse was provided with window blinds, and a chimney stood at each end. No brick buildings appeared in Carrollton until after the Civil War.[22]

Many of the original town lots were still unsold ten years after the county was organized, in 1837. At this time an observer reported seeing five deer in a clearing on the Bowdon road about two hundred yards from the Square. Wolves abounded in the vicinity and now and then a bear could be flushed from the swamps. Carrollton at this time had only "eight or ten houses" and two stores, in addition to the courthouse and jail.[23] There were only six post offices in the county. The first of the county's post offices established in March, 1827, was known as McIntosh Old Place. The second was Carroll Court House established later in the same year. Both were discontinued in 1829.[24]

For many years the county was without roads other than trails cut through the wilderness. Long before the region was settled, two or three Indian trails had been widely used, the most famous of which was the McIntosh trail. This trail originally ran from Augusta through Indian Springs to the Creek town of Okfuskee in Alabama. It crossed the Chattahoochee at the William McIntosh ferry. From there it ran across what became the southern half of Carroll County to Alabama. Near the future site of Sharpsburg this trail had a fork which bore southward and crossed the Chattahoochee at what later was Philpot's ferry south of Franklin. This was the Grierson (Grayson) Path to the Hillabee villages west of Heard County.[25] There was another road which began in Florida and ran parallel to and just west of the Chattahoochee River, extending to the Cherokee Nation and thence into Tennessee. At a point north of Franklin this road began to veer slightly west of the river as it ran northward to gain a high ridge in the vicinity of Whitesburg.

The McIntosh trail was designated as a public road by the Carroll Inferior Court in 1829 and now was labeled the Alabama Road. Most portions of this oldest official roadway in the county had been paved in 1970 and appeared on the highway maps as Route 5. The old road along the west bank of the Chattahoochee was also in use in 1970, being known as the Old Five-Notch Road. Such designations as five-notch road, three-notch road, and two-chip way suggest the frontier method of numbering and designating roads by cutting notches on trees.[26].

Roads and transportation provided one of the main items of business for the early justices of the Inferior Court. While meeting at old Carrollton, in the present vicinity of Sand Hill, the justices ordered the cutting of three roads. The first of these was to run from old Carrollton to the Little Tallapoosa River below Hickory Level and thence westward across the northern part of the county to Cate's store on lot number 12 in the Eighth District (near the future city of Tallapoosa). Another road ran eastward to Baxley's ferry on the Chattahoochee, and the third ran southward to Peter's Point on the same stream. Commissioners appointed to lay out and cut the last road were Carrington Knight, James F. Garrison, Thomas Bonner, and Robert Shaw. They were required to take an oath to locate the road "without favor or affection to any person or persons whatever," a charge they must have found difficult to follow since all of these commissioners lived in the southeastern section of the county through which the road was to pass.

When the county site was moved to its future location in the Tenth District, a road was opened immediately from Carrollton to the McIntosh Reserve. There was also a road to Peter's Point, one to Pumpkintown (Hammond's Ferry) on the Chattahoochee, another to Terry's Ferry, and still another to the Alabama line. Finally, a road was designated to intersect Phillips' Road at the Campbell County line. In January, 1831, Hiram Sharp and Aaron Jones were directed to lay out a road to Sally Hughes's place in the Cherokee Nation and also to mark the best route to Campbellton.[27] As late as 1840 there was no public transportation anywhere in the county. The nearest stage route was that from Columbus to Newnan, which passed through Hamilton and Greenville. It was not until after the Civil War, when the first railroad reached Carrollton, that the community possessed its first easy access to the outside world.[28]

Carroll County originally embraced an area greater than that of any of its contiguous neighbors. Because of transportation and communication problems, it was inevitable that its size would soon be diminished. By the end of the first year, on December 14, 1827, the southern tip of the county containing a community originally known as Franklin (later renamed West Point) was removed from Carroll's jurisdiction and added to Troup County. In the following year Campbell County was created, which took away the northeastern portion of Carroll. This was an area which still later became Douglas County. It was this dismemberment of its eastern territory, together with the rapid development of the western part, which in the following year made it desirable to move the county's seat several miles westward to its permanent location. In 1830 Heard County was created from portions of territory taken from Troup, Coweta, and Carroll counties. All of Heard's territory lying west of the Chattahoochee, fully two-thirds of its total area, came from Carroll's original lands. Finally, in 1856, Carroll lost all of its northwestern territory which now became the southern part of the new county of Haralson.[29] Fully three-fourths of Haralson's total area came from Carroll, while the remainder was part of the Cherokee cession.

In the meantime Carroll's territorial jurisdiction was immeasurably increased in December, 1828. In an effort to dislodge the Cherokees, the Georgia legislature extended its laws throughout that part of the Cherokee Nation which lay within the chartered limits of the state. "Cherokee Georgia," as it was called, was placed under the jurisdiction of the five counties lying adjacent to the region. These were Carroll, DeKalb, Gwinnett, Hall, and Habersham. Carroll's jurisdiction extended from Buzzard Roost on the Chattahoochee northward to Sally Hughes's place just north of the Etowah River near Cartersville, and thence westward to the Alabama line just north of Rome. (This law was reenacted a year later.) This territory was added to Carroll for court jurisdiction only and was never an organic part of her territorial domain. All expenses incurred in the form of prison fees and officers' fees in prosecution of crimes committed in the territory were paid from the governor's contingency fund.[30] In October, 1831, James Hemphill was appointed justice of the peace over the Cherokee area which fell under Carroll's jurisdiction.[31]

Being thus wedged between the now hostile Cherokees on the north and the Creeks on the west, Carroll was the most exposed region of the state and it now had the longest Indian frontier of any Georgia county, running a distance of about 180 miles. Under these conditions, it was called upon to exercise police power over an extensive area occupied by her Cherokee neighbors.

Trouble with the Cherokees soon appeared. On November 15, 1830, Isaac Wood and ten other Carroll citizens wrote to Governor George R. Gilmer complaining of the defenseless condition "of a small population thinly settled on the frontiers, daily exposed to the wild depredations and ravages of an enraged people. . . ." They reported the incident of a citizen on his way to Tennessee who had been murdered and burned to ashes by the Cherokees. They stated that William Young had been shot from his horse on the road from Carrollton to Sally Hughes's place. "A few days since," they wrote, "Mr. Curtiss, the sheriff of this county accompanied by Major Boggess . . . went into the Nation to levy some executions on property. . . . Having stopped for the evening at an Indian house, they were awakened about midnight by the clash of arms & found themselves surrounded by a band of hostile Indians. . . ." [32] In December following, a group of twenty-five Carroll citizens, headed by Jiles Boggess, then a major of a county battalion, asked the governor to form a company of cavalry to assist civil officers in carrying out their duties in the Cherokee country. They complained that infantry militia was inadequate to cover so great a distance and "that offenders can scarcely be apprehended." [33]

A small number of the offending Cherokees were apprehended, however, and brought to Carrollton for confinement and trial. Major Boggess was able to arrest six of the twenty who assaulted him and Sheriff Curtis in November, 1830. He brought before the Inferior Court the Indians Old Field, Sam Roe, Bill Walking-Stick, Crow, Lee, and Spirit, charging that they had damaged him to the extent of $10,000. They had, he petitioned, "with arms made assault upon him & laid hold of him pulled & dragged him about, bound his hands & took from [him] his mare & forced him to go 5 miles on foot when he was lame & jerked & drew him about with cord, threw him into a branch, kept him tied for 2 days, then beat & bruised him & tied him with a rope."

These Indians were lodged in the Carrollton jail to await a trial which was held in July, 1831. They were represented by attorney Thomas A. Lothaw, who claimed that as citizens of the Cherokee

Nation they were not residents of Carroll County and were not bound by Georgia laws. The defense cited existing treaties between the United States and the Cherokee Nation and also invoked the Constitution and acts of Congress to show that the law of Georgia passed on December 19, 1829, was unconstitutional. Despite these claims the Inferior Court fined the Indians $1,500 and costs.[34] Thus a handful of backwoods justices dealt a blow for states rights against the emerging power of federal authority.

The local court at Carrollton continued to be concerned with Indians and their anomalous relationship to the white man's justice. In June Boggess brought a similar suit, this time against Jesse Beanstick and Cannouk for assault upon his person. In addition, Rattling Gourd was charged with arson. Rattling Gourd and Cannouk apparently were released, but Beanstick was "confined to dungeon" until July 30 of the following year when he paid $27.76 assessed as costs.[35] These cases occurred at the time that other and more famous cases of this type were being heard in the United States Supreme Court. These were *Worcester* v. *Georgia, Cherokee Nation* v. *Georgia,* and *Tassel* v. *Georgia,* all of which brought into sharp focus the growing conflict between state and national authority. In all these trials under Georgia law the Cherokees were greatly handicapped in securing even-handed justice because of a state law of 1828 which declared that no Indian or a descendant of an Indian residing within the Creek or Cherokee nations could be deemed a competent witness "or a party to any suit to which a white man may be a party." This statute remained in force in Georgia for more than a century and a quarter.[36]

Carroll County's extensive Indian frontier contributed to another problem which threatened to have grave consequences. The county became the base of operations of a well-organized gang of horse-thieves, renegades, and outlaws whose operations extended all the way from Alabama on the west to South Carolina on the east. Known locally as the "Pony Club," this group of thieves brought real terror to the county during the early 1830s. They were difficult to convict because of the clandestine character of their occupation and their close organization. *Habeas corpus* and other proceedings in 1830 show numerous prisoners released from custody because of perjury witnesses, alibis; also some of those seated on the grand jury which released them were members of the gang. The principal rendezvous for this gang was on Hominy Creek (below Hickory Level on lot 22), near where it flows into the Little Tallapoosa, on a farm later

owned by John D. Morgan. This was an area of swamps and
dense thickets. Barnes Williams once reported seeing "twenty-five or
thirty" of these renegades sitting on a fence in the sunshine. Upon
discovering the visitor "they dropped like turtles off a log" and retreated to their lairs in the swamp.[37]

George Sharp, an early settler in the county, stated that this band
of cattle thieves dominated the first election of district magistrates
in the county. He reported seeing during 1831 or 1832 a group of
three men driving a herd of cattle near his father's house in the
northern part of the county. A short time later two white men,
Hawkins Phillips and John Goodlin in company with four Indians,
stopped for the night at Sharp's home. On inquiring about some
cattle that had been stolen from Indians in Alabama they were told
that they could probably find them in Almon's pasture, a fenced-in
canebrake near the future site of Temple. On finding the cattle and
identifying them, they permitted the Indians to drive them back to
Alabama. Almon refused Goodlin and Phillips the hospitality of his
house for the night but he rode with them to Villa Rica, "the nearest
honest settlement." Before arriving there, however, they met a number of cattle thieves and in an encounter which followed one of the
thieves was shot to death.

Honest citizens, known locally as "Slicks," and who bore no
aliases, could be spotted easily. Soloman Wynn and George S. Sharp
each headed a group of vigilantes who caught many horse-thieves,
whipped them, and then ordered them to leave the county. The
Pony Club did not relinquish its political control of the county without a struggle. In an election of 1832 gang members engaged in a
desperate street fight with citizens on the public square at Carrollton.
The representatives of law and order, led by Jiles Boggess, who was
then sheriff, were victorious. At the next session of the grand jury
some members of the defeated ring charged Boggess and his associates
with assault and intent to murder. Instead of bringing in true bills,
however, the jury expressed gratitude to Boggess for his efforts to
banish crime in the community. In their presentments they cited
lawyers John A. Jones and Allen G. Fambrough as being in league
with the Pony Club. The youthful Judge Walter T. Colquitt attempted to have these references to the two lawyers stricken from the
record, claiming that as members of the court they could not be
intimidated in this manner. The foreman of the jury, William G.
Springer, is said to have jumped to his feet and openly defied the
judge, whereupon Colquitt then consented. Springer reportedly

weighed four hundred pounds. The 1833 grand jury presentments included a sly observation that "Custom has made it necessary . . . that we should compliment the judge and solicitor which is sometimes irksome from the fact of their not deserving it. But at this time we give judge Grigsby E. Thomas [who had just succeeded Colquitt] our thanks for his arduous attention to duties . . . and to Solicitor [James P. H.] Campbell. . . ."

In the same presentments the grand jury indicted Thomas Mederis for keeping a drunken and disorderly company about his house, allowing "fiddling and dancing" and for making whiskey on the Sabbath, and "for menacing voters" in the 682nd District. Thomas Hogan was also indicted "for assaulting and violently beating Absalom Adams on election day in the 649th District," and also "for threatening to beat . . . Thomas Wynn and having pistols and rocks to annoy the good people of the said 649th district." Joseph Davidson and Daniel Sparks were indicted "for fire hunting at night to the great annoyance of their neighborhood." Joe Hicks was indicted for keeping a gambling house at the Villa Rica gold mines.[38]

This band of early outlaws rapidly diminished after 1832. A few are known to have remained in the county to become respectable citizens. Since the thief was now more likely to be apprehended and punished, horse-stealing became rare. In May, 1834, John Killian, after being convicted for this offense, was publicly whipped on three successive days and also confined in the dungeon for three months. In addition he had to pay the county $45.34 for the cost of keeping him in jail and a fee of $3.75 to cover the cost of administering the public whipping. When his wife Charity attempted to effect her husband's escape, she also was whipped and sentenced to forty-two days in jail.[39]

Except for Indian problems and the apprehension and punishment of cattle rustlers and horse thieves, local government in this period was simple. Only the superior court judge and the solicitor received a fixed salary, the former receiving $2,100 annually and the latter only $225. Originally the Carroll Superior Court met on the first Monday in February and August, but because of bad February weather and impassable roads the sessions were later changed to April and October. Carroll was originally part of the Chattahoochee Circuit but in December, 1833, the legislature organized the Coweta Circuit from parts of the Chattahoochee, Flint, and Cherokee circuits. Carroll was an original component of this new circuit, which reached from Meriwether on the south to DeKalb, Cobb, and Paulding counties on the north.[40]

As already noted, Walter T. Colquitt was the superior court judge during Carroll's formative years. He was elected judge of the Chattahoochee Circuit in 1826 at the age of twenty-seven. This job required a young and vigorous judge, for Colquitt had to ride a frontier circuit extending from Columbus to the Cherokee Nation. Travel was by horseback and there were no bridges across most of the streams. Although a graduate of Princeton, where he had arrived wearing a rabbit skin hat, Colquitt was a genuine product of the Georgia frontier. He had the distinction of being made a brigadier general in the state militia at the age of twenty-one. Later in life he became a United States senator and was prominent in national affairs.[41]

Education in early Carroll was not neglected, although schools were few and of poor quality. As early as 1829 the Carrollton Academy was incorporated under a self-perpetuating board of trustees who had authority to fill future vacancies by appointment. The first school building, erected at a cost of $815, was a two-story frame structure which stood on the west corner of what later became Dixie Street at its juncture with Newnan Street. Three years later the board was increased to seven members when Jiles Boggess and Henry Curtis were added to the group. During the first year of operation the academy drew only $118.65 from state funds, that being the county's share of the Poor School Fund. In 1835 only five persons in the county benefited from this fund, four of whom were widows. The academy in 1832 reported only twenty-five male and fifteen female students and its total receipts from all sources over the first three years was $764.30. By 1835 the school was reduced in enrollment to sixteen students, and in that year its corporate structure was amended. Jiles Boggess, Appleton Mandeville, Henry Curtis, and Thomas Epsey were made commissioners to open subscription for students and to hold an election for five trustees, each of whom was to hold office only one year. In the election the subscribers were entitled to one vote for each student pledged. By 1837 the academy reported 121 male and 24 female students, and the board had $400 on interest.[42]

Decreasing enrollments at the Carrollton Academy followed the opening of other schools in the county. In 1831 the Lyceum Academy was opened at Carrollton. A year later the trustees of this institution reported that they had engaged the services of Mr. Richard K. Hill and "Mr. Thompson, a good English scholar" of considerable experience who had been "raised in the South *with all our feelings.*" The Villa Rica Academy was opened in 1835. After two years its enrollment equalled that of the Carrollton Academy. The Union Academy appeared in 1837, and one called Liberty Plains opened in the following year. The former stood on lot 94 in the Sixth District, three and a half miles northeast of Hickory Level. By 1840 Georgia had inaugurated the Common School Fund, of which Carroll received in the first year of its operation a total of $1,041.83.[43]

Somewhat typical of the early educational experience in frontier Carroll was that of William Washington Merrill, whose father moved to the county in 1832 when William was seventeen, settling on Turkey Creek some ten miles from Carrollton. In 1836, at the age of twenty-one, William was enrolled in the Carrollton Academy, living with Thomas P. Wilkins for whom he worked for his board, laundry, and lodging. His teacher was Grisham Durham, whose daughter he later married. His principal studies were arithmetic, spelling, writing, and geography. His schooling abruptly ended with the Creek uprising of 1836, which demanded his service in the militia.

William Merrill's autobiography reveals other aspects of frontier life during the 1830s. At his settlement on Indian Creek the family had few neighbors, all of whom were poor and ignorant. Their livestock grazed on the open range, and the people spent their time in hunting wild game and tending a small field of grain. There was little to sell except animal skins and venison hams, and bread was scarcer than meat. Once he had to go twelve miles to buy corn and then carry it eleven miles in the opposite direction to get it ground into meal. He hired out as a carpenter to build a cabin and a mill in Cobb County, after which he went to Jacksonville, Alabama, to hew timber for a frame hotel. He saved his earnings, bought a sow and pigs, and finally a cow. From the increase of these he raised a stock of hogs and cattle. His mustering-out pay after the Creek uprising was forty dollars, which he exchanged for a horse.[44] During 1837 he worked for eleven dollars a month for Isaac Cobb, who lived on the corner where the First Baptist Church later stood. Then, despite his own educational limitations, he taught school for three months in a house where N. D. Reid later lived.

The crude conditions of life in the area west of Bowdon was observed by George R. Gilmer in 1836. He spent a night at the one-room cabin of a family with sixteen children. The house was without a loft, so the younger children slept on the floor before the fireplace. The former governor and his lady slept on one of the three beds in the single-room cabin. Their bed was between that occupied by the older girls and the one in which their parents slept. "We insisted on sleeping in a wagon under the shelter, but the very proposition hurt our hostess so much, that we could not urge it," wrote Gilmer. In the morning he rose early, went "to a most beautiful spring of water at the foot of a hill" to wash up. Returning to the house he asked his hostess for a towel for Mrs. Gilmer. Somewhat embarrassed, the woman went to a pile of clothing stacked on a plank in the corner of the room, took a boy's shirt, and tore off the tail. When Mrs. Gilmer got up, she washed and dried herself with the rag "without suspecting its previous use," wrote Gilmer, who expressed an aristocratic gratitude for such generous hospitality from simple people.[45]

George Sharp recalled his early experiences in the northern part of the county near the Indian boundary, where his family settled in 1828. The Cherokees, who were friendly at that time, would call at the cabin occasionally to barter or trade. Their visit was always unannounced and informal. Their presence often was first noted when they were seen peeping through the log cracks of the house. The Indians would burn leaves in the fall to facilitate nut-gathering, resulting in a shroud of haze which, according to Sharp, produced the name "Indian Summer" for the fall season.

Sharp noted that chestnuts were abundant throughout the fall until Christmas. Large huckleberries filled the woods in the early summer, but blackberries were rare. There were few redbirds and bluebirds in this period; but quail, whippoorwills, and woodchucks were plentiful as were also migratory wild pigeons. Sandhill cranes and wild geese passed over in great numbers in the fall, going southward, and they returned in the spring on their north-bound flight. Horses were often frightened by their noise.

In 1831, the firm of Majors and Coltharp sold goods at a little store on the headwaters of the Little Tallapoosa near Hart Town. They brought their goods from Augusta in a wagon with wooden axles, with a tar bucket hanging underneath to provide lubrication. They obtained a high price for their goods; a 200-pound sack of salt brought five dollars. All plows, axe-heads, gun barrels, horseshoes, and wagon irons were forged by local blacksmiths, and any metal accessory was scarce and expensive. A finished rifle cost twenty-two dollars and weighed from 12 to 14 pounds. All cooking was done without stoves on an open fire. Shoes were sewn together from homemade leather, the uppers being of buckskin and coon hide. There was little variation in size and there were no "rights" and "lefts." Sugar, coffee, salt, and iron were the principal commodities supplied by the frontier merchants. An occasional sack of Irish potatoes appeared as their only stock of groceries. These were brought from New England, since none was grown in Georgia at this time.

Sharp's father in September, 1832, seeded 10 acres in wheat using three-fourths of a bushel per acre. Deer and turkey almost destroyed the crop, leaving a harvest of only 160 pounds. The northern part of the county abounded in wolves, catamounts, foxes, and polecats, and there were a few bears. Once a 10-foot panther was shot in the act of killing one of the hogs.[46]

The agricultural life of Carroll County began under capricious weather conditions. The winter of 1827 was an unusually cold one. In January the rivers as far south as Milledgeville and Macon were frozen over. The first part of January, 1828, was unusually mild with temperatures ranging up to seventy-six degrees. Fruit trees began to bloom and meat in smokehouses failed to cure and was lost. Then on April 5 the mercury plummeted to 20°F and streams were again frozen over. Corn and other crops were killed and a few trees succumbed to this low temperature. Again during the fall and winter of 1828–1829 the weather was unusually mild until January 11, when the mercury fell from seventy-six degrees to 16°F. The winter of 1831 was characterized by unusually low temperatures with heavy snowfalls. For two months the ground was almost constantly frozen. During the middle of April a late frost killed the vegetable crops. Frigid weather and heavy snows also characterized the winters of 1832 and 1835. On January 8 of 1835 there were 8 inches of snow, and a month later the temperature fell to 3°F.[47]

The economic life of the people during this period is revealed in farm inventories. The property of Robert Beal included one piggin, a spider, shoe knife, a pair of cards, two "beef hides," a deerskin, and an oven and lid.[48] Joseph Little had a branding iron bearing the letters "J L" with which he identified his cattle. Corn, pork, venison and a small quantity of wheat were the principal food items.[49] Little cotton was grown except for home use. No cotton gin or wheat thresher appeared on any farm inventory until 1833.[50]

The absence of extensive cotton-growing in the frontier period was largely a result of the great distance from markets and poor roads. Heavy freight was impracticable to move except by water and the principal market in 1837 was the relatively new town of Columbus at a distance of eighty miles. At this place also was the nearest newspaper and banking agency. Indicative of the importance of water transportation in this region was an act passed by the legislature in 1834 requiring that the Centralhatchee Creek in Heard County be kept open from its junction on the Chattahoochee River to Tompkins's Mill "for the free passage of lumber boats and other water craft." [51] In 1832 only six people in Carroll County listed a carriage on their tax returns. Travel was almost entirely by horseback, and ferryage was high. A trip to the state capital at Milledgeville and return normally required ten days.

The accessibility of the Chattahoochee River for both travel and transportation helps to explain the fact that the eastern part of the county was the first to develop an agricultural economy based on cotton and slavery. As late as a century after the opening of the county this area still had the highest percentage of Negroes. In the antebellum period most of the cotton was grown within five miles of a navigable stream.

Rural isolation, whether in the highlands of Scotland or the foothills of western Georgia, tends to perpetuate antiquated figures of speech. Many colloquialisms were recognized by visitors to Carroll County for more than a century after its founding. The pronouns "we-uns" and "you-uns" were frequently heard as recently as World War I. The suffix *uns* was derived from a word common to Gaelic and Celtic which meant "person." The words "our'n" and "your'n" were old Germanic forms. Many early word-forms undoubtedly were influenced by cockney English which has long since disappeared from the region but which has left its flavor in the h-sound before words beginning with E, U, or T. Examples are *hoochee* for the original *uchee* (in Chattahoochee) and Hightower for the original *Itowah* or *Etowah*.

Other local place names appeared to remind later generations of their link with the past. The names of the county's rivers and creeks are among the oldest. The rivers, Tallapoosa and Chattahoochee, still bear their original Indian names. The latter was an early Indian town whose name was also given to the river on whose banks it stood. Since this village was transitory, its various locations are unknown. Benjamin Hawkins, traveling along the Five-Notch Road, noted its presence in 1798 as somewhere near the present town of Franklin. He noted that "The name of this river is from Chat-to, a stone; and

39

ho-che, *marked* or *flowered;* there being rocks of that description in the river . . . at the old town Chat-to-ho-che." [52]

This explanation was repeated by Eleazer Early, who published a map of Georgia in 1818 on which he placed Chattahoochee town at the approximate location of the home of Chief McIntosh on the west bank of the river in what later became Carroll County. Early's map repeated Hawkins's explanation that the word meant "flowered rock." Subsequent writers of Georgia history have accepted this version almost without question.

It appears, however, that the Creek word *Uchee* meant "corn," and *hochee* meant "pounded or beaten." The word Chattahoochee therefore must have meant one of several closely related terms from which any one may choose. Three or four of these are: "Corn rock," "pounded rock," "meal rock," or "flour rock." [53] The last probably is what Hawkins meant to write in 1798. The numerous extant manuscripts in Hawkins's handwriting reveal that he invariably used the old spelling "flower" for flour.[54] Thus he was referring to rocks marked with white flour, or perhaps corn meal, which also was often referred to as flour. Such rocks with mortar depressions wrought by erosion from river currents appear in the stream at the McIntosh Reserve, and there are other rocks with depressions wrought by hand on the banks of the stream a short distance away. Also in this immediate vicinity are several hundred acres of rich bottomland capable of yielding great quantities of corn which the Indians brought to this spot for primitive processing into meal. The original location of old Chattahoochee town at this point is substantiated by the fact that McIntosh as late as the early 1820s often datelined his letters "Chattahoochee."

Nearly all of the streams in the county were named by the early surveyors who marked them on the original land maps. Whitewater Creek, in Heard County, for example, appears on the surveyor's notes as Wehutkee, a Creek word meaning "white water." Apparently this name was derived from the fact that the numerous shoals of the stream gave it a frothy appearance. Yellowdirt Creek appears on Reuben Ransom's original land map as "Yellow land creek." The name could be a translated Indian title *fokelani,* the name of a well-known Creek Indian which meant "yellow dirt." The Creek word for a small stream was *hatchee,* or more appropriately, *hachi.* Thus Hillabahatchee, a creek in Heard County, literally means Hillabee Creek, and it derived its name from the fact that its headwaters were around the Hillabee villages just west of the Heard County line in

Alabama. Centralhatchee, which means "middle creek," probably derived its name from the fact that it flows between Pink and Hillabahachee creeks. Farther north, surveyors inserted the names Buck, Buffalo, Indian, Turkey, Whooping, Snake, Hominy, and Hurricane creeks to the early land maps. Some of these perhaps were English renditions of their original Indian names. Turkey Creek may have been an English translation of the Creek word, *Pinehootee hatchee,* and Whooping Creek possibly was derived from *Wetumcan,* meaning "rumbling water." Snake Creek obviously derived from its crooked course. Hurricane Creek probably received its name from the fact that surveyors observed that timber had recently been unrooted along its course by a tornado.[55]

The early Carroll settler expressed the severe illness of a neighbor by saying that he was "lying mighty low," and a young man indulging in faithful and constant courtship was said to be "tying his horse to the same tree." Two other expressions heard in early Carroll County but which have long since disappeared are "Aaron alone" and "School butter." The former was frequently heard as late as the 1890s, although the exact context of its use has become lost. The expression is said to have originated when one Aaron Jones, a Carrollton merchant, employed a sign painter to place the single word "Aaron" over his shop—"Just Aaron alone," he instructed. The sign-painter actually wrote AARON ALONE, much to the dismay of Jones and the mirth of his neighbors.[56] "School butter" was a challenge to fight which any bully or self-appointed champion might hurl at any group of young men, or perhaps to any one of the group who wished to represent them. The expression is said to have derived from "School better," which meant "I am better than anyone in your school." Rarely did a stranger fail to find an antagonist in any group which he challenged in this manner.[57]

The old expression "water-bound" is seldom heard in the modern age of paved roads and concrete bridges, but in early Carroll heavy and prolonged rainfall might make this condition pandemic, isolating individual farmsteads for days or even weeks. To be water-bound for a long period might produce serious consequences. This expression had all but disappeared by 1930, at which time a suitor living at Whitesburg used the expression to explain his failure to keep an engagement with a young woman living on the east side of the river. Because the expression was unknown to her, she attempted to guess at its meaning. She wrote to him expressing concern over his illness.

There were a few colloquialisms heard only in the vicinity of Carrollton. One of these originated soon after the Civil War, when Andrew Hallum was the town marshal. One night some boys tied a goose to the top of the well-shelter in the southeast corner of the Square. When Hallum untied it the next morning the goose, whose vocal cords had been strained during the night, flew away emitting a sound strangely resembling "Hallum! Hallum!!" For many years afterward men lounging on the Square used this word as an expression of disbelief.[58]

Many rural communities in the county bear names which suggest a frontier origin such as Hickory Level, Buckhorn, Cross Plains, Sandhill, Plowshare, Laurel Hill, and Shady Grove. Buckhorn Tavern was a large double log house with a breezeway down the center. On the walls were buckhorns where travelers hung their hats, coats, and saddle bags. Located west of Villa Rica, this tavern was on an early stage route to Alabama. Here horses were fed, watered, and changed.

Other place names suggest the site of a country store where farmers were cheated, denied credit, or perhaps dealt with in more generous fashion by merchants who operated them. Lowell was originally known as Trickum, a word possessing a venal connotation, while Fairplay possessed the opposite significance. Sackville, Plug, Ditto, and Dot suggest country stores; Bowenville derived its name from its first postmaster, William Bowen. The name Rotherwood in the eastern section of the county has an unusual origin. It was the site of an early post office established on February 27, 1829, with William G. Springer as postmaster. As already noted, this site was known by the Creeks as Lockchau Talofau and later was referred to simply as the McIntosh Old Place. The land in that vicinity was owned by William Green Springer, son of the Reverend John Springer, a Presbyterian minister of Wilkes County, and his wife Anne Green. The name Rotherwood is said to have been given to the Springer home by an English lady who, on an early visit to the Springers, noted the similarity of the Carroll countryside to that described in Scott's novels. In February, 1829, the post office was moved from Wagnon's house to the Springer home and William Springer became postmaster. Rotherwood remained a post office until 1868, when it was discontinued for a few years and then reopened under the name Ratherwood. It was finally discontinued in 1897 when the mail was routed to Plug.

Carrollton was the fourth post office established in the county. It opened on March 16, 1829, and has had the longest continuous history of any office in the county. Its first postmaster was Isaac Wood. During the 1830s four additional post offices appeared: Villa Rica, Tallapoosa, Laurel Hill, and Hickory Level. Only two appeared in the 1840s. These were Cerro Gordo (later Bowdon) and Burnt Stand in the extreme northwestern part of the county.[59]

III

The Receding Frontier

THE Indians remained on the borders of Carroll County until 1838, when General Winfield Scott was ordered to remove by force the last of the Cherokees remaining within the chartered limits of Georgia. To prevent their escape, the soldiers were instructed to move simultaneously in small squads over the territory and to give no warning of their purpose. Men at work in the fields were seized, women were taken from their spinning wheels, and children from play. A few lawless white men followed the soldiers to loot the abandoned homes and rob Cherokee graves of silver pendants.[1] The land on which the Cherokees resided had been distributed, in 1832, in the last of the Georgia land lotteries. Thus for five years before Scott's troops arrived, the Cherokees literally had been overrun and dispossessed by Georgians, despite guarantees which the Indians claimed the federal government had given them.

By autumn of 1838, the Indians were gathered by federal soldiers in a concentration camp near Chattanooga. From this point they began what has been called the "trail of tears," a trek of suffering and death which took them beyond the Mississippi. This exodus, involving nearly fifteen thousand Indians, was perhaps the most tragic which has ever occurred on the North American continent. In a journey lasting four months, there were only about 10,000 survivors.[2] The dramatic character of the "trail of tears" has become well known, partly because of the advanced stage of Cherokee culture at

44

the time and also because these Indians had many white American sympathizers who publicized their suffering.

The story of an earlier migration in which the Creeks were the victims has been somewhat neglected. Their departure was no less dramatic than that of the Cherokees. As already related, the assassination of William McIntosh in 1825 climaxed the long-standing feud between the Lower Creeks along the Chattahoochee and their more primitive kinsmen living on the Coosa and the Tallapoosa rivers. After the final cession of their Georgia lands, the less numerous Lower Creeks showed considerable reluctance to abide among the hostile Upper Creeks. The former sought to obtain permission to occupy a reservation in Georgia extending from the Chattahoochee eastward and including the Pine Mountain region and Warm Springs. Failing in this effort, a group of Lower Creeks known as the "McIntosh party" made the first of several Creek migrations to Arkansas, some leaving as early as 1829. Others, largely of the group known as Upper Creeks, remained on Carroll County's western boundary until 1837. In the meantime Alabama, which had achieved statehood in 1819, had her white settlements confined to the western portion of that state, with the Creeks occupying a belt between them and the line of the Chattahoochee River. Following the precedent set by Georgia in dealing with the Cherokees, Alabama now extended its laws and jurisdiction over the remaining Creek lands of eastern Alabama to the Georgia boundary. Deprived of hunting grounds sufficient to sustain them and not yet skilled in the arts of civilization, the Creeks were in a more miserable condition than that of the Cherokees. Often forced to live on roots and bark, poorly clad, browbeaten and cowed by white men who had settled among them, they were driven to desperation. "You cannot have an adequate idea of the deterioration which these Indians have undergone during the last two or three years," wrote an observer in 1833. "From a general state of comparative plenty to that of unqualified wretchedness and want . . . and the corn crop of this season will not feed more than a quarter of them," he continued.[3]

These conditions culminated in the Creek War of 1836, which was among the last of the Indian uprisings east of the Mississippi River. One event which immediately provoked this uprising occurred just northeast of Carrollton when a company of Georgia militia fired upon a group of fifty Creeks camped on the Georgia side of the Coosa River. Soon afterward the Georgians killed some defenseless Indians who were picking cotton near the Chattahoochee River.[4] On May

16, 1836, a group of fifty or sixty Creeks, in retaliation against such attacks by white men, stopped a mail stage about twenty miles west of Columbus on the road to Tuskegee. They robbed and burned the stage and killed some of its passengers. Panic-stricken whites living in the area fled to the white settlements. Governor William Schley reflected the attitude of most Georgians when he complained that the Indians had started the war. He characterized them as "idle, dissolute vagrants, many of whom had for a long time, been subsisting on provisions stolen from the people of Georgia living on or near the Chattahoochee." Governor Clement C. Clay of Alabama was more realistic in his judgment of the matter, claiming that the uprising resulted from "the destitute, and almost starving condition" to which the Indians had been reduced by the frauds and forgeries perpetrated upon them by a venal class of white men.[5]

The people of Carroll County were thrown into a panic by this Creek uprising. Rumors were abroad that the Cherokees were planning to join the Creeks in a last desperate resistance to the encroachment of the white men, and Carroll's borders were exposed to both groups of Indians. As a result of this danger a volunteer company was raised at Carrollton on May 21, offering its services to the governor. While agreeing to serve at any point, they suggested that "our frontier is as defenceless as any part of the state can be & [we] would consider it a favor in your excellency if our services Should be ordered to be given on the Said Frontier." This company, under the command of Thomas Bonner, was composed of sixty-six enlisted men and twelve commissioned and noncommissioned officers who formed part of the Seventy-fourth Regiment of the Georgia Militia.[6]

On June 7 these volunteers directed another message to Governor Schley requesting him to place an entire battalion on the Alabama line with headquarters somewhere between Carrollton and Franklin. They pointed out that, except for two or three companies at West Point, there were "no troops and no rallying point in case of a sudden excursion on the whole line from Columbus to Nikajack. . . ."[7] About two weeks later, citizens living in the northwestern part of the county assembled to make an appraisal of their unusually exposed position, in a narrow wedge between the Creeks and Cherokees. They asked the governor to send "a sufficient Guard should any hostilities or depredations be committed as we are placed in a defenseless situation as our troops are called off and . . . Alabamians are flying and taking refuge in the old settlements and leaving the Inoffensive to the mercy of the savage. . . ." They told of information received hourly of hostilities aimed at the vicinity in which they lived. They also reported observing Creeks crossing over the Cherokee line from Alabama and reconnoitering to the north of them. "It will be necessary to build a fort 20 miles west of Carrollton . . . and [we] pray that a sufficient force of arms and ammunitions be sent us," they concluded.[8]

George R. Gilmer, a former governor of Georgia, was on a visit to western Alabama when this uprising began. He later wrote of the dilemma he faced in choosing a return route to Georgia. "I had to determine whether I would venture among the enraged Cherokees, or cross over to Carroll County, through the Creeks," he wrote. He took the latter route, hoping to reach Carroll County on the following day. Everywhere along the rough road he found people frightened and many in flight because of rumors that the Indians would attack that night. Hoping to halt for the night at the Tallapoosa River, he found cabins empty with doors open and spinning wheels in the yard, and he was forced to travel six additional miles before he found a lodging place. "We . . . had for our supper sobbed Irish potatoes, and coffee, with a grain to a gallon of water, without milk or sugar," he reported. When he arrived at Carrollton the next day, he found everyone on guard against an Indian attack.[9]

Despite all this excitement, not a single cabin in the county was attacked in this uprising. Hostile action consisted only of an exciting invasion into southwestern Georgia by a group of Creeks who were attempting to join the Seminoles in Florida. They burned the village of Roanoke and seized a few vessels on the Chattahoochee before General Scott subdued them. The uprising was over by the middle of July, and its instigators captured and brought in irons to Fort Mitchell, which was located just west of Columbus. The leaders and their sullen warriors, manacled and chained, were then marched off in double file to Montgomery, where they were placed in boats and sent to the West. Among this group was the eighty-four-year-old chief, Eneah Emathla, who was forced to march with the others. One of his wounded warriors who was being transported in a wagon drew a knife and cut his own throat. Another killed a guard with a hammer and was shot dead in his tracks. A third was bayoneted by a guard. "To see . . . a once mighty people fettered and chained together forced to depart from the land of their fathers into a country unknown to them, is of itself sufficient to move the stoutest hearts," wrote an eyewitness to this last Indian exodus from the region of the Chattahoochee.[10]

Unlike the Cherokees, the Creeks were moved in numerous small groups at different periods from 1829 to 1838. To get the full impact of this event, one must examine each of these expeditions in detail and study a voluminous body of literature dealing with it. When fully assessed, this journey is seen to equal if not to surpass the Cherokee "trail of tears" in its tragic consequences. In 1837 several Creek mothers, rather than deliver their children to the emigrating agent, killed them with their own hands.[11] Captain John Page commanded one removal party of 630 Creeks. Destitute of clothing, the Indians nevertheless were forced to begin their march in December at the onset of a severe winter. Almost every day, through rain, snow, and freezing temperatures, the journey began at four in the morning in order to make six to ten miles before dark. "I have to stop the wagons to take the children out and warm them and put them back again six or seven times a day," wrote Captain Page. "I send ahead and have fires built for this purpose. I wrap them in tents and anything I can get hold of to keep them from freezing. Five or six in each wagon crying. . . . I am sometimes at a stand to know how to get along under existing circumstances." The journey ended on March 24, with only 469 survivors.[12]

Few, if any, white men who participated in this forced exodus were indifferent to the suffering of the Indians. "No portion of our American history can furnish a parallel to the misery and suffering at present endured by the emigrating Creeks," wrote one of these observers in 1836. "Thousands of them are entirely destitute of shoes . . . are almost naked, and but few of them [have] anything more on their persons than a light dress calculated only for the summer. . . ." In this condition they had to wade in cold mud or were hurried onward over frozen ground. Many who fell by the wayside died and were covered only with brush, where they remained until devoured by wolves. Vultures followed their route by the thousands and it is said that their trail, marked by human bones lying on top of the ground, could be followed for many years afterward. The Creeks were involved in a variety of minor tragedies. One group of 611 were boarded on the aged steamboat *Monmouth* heading up the Mississippi River. Through negligent handling, the ship collided with a tow-boat and was cut in two with the loss of more than half of those on board.[13]

Most of the last of these emigrating Creeks belonged to the hostile group known as Upper Creeks. When they approached their new homes in western Arkansas (an area which later became Oklahoma) with only a remnant of their leaders, the small faction of "McIntosh Creeks" who had preceded them at an earlier date became uneasy and frightened. Federal supervisors called upon the governor of Arkansas to furnish ten companies of militia to discourage any renewal of a Creek internecine war. However, a meeting was arranged between Rolly McIntosh and a group of Upper Creeks, including Eneah Emathla; the Upper Creeks were warned that government annuities would be withheld unless they met the standards of behavior set by federal authorities. The McIntosh Creeks left their lands on the Vertigras River to the newcomers and moved farther up that stream, where they appropriated the better lands around the site of Tulsa.[14] Several decades later the descendants of the McIntosh faction found themselves occupying extremely valuable oil land. They grew increasingly wealthy and many of them later became leaders in Oklahoma.

The antagonism between the two Creek factions, which began as early as the American Revolution, did not end with their removal to Oklahoma. During the Civil War the Lower Creeks cast their lot with the Confederacy. On the other hand, many of the more influential leaders of the Upper Creeks were Unionist in their sympathies. Among these was the aging Opoethala Yoholo who was at Indian Springs in 1825 and later had urged the death sentence of Chief William McIntosh for signing the treaty of removal. This venerable chief now assembled a group of his followers, consisting of 6,000 people, to remove them from Oklahoma to the free territory of Kansas. Ironically, the Confederate Creeks were largely under the control of three members of the McIntosh family. The highest ranking Creek officer in the Confederacy was Daniel Newnan (Unee), the youngest son of Chief William McIntosh. His brother, Chilly, was a lieutenant colonel; a cousin of these two, James McIntosh, also held the rank of colonel.

Unee now set out in pursuit of Opoethala Yoholo and his followers. He overtook the fugitives and administered to them a severe defeat, scattering them into small groups. As the weather turned cold they were without supplies and equipment, and only a few succeeded in crossing into Kansas. Opoethala Yoholo himself died in camp after a few months, and with his death the vengeance of the McIntoshes must have seemed complete. These events served only to rekindle the fires of the old tribal feud and it survived in some degree to the twentieth century.[15]

In this cauldron of feudal strife and stark tragedy of the 1830s

Carroll County ceased to be an Indian frontier. However, the frontier traditions lingered for many decades afterward. In 1840 the county's population was 5,247 of whom only 522 were Negroes. The frontier pattern of an excess of males over females and an extremely youthful population was still in evidence. Only 10 percent of the white population was over forty years of age, and only twelve individuals were over eighty, three of whom were Revolutionary War pensioners. There were no blind persons in the county and only one insane person was under public charge. Only a total of eighty-seven were engaged in manufacturing and the trades, nineteen of whom were merchants. There were only fifteen professional people (physicians, lawyers, ministers, and teachers). Agriculture was the occupation of 84 per cent of the people, and the second largest occupation was mining.[16]

Carroll's mining history began in 1830, soon after the county was settled. In that year gold was discovered at Pine Mountain, a short distance north of the future site of Villa Rica. This community was originally known as Hixtown, named for William Hix, who had operated a tavern and a general store there before 1830. By 1832 several hundred men were employed annually in the mines, which produced an annual average of 25,000 pennyweights of gold for the next few years. (A pennyweight was 1/20 of an ounce and valued at approximately one dollar.) The principal mining belt was situated on lots 155, 165, 166, 192, 193, 194, and 195 in the Third (land) District. The ore-bearing veins were numerous, varying from a few inches to several feet in thickness. These often expanded into pockets containing many tons of high-grade ore.[17]

Later the Carroll gold belt was found to extend from this point in the northeastern corner of the county diagonally to the southwest corner, passing east of Carrollton through Oak Mountain, on which some deposits were found. The most significant of the later discoveries was on the 1,215-acre plantation of Zadok Bonner, located eight miles southwest of Carrollton. The Bonner mines, which began operation about 1840, were situated on a number of small streams flowing into Buffalo Creek, on lots 94 and 95 in the Eleventh District.

The mining process used before the Civil War was the simple placer method with hand rockers, in which unskilled Negro labor was employed. Each hand averaged from two to twenty pennyweights per day. The "Big Cut" near the Bonner residence was by 1860 350 feet long and 20 feet deep. More than a half-million dollars' worth of gold was extracted from this vicinity before 1860. In addition to the Bonner mine, others in the county were the Hixon mine, the Lassetter mine, and the Chambers mine, all of which were in the Sixth District. Near these were the Hart, Davis, Clopton, Stacy, Astinal, and Jones mines.[18]

Closely identified with Carroll's mining history was the town of Villa Rica, a Spanish phrase which literally means "rich village." The town was incorporated in 1842 on lot 193, a short distance north of its later location on the Southern Railroad. Ezekiel S. Candler, whose descendants were to achieve an unusual degree of prominence in Georgia, was among the original commissioners of the town.[19] However, the old town was known more for its vices than for the prominence of its citizens. Many street fights and violent deaths occurred on its noisy old streets, which later reverted to silence and decay. One early settler recalled seeing forty men engaged in a drunken street brawl. Here John Murrill, the noted gambler and highwayman, is said to have dwelt for some time. It was here that old man Chatmans, while sleeping off a drunk, had his throat cut by a midnight assailant. Here also the old circus master, John Roberson, once spread his tent under which the world-famous clown, Dan Rice, shook the lively miners with laughter. In 1850 Charles J. McDonald came to old Villa Rica to champion states' rights against Howell Cobb in an open-air debate, after which was held perhaps the first political barbecue in the county.[20]

The area around Villa Rica in the first three decades of the county's history was somewhat more densely populated than that in the vicinity of Carrollton. In addition to mining, land in the Villa Rica area provided excellent range for livestock, and it was also a hunter's paradise. Land was generally so cheap that only the highest quality was used for farming. The first white child born in the county is said to have been Benjamin M. Long, who in 1827 was born at Hart Town, three miles southwest of Villa Rica. This community was settled by a resident of the Indian Country named Samuel Hart, who built a two-story house there even before the county was organized. This house, still standing in 1970, was sold in 1827 to John Long who had arrived from Tennessee.[21]

Some idea of life in this vicinity in the decade before the Civil War is revealed in the letters of Mary Ann Stevens, who moved from Putnam County to a farm near Villa Rica a few years after her marriage to James R. Turner in 1838. Writing to her sister near Eatonton, she spoke of drudgery and toil, the sickness and death of her brother-in-law, Thomas Turner, who left a wife and eight children.

Once her oldest son was injured in a mine blast and almost lost his eyesight. Often giving way to gloomy feelings, she longed for the more settled life of Old Putnam. "Oh how glad I would be to see my sister once more," she wrote, "but as fate has separated us in this world let [us] try to live so as to meet in that better world where there will be no more toiling and suffering and parting. . . . I do not like Carroll much yet." [22] Again she wrote of going a full week without undressing because of a siege of illness in her family. She spoke of Carroll as "a strange country" inhabited by queer people. "[They] are the most slovenly women in there [*sic*] dress I ever saw," she said. "[They] go barefooted and every other way that looks bad. I saw one not long since in a main road with no shoes on and her underskirt on her arm." She admitted that there were a "few good looking ladies in Carroll as anywhere, but the most of them look worse than common." [23]

Mary Ann's husband, to whom she always referred as "Mr. Turner," supplemented his income by teaching school. The number of teachers in the county increased from a half-dozen in 1840 to sixteen ten years later. With one exception, all of these were men.[24] Classes were generally held in one room houses. The Carroll County Academy was opened in 1845, followed in 1850 by the incorporation of the Carrollton Male Academy under five trustees. In 1854, they were authorized to sell this property and invest the proceeds in a new institution, which opened two years later under the name of the Carrollton Male and Female Academy.[25] This apparently was the first attempt at coeducation on the academy level in the county and it was perhaps the first school to occupy more than one room. Yet classes were held in two single-room buildings located near the future site of the railroad depot. In the meantime, in 1852, another school building was erected from popular subscription on what became College Street and, in the following year, is was given in trust to the Carrollton Masonic Lodge. This school became known as the Carrollton Masonic Institute.[26]

Collegiate education also had its beginning in Carroll in the antebellum period. This movement was closely identified with the history of the Bowdon community in the western part of the county. In 1849, Nathanael Shelnutt moved with his family from Campbell County to the future city of Bowdon and established a store which he operated in conjunction with farming. At about the same time Joel Fain and Alexander Gardner established stores in the general vicinity, although two or three miles apart. The community was

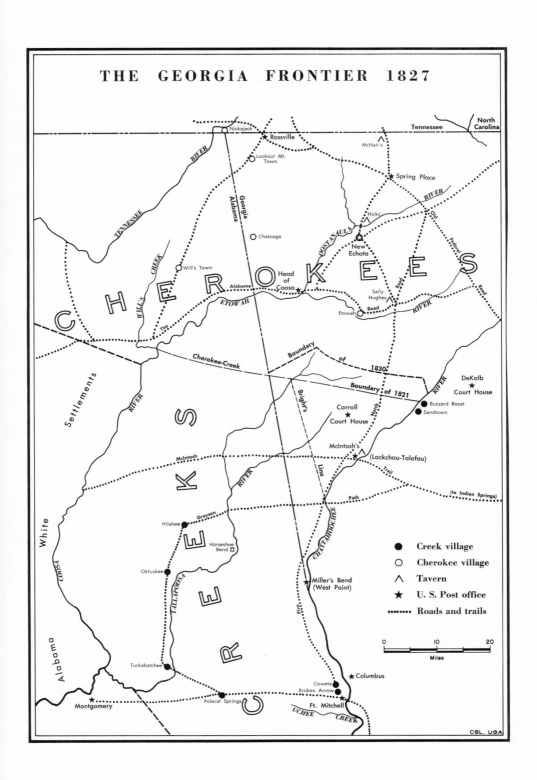

THE GEORGIA FRONTIER 1827

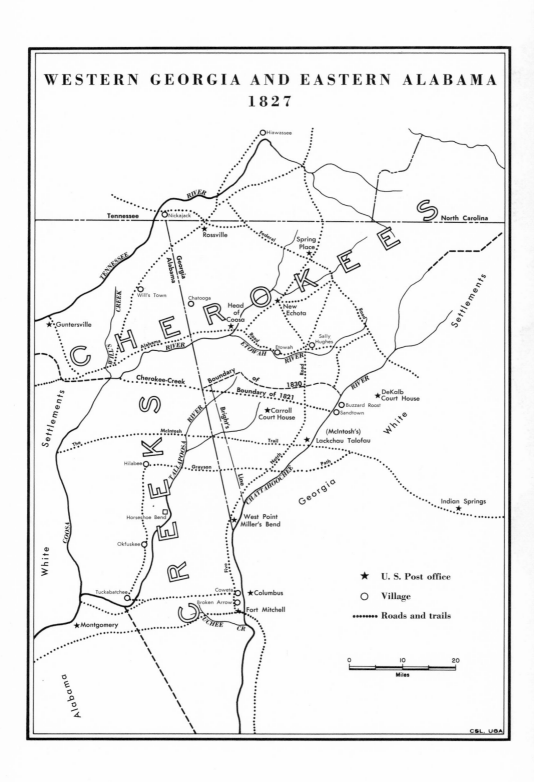

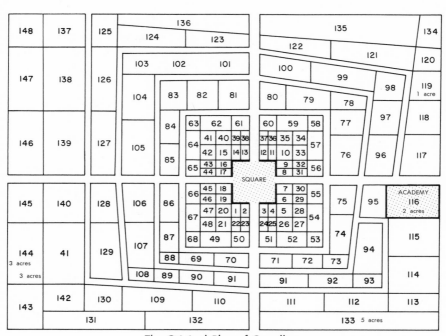

The Original Plan of Carrollton
The central portion has remained largely unchanged

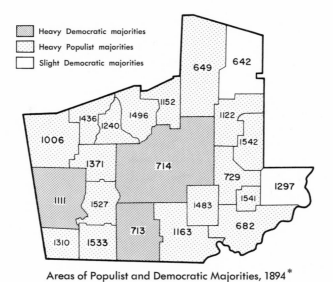

Heavy Democratic majorities
Heavy Populist majorities
Slight Democratic majorities

Areas of Populist and Democratic Majorities, 1894 *

*Minor Civil Division Boundaries, 1930

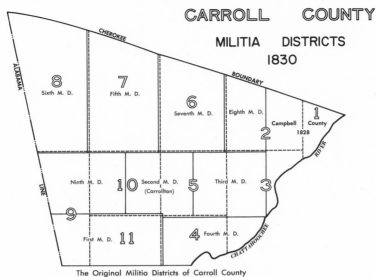

CARROLL COUNTY
MILITIA DISTRICTS
1830

CHEROKEE

BOUNDARY

ALABAMA

8
Sixth M. D.

7
Fifth M. D.

6
Seventh M. D.

Eighth M. D.

1
County
1828

2
Campbell

RIVER

LINE

Ninth M. D.

10
Second M. D.
(Carrollton)

5
Third M. D.

3

9

First M. D. 11

4 Fourth M. D.

CHATTAHOOCHEE

The Original Militia Districts of Carroll County

Nine militia districts as described above were laid out on August 12, 1830. The
western half of the county comprised the First Battalion and the eastern half
comprised the Second Battalion. The two battalions, or nine militia companies,
formed the Seventy-fourth Regiment of the Georgia Militia. Numerals and broken
lines indicate land districts.

CARROLL   COUNTY
MILITIA   DISTRICTS
1930

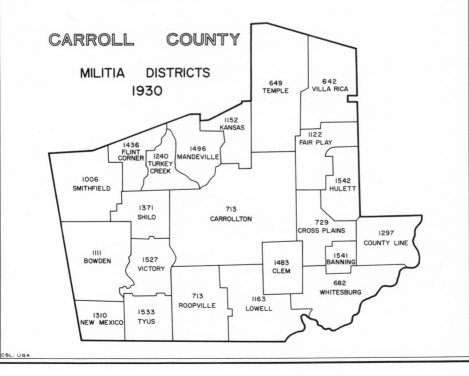

649
TEMPLE

642
VILLA RICA

1152
KANSAS

1436
FLINT
CORNER

1240
TURKEY
CREEK

1496
MANDEVILLE

1122
FAIR PLAY

1006
SMITHFIELD

1371
SHILO

713
CARROLLTON

1542
HULETT

1111
BOWDEN

1527
VICTORY

729
CROSS PLAINS

1297
COUNTY LINE

1483
CLEM

1541
BANNING

682
WHITESBURG

1310
NEW MEXICO

1533
TYUS

713
ROOPVILLE

1163
LOWELL

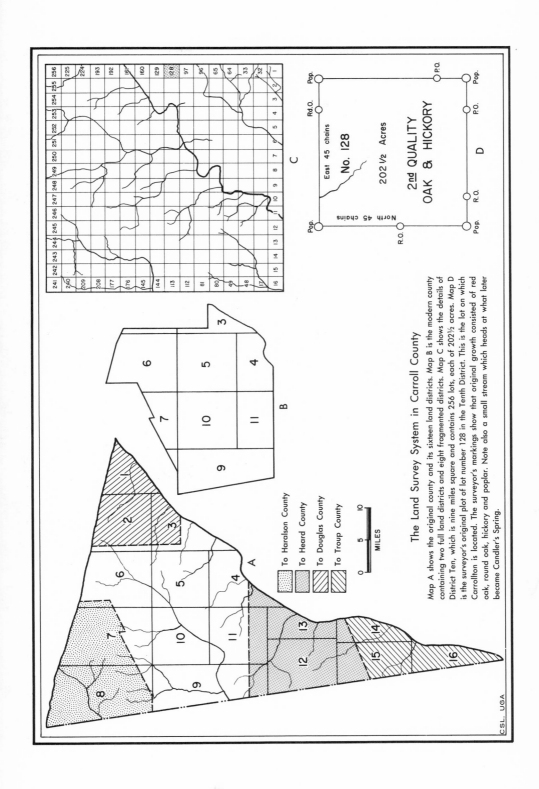

The Land Survey System in Carroll County

Map A shows the original county and its sixteen land districts. Map B is the modern county containing two full land districts and eight fragmented districts. Map C shows the details of District Ten, which is nine miles square and contains 256 lots, each of 202½ acres. Map D is the surveyor's original plot of lot number 128 in the Tenth District. This is the lot on which Carrollton is located. The surveyor's markings show that original growth consisted of red oak, round oak, hickory and poplar. Note also a small stream which heads at what later became Candler's Spring.

To Haralson County
To Heard County
To Douglas County
To Troup County

MILES
0   5   10

C

No. 128

East 45 chains

North 45 chains

202½ Acres

2nd QUALITY
OAK & HICKORY

D

Pop.   Rd.O.   Pop.
Pop.   P.O.
P.O.   D
Pop.   R.O.   Pop.
R.O.   P.O.

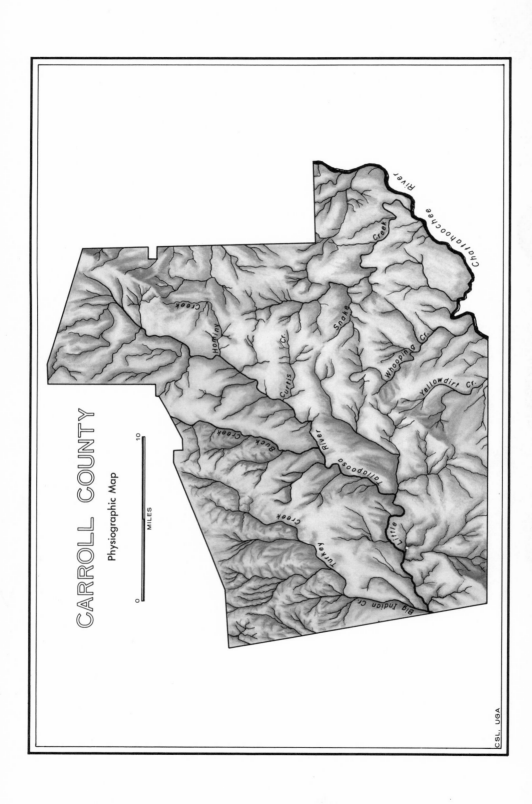

CARROLL COUNTY

Physiographic Map

MILES

0   10

Chattahoochee River

Creek

Hominy Creek

Snake Creek

Curtis Cr.

Whooping Cr.

Yellowdirt Cr.

Buck Creek

Tallapoosa River

Turkey Creek

Little Creek

Big Indian Cr.

CSL, UGA

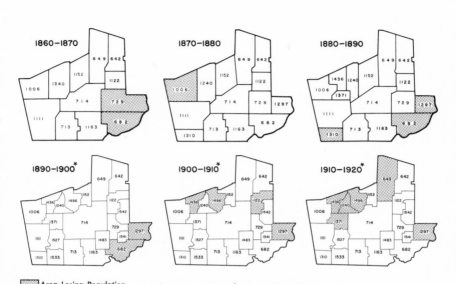

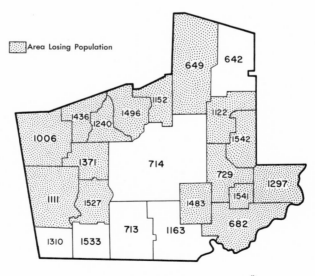

Areas Losing Population, 1870-1920

Area Losing Population

Areas Losing Population, 1920-1930*

*Minor Civil Division Boundaries, 1930

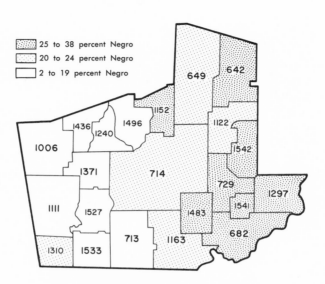

Negro-White Population Distribution, 1930

25 to 38 percent Negro
20 to 24 percent Negro
2 to 19 percent Negro

649 642
1152
1436 1496
1240 1122
1006 1542
1371 714 729 1297
1111 1527 1483 1541
682
1310 1533 713 1163

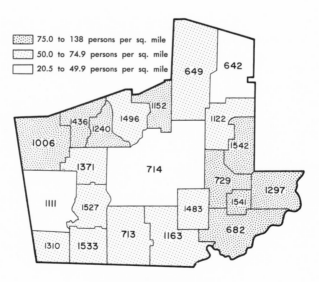

Population Density, 1930

75.0 to 138 persons per sq. mile
50.0 to 74.9 persons per sq. mile
20.5 to 49.9 persons per sq. mile

649 642
1152
1436 1496
1240 1122
1006 1542
1371 714 729 1297
1111 1527 1483 1541
682
1310 1533 713 1163

originally known as Cerro Gordo from the name of a post office established there in September, 1847. In July of the following year the name of this office was changed to Bowdon, in honor of Franklin Welsh Bowdon, a South Carolina congressman who grew up in nearby Alabama. In 1853 a meeting of about thirty citizens was held for the purpose of selecting a new town site. They chose a site on land belonging to William F. Johnson, who had it laid off into lots along two streets and sold to the highest bidder. The highest price bid for a one-fourth acre lot was $10.50. By 1856 the village had five stores, two barrooms, several shops, and a primary school.[27]

Under the direction of William W. Fitts the school flourished from the beginning. To assist him in his rapidly growing enterprise, Fitts secured in 1855 Charles A. McDaniel, a first honor graduate of Emory College. In 1856 Fitts left the Bowdon Seminary, as it was now called, to pursue the study of medicine in Atlanta, from whence he later returned to practice in Carrollton. To replace him in the seminary, the trustees secured John M. Richardson, who had previously taught with McDaniel at Perry.

Richardson possessed a remarkable academic background. He had studied at the Citadel and at the University of Virginia, where he became an excellent student of mathematics and science and a master of the French language. In 1853–1854 he had studied engineering at Harvard, graduating *summa cum laude*. Both Richardson and McDaniel had experienced personal difficulty in acquiring a college education, and together they conceived the idea of converting their seminary into an institution of college rank to serve the underprivileged people of western Georgia.[28]

In 1850 there was no college in the western part of the state and only thirteen colleges in Georgia. The state's total college enrollment was slightly in excess of 1,500 students, the University of Georgia claiming only 117 of these. The total endowment of Georgia's colleges was less than $25,000, and only $500 annually was drawn from public funds.[29] Finances apparently did not present a serious problem in establishing a college in those days before accreditation. The principal requirements were vision, leadership, and the ability to secure competent professors who were willing to teach for a salary that would afford them only the barest essentials of life. These conditions were abundantly present in Charles McDaniel and John Richardson. They began their college in a two-room log house in 1856. One room was used for academic subjects and the other was devoted entirely to laboratory activities. Indeed, it was the latter which largely distinguished the college from the academy in the antebellum period. Admitting both men and women as a practical necessity, the Bowdon Collegiate Institute was perhaps the first co-educational college in Georgia.

On Christmas afternoon, in 1857, a short time after the college was chartered, the citizens of the Bowdon community, as yet unincorporated, met at the log college to discuss plans for erecting a larger building.[30] A new tract of land was given by William T. Colquitt and subscriptions were raised for the construction of a two-story frame building, 72 by 60 feet, with a 12-foot veranda. Completed in 1859, this building possessed a belfry in the center of a neat, pyramidal roof. Each of the rooms was heated by a fireplace.

The college catalogue of 1858–1859 listed 177 students, of whom 85 were in the "primary and Female school." Three states and twenty Georgia counties were represented in the total registration. Most of the students arrived on foot and on horseback. They paid a total annual cost of $125 and $130. Board was provided in private homes at a cost of $8 per month, including fuel and laundry. A few lived in tenant houses and did their own cooking, some producing their own vegetables. Students brought from home such items as poultry, cured meat, grain, and livestock in exchange for board. The school term began in August immediately after crops were laid by, and at the end of October a recess permitted students to return home and harvest their crops. Commencement was held around the first of July.[31]

The early catalogues of the college reflect a stern, puritanical atmosphere in its regulations. "We have no taste for the 'fast young man' and we trust that he will not be sent here," stated the 1858–1859 prospectus. All students were required to attend "Divine Services" at least once every Sabbath. "Lounging about the village, or engaging in idle sports, or noisy conversations on the grounds, or in their rooms during the study hours" were not to be tolerated, nor the use of spiritous liquors, the carrying of deadly weapons and gambling.[32]

The college opened with departments of English, Latin, Greek, French, Natural Science, and Mathematics. Included in the last were courses in surveying and astronomy. Calculus and analytical geometry were required in the senior year. The Natural Science Department included philosophy, chemistry, geology, and mineralogy. The Department of English included a study of Paley's *Moral Philosophy*, Albert T. Bledsoe's *Liberty and Slavery*, Weyland's *Political Econ-*

omy, and Story's *Constitution of the United States.* There were no novels to be read and there was no mention of English literature as such. The Greek and Latin departments fulfilled all the requirements in humanities, as students became familiar with the works of Thucydides, Herodotus, Sophocles, Tacitus, Cicero, Horace, Livy, Caesar, and Juvenal.

Courses could be arranged into two separate groupings or programs of study. The program with a concentration in humanities was called the Collegiate Course, and the math-science concentration was known as the Engineering Course. Tuition for the latter was fifty dollars per year, or ten dollars more than the former. "In making our reports," stated the college bulletin, "the utmost frankness will be observed, and should the student . . . appear to be better fitted for an apprenticeship to the plowhandle than to literature and science, his parents . . . will be advised to employ him in that field for which he is best qualified. . . ." [33]

In this period the library consisted of no more than a hundred volumes, and most of these were well-chosen references. Included were Adam Smith's *Wealth of Nations,* Sir Charles Lyell's works on geology, Brande's *Encyclopaedia,* and such periodicals as *Russell's Magazine, DeBow's Review,* and the *Southern Literary Messenger.* Books defending Southern institutions and the South's position on slavery were high on this list. A debate between the Calhoun and Clay literary societies considered the question "Resolved; that the Negro has a soul," in which the affirmative was victorious.[34]

The college had a military department almost from the beginning. This was in part the result of a martial spirit which ran strong in this last of the frontier communities, but the firm knowledge of military drill and tactics acquired by Professor Richardson at the Citadel was the basic factor in the inauguration of this department. The state armory at Milledgeville provided the college with a hundred muskets and cavalry swords for use in the drills that were held from three to five times each week. At the outbreak of the Civil War the college had on its rolls 140 cadets, each of whom had provided himself with a uniform specified by college regulations. While participation in the military program was not mandatory, apparently all able-bodied males were members of this organization. Bowdon College probably was the first private institution in the state to have such a program.

Thus the people of this backwoods community, with limited resources and the vision of two dedicated educational leaders, displayed rare courage in establishing a thriving college in the wilderness. It was an achievement unmatched anywhere in Georgia at that time. Many farmers of the surrounding area moved to the village to give their children the advantages of these educational opportunities. As a result, the town literally grew up around the college. It was incorporated in 1859, only two years after the college was chartered. The original charter of the town of Bowdon intimately reflected the presence of the college. It not only placed a modified ban on the selling of intoxicating liquors but stated "That no person shall under any pretense" furnish a student "with any kind or quantity of spiritous or intoxicating liquors." [35]

By 1860 Bowdon seemed headed for prosperity. It had ten stores, two livery stables, two tanyards, and a large number of shops. During the latter part of 1860, however, a disastrous fire swept through the town and destroyed three-fourths of the business houses. At this time its population was 304, all of whom were white except two free Negroes. Carrollton's white population exceeded that of Bowdon by only seventeen persons.[36]

To compliment its educational establishment, the community of Bowdon was supplied with ample religious accommodations. At the time of its incorporation in 1858 it had a Methodist Episcopal Church, a Methodist Protestant Church, and a Missionary Baptist congregation which had been inaugurated under the leadership of the Reverend James Barrow, who had previously founded the Eden Baptist Church near the town. Eden was the first church of that denomination in the western part of the county. The Bowdon Baptist Church was not organized until 1860. A resident of Bowdon, William Goggans, who was wounded in the battle of King's Mountain during the Revolution, was said to have been the first member of the Baptist denomination in the county.[37]

In the county as a whole as well as in Bowdon, the Methodists far outnumbered the Baptists during the period before the Civil War. Founded in 1828 as part of the Coweta and Carroll Mission, Concord Methodist Church was perhaps the first organized religious group in the county. Its prime mover was James Baskin, who had been born in South Carolina and served as a Methodist minister in Jackson County.

By 1850 there was a total of twenty-eight churches in the county, twenty of which were Methodist. Only eight were Baptist. Methodist church property had a total value of $6,000; the Baptist property was slightly in excess of $2,000. The Methodists were the first to organize a church in Carrollton, holding their services in the courthouse until 1847, when they completed a building on the north side of Alabama Street where the first community cemetery later was established. Among the early Methodist circuit riders was James Lupo, whose home was near Stripling's Chapel (a church south of Carrollton named for another circuit rider, David Stripling). Traveling by horseback, he required four weeks to complete his circuit, after which he remained at home with his family only a few days before beginning a new tour.

Another circuit rider, Bill Timmons, lived near Old Camp a few miles west of Carrollton, although he lies buried at Smyrna, in another community. Timmons was particularly noted for his great piety. Among his self-imposed ascetic rules was his refusal to eat bread baked with soda. All six of his sons followed in their father's footsteps and became Methodist ministers.[38]

Only rarely could these early Methodist ministers devote their full time to preaching. Augustus C. Reese was an ordained Methodist minister who devoted his life largely to teaching school. J. M. Blalock was a successful merchant and at one time held the office of Ordinary. Matthew Griffin at times held the office of clerk of Superior Court.[39] Others engaged in farming and preached on Sundays and during summer revivals which were invariably scheduled for August after their crops were cultivated.

The Baptists have left far more numerous records which reflect early religious activities than have the Methodists. Because of their congregational organization, the minutes of their monthly conferences give a vivid description of the character of religious society in a frontier community. About the time that Carroll was organized, a schism developed among the Baptists in Georgia which, in 1837, resulted in two distinct groups of this sect. These were the Missionary Baptists and the Primitive or "Hardshell" Baptists. The latter group was opposed to making contributions to foreign missions and they held no brief for an educated ministry, believing that God called men to preach irrespective of their occupation and learning, and that the Holy Spirit instructed and inspired the preacher at the time he delivered himself of the sermon. Their opposition to foreign missions was based largely on practical economics and they would not even support the Baptist Indian Mission at Withington, in the Alabama Creek country. One Baptist minister stated that, before 1813 when missions came into vogue, he could make a tour of his churches and collect fifty to sixty dollars a year for his services, but now he could collect nothing. A few people were opposed to missions because they belonged to the general category of benevolent societies which often were identified with the abolition of slavery. This "anti-missionary spirit," as it was called, raged during the 1830s and was kept alive throughout the antebellum period. It tore Baptist congregations apart, destroyed friendships, and broke asunder many long-standing Baptist associations.[40]

One of the earliest Baptist associations of which Carroll's churches were a part was founded at LaGrange in 1829 and was known as the Western Association. It originally comprised a total of sixteen churches. Despite the pro-missionary leadership of James Reeves, the first moderator, and John Wood, clerk, this association showed an early reluctance to exchange communications with the Georgia Baptist Convention. Later, in 1836, it adopted by a close vote a resolution of non-fellowship with "all benevolent institutions." During the following year some of the churches broke away and formed a separate association. The Tallapoosa Association, of which Carroll became a component, was formed in 1838, but it was not brought into the Georgia Baptist Convention until ten years later. By 1848 there were eight Baptist churches in the county. The Bethel Baptist Church near Temple was among the first of that denomination in the county, having been founded before 1830. The Eden Baptist Church near Bowdon was incorporated in 1835. In the following year Indian Creek and Bethesda began as Missionary Baptist churches. In 1847 Baptist churches were organized at Pleasant Grove and Macedonia. The Upper Tallapoosa Baptist Church also came into existence at the same time. Later, in October, 1848, the Upper Tallapoosa Baptist Church was moved to Carrollton, becoming the first church of that denomination in the town and the parent of the First Baptist Church of the modern city of Carrollton.[41]

The Upper Tallapoosa Church was constituted on August 9, 1847, by a presbytery consisting of James Reeves and one other person. The charter members were John Barrow, John T. Meador, William and Nancy Beall, Melinda Chappel, Allen and Elizabeth Edea [Eady?], and Sara Benson. Amelia Green was received by letter at the time of organization. William Beall was made deacon, and James Barrow was the first minister. On February 12, 1848, James Davis was invited "to the pastoral care of the church." After the removal of the church to Carrollton, the title of the organization was known for a brief period as "The Baptist Church of Christ at Carrollton." [42]

When the church moved to Carrollton and adopted its new name, its meetings were held in the Methodist Church until a frame building was constructed on the east side of Depot Street, where the Central of Georgia tracks later were located. The church building apparently was not completed until November, 1852, when the building committee was discharged. The deacons then were authorized "to employ a housekeeper and furnish the house with lights on all proper occasions." Later John T. Meador presented an account of $3.10 for candles and a door lock and a subscription was authorized to buy a church bell. But the deacons had not yet troubled themselves to secure a deed to the land on which their building stood. This was not acquired until September, 1854.[43]

After the railroad was built, in 1874, worship was conducted for several years in a frame building also located on Depot Street but near the Square. The church's final move was to another frame structure located on the corner of Dixie and Newnan streets.[44]

By the end of 1850, a total of forty-eight Baptists had been accepted into the fellowship of the Carrollton church, of whom fifteen had been discharged. Of the latter group fourteen had left the community and one had been expelled from the congregation.

During this early period church services were held on Fridays and Saturdays so that they would not conflict with the Methodists' use of their own meeting house. In 1852 meetings were held on the "first Sabbath and Saturdays before." In March, 1851, T. W. Burton was chosen pastor at fifty dollars per year and his contract was renewed at the same stipend for a second year, after which he was succeeded by James Rainwater. At this time the church contributed only five dollars annually for home missions; nothing was recorded for foreign missions. It may safely be assumed that the church belonged to the missionary group, yet there was certainly no evidence of a strong allegiance to the traditions of that branch of the church. It was not until 1861 that money was allocated for a Sunday school library, which was a definite feature of the missionary churches.[45] However, certain Primitive Baptist ideas were slow to disappear. As late as 1864 a resolution was proposed that the congregation adopt "the practice of washing each other's feet at the same time and as often as we take the sacriment of the Lord's Supper." In the tabling of this resolution the church apparently made the final break with the traditions of the older branch of the church.[46]

Throughout the antebellum period Negro slaves were taken into both the Baptist and Methodist churches and accorded the same

Christian fellowship as that extended to white members. The first recorded slave admitted to the Baptist Church at Carrollton was a female named Silvey, "the property of Laban Pilkenton." Often these Negro members were referred to as "colored brothers" or "colored sisters" and sometimes as "servants" but almost never as slaves. On Sundays designated for church services there were usually three sermons each day. At the morning service the white members occupied the front rows and the Negroes sat on the back rows. At the afternoon meeting this arrangement was reversed, and at "early candlelight service" only white members were expected to attend, apparently because slaves were required to observe the curfew law against assembling after dark. However, this rule does not seem to have been rigidly enforced. At a Saturday night prayer meeting in September, 1856, for example, the door of the church was opened and seven slaves were received into membership. These were "John Thomas James & Jorden a black brother property of Nancy Beall & Sara the property of Thomas Chandler & Liza the property of Thomas Bonner all by Experience . . . and Messiah a black sister the property of Thomas Chandler." [47]

Reflecting the stern admonitions of John Calvin, the sexes were segregated more incisively in these early church services than were the races. It was not until two decades after the Civil War that men and women occupied the same pews.

Despite their differences on doctrinal issues, the Methodist and Baptist churches in Carrollton showed an admirable spirit of co-operation in most matters. They not only shared the same meeting house for a number of years, but always arranged their services so as to permit attendance at both. That there was some transfer of loyalty from one to the other is also evident. In 1854, for example, the Baptists voted without dissent to withdraw "there fellow ship from sister Marth[a] Brock for joining the Methodes [*sic*] church." [48]

The rigid discipline exercised upon the personal lives of church members must have been equally impressive in both denominations, but only the Baptists have left adequate records on these matters. The fact that Henry Edea [Eady?] was a son of one of the founders and pillars of the church did not prevent his excommunication in October, 1849. The church conference charged him with intoxication and "with quarrelling, drawing his knife, threatening to cut any who might approach him also with swearing." Church members were not permitted to absent themselves from the monthly conferences held on the Saturday preceding the Sunday service. Because "Broth-

[er] Heptinstall" had missed three consecutive conferences, he was dismissed despite the fact that "the commity appointed to see him Reported that they had labored with him." [49]

W. B. Conyers, a prominent member of the church building committee in 1850, had become a backslider six years later when a charge was made against him for "Attending the Ballroom and Dancing Commity." Conyers acknowledged the truth of the charge and expressed regret "that he had wounded the feeling of his Brotheren by Visiting the Ballroom and Dancing and that he would Dance no more though he did not feele that he committed a sin in the art of Dancing." Conyers did not give up his enthusiasm for skylarking. He was again cited for misbehavior and finally excommunicated in November, 1859. [50]

In June, 1857, the congregation was shocked by the reported bad conduct of one "Sister Sarah Jeames [James?]" and sent a special committee to see her. This committee was composed of two women, "Sisters Smith and Milligan," who reported that the accused sister was indeed "in the family way." Subsequently she was "Excluded from the fellowship of the Church." In the meantime, however, she called for her letter stating her intention to remove to another community where she hoped to mend her behavior. The request was declined. About the same time one Graham had been faced with a report that he was a refugee from justice because of counterfeiting. Because no proof was given to support these charges, he was permitted to remain within the church. [51]

Charges against Negro members were numerous but their offenses were far less sophisticated than those usually lodged against white members. In March, 1856, for example, a charge of stealing was preferred against "Tilman servant of Mr. Thomas Bonner," whereupon the conference voted unanimously for his exclusion. Later a charge of fornication was brought against "Brother Nelson Bonner Col[ored]" and "Brother Howard Wells Col" and a committee was appointed to investigate these charges. This was in June, 1867, two years after the slaves were freed but before the black members had withdrawn to establish their own church. Apparently the dropping of these charges was a result of the withdrawal of most of the black members to form a separate congregation. [52]

No treatment of the early Baptist Church in Carroll County would be complete without a discussion of Reverend James E. Reeves, who was among the more notable Baptists in the early history of western Georgia. Born in 1784 in Guilford County, North

Carolina, Reeves removed to Georgia where he was ordained in Jasper County in 1814. He had practically no formal education, yet he came to be recognized as perhaps the best biblical scholar in the entire Georgia Conference, and he was a great advocate of Sunday schools. As the frontier receded and its perimeter widened he moved westward, settling consecutively in Butts, Henry, Campbell, Coweta, Troup, Heard, Carroll, and Paulding counties; and finally in eastern Alabama. Hence his pastoral life was spent entirely on the frontier, where he was a leader in the struggle against the anti-missionaries and against all types of frontier intemperance. He was married twice and fathered a total of fifteen children, all of whom he raised to maturity. He also had seven step-children. He owned several slaves whose Christian and spiritual training he attended as arduously as that of his own numerous offspring. Before his death in 1854, he is said to have founded more churches in western Georgia than any other Baptist leader.[53]

Reeves was no less prominent in the controversy over slavery which led to the separation of the churches than was the Georgia Methodist, Bishop James O. Andrew. In 1844 an application was made by the Georgia Baptist Convention to the American Baptist Home Mission Board in Boston, asking for Reeves's appointment to a missionary post in Carroll County within the Tallapoosa Association. At this time the Northern Baptists shared a general hostility toward slavery, and the Triennial Baptist Convention, which included the Missionary Baptists of the entire country, declined to approve Reeves's appointment on the ground that he was a slaveholder. The executive committee of the Georgia Baptist Convention then instructed its treasurer to discontinue payments to the National Home Missions Board. The state convention, meeting in Forsyth later in the year, fully approved this action and voted to join the Southern Baptist Convention, which was then being formed at Augusta. A charter to the new Baptist organization was granted by the Georgia legislature in December, 1845.[54]

Thus the first two or three decades of Carroll's history was a period in which both Creeks and Cherokees were removed from its borders and the rawness of its frontier character was modified through both religion and education. But no sooner had the community attained some degree of moderate stability than it was thrown into the holocaust of the Civil War. From this conflict it emerged with scars which were slow to heal and which retarded its normal development toward a settled economy and a gentler way of life.

IV

The Coming of the Civil War: the 1850s

CARROLL County experienced rapid growth in the two decades preceding the Civil War. By 1860 its population of approximately 12,000 included only 1,875 Negroes. It was now among the first thirty-seven larger counties, each of which was accorded two representatives in the lower branch of the legislature.[1] Its size had been achieved despite the fact that the northwestern part of the county had been truncated in 1856 to form the southern half of Haralson County.

In addition to this major decrease in its territory, several other subtractions and an occasional addition of small areas occurred from time to time after 1830. Throughout the antebellum period, citizens living on the county line frequently had their farms removed from the jurisdiction of one county to another by a special legislative act. For whimsical reasons lots number 1, 162, and 163 in the Fourth Land District were added to Heard County in December, 1831.[2] Three years later lots 158, 159, and 160 in the same district were also transferred to Heard. On the other hand, Carroll in 1847 received three lots from Paulding, and three years later a small area on which stood the residence of John Low was transferred from Carroll to Paulding. In 1856 four lots which earlier had been transferred to Heard County were returned to Carroll. One of these was that on which stood the residence of Benjamin H. Wright, who had recently represented his district in the state senate. Wright arranged this transfer because of certain lawsuits pending against him in Heard County at the time. A resulting legal controversy was settled by a special act of the legislature in 1860, which transferred these suits to the jurisdiction of the Carroll Superior Court.[3]

An area which was long a center of controversy was that in the vicinity of Reid's Mountain near the Carroll-Haralson line. Matthew Reid, who lived in that area, had served Carroll for three terms in the state legislature, between 1841 and 1854. When Haralson County was formed in 1856, the land on which Reid's residence stood was included in the newly created county, and his long and somewhat successful career in Carroll's politics abruptly ended. In 1859 he succeeded in obtaining a legislative enactment returning to Carroll County lots 278 and 256 in the Seventh (Land) District, where his residence was located. For reasons which are not clear, the law failed to get the signatures of the presiding officers of the House and Senate. Despite this legal omission, however, Reid began voting again in Carroll County, whereupon he was charged by his political enemies with irregular voting. Dissatisfaction of other residents in this general area, in 1873, resulted in the return to Carroll of more than 5,000 acres lying a distance of ten miles along the southern boundary of Haralson County.[4]

Such political shenanigans along the boundaries of the county continued until 1879 when a state law removed such local matters from legislative control. Changes in county boundaries were still possible, but the law stipulated a complicated procedure which required the consent of local authorities in both counties involved in any transfer of territory.[5]

Population growth was reflected in the creation of new militia districts. Carroll in 1850 had eleven of these units. In the order of their creation these were units 642 in the Second (Land) District, 649 (Sixth), 653 (Eighth), 681 and 682 (Fourth), 713 (Eleventh), 714 (Carrollton) and 729 (Fifth), 741 (Tenth), 754 (Ninth), and 813 (Seventh).[6] The most rapid population growth since 1840 was in the Fifth and Sixth districts, representing the middle portion of the county extending from south of Carrollton to Villa Rica. Two additional election precincts were formed in this area during the early 1840s. In 1854 an additional militia district was created east of Villa Rica, which became part of Douglas when that county was created in 1870.[7] Earlier, in 1856, Carroll had lost militia districts 653 and 813 to Haralson County. In 1853 all militia districts at "the places where justice courts were held" were declared to be election places.[8]

Each Georgia county had one senator until 1845, when forty-seven senatorial districts were created, Carroll and Campbell forming the Thirtieth Senatorial District. In 1852 the older system of electing one senator for each county was resumed until 1861, when Carroll became part of the Thirty-seventh District. It was to remain in this district for more than a century.[9]

In the year that Haralson County was created, Carroll became part of the Tallapoosa Superior Court Circuit. In addition to Carroll, this circuit comprised the counties of Haralson, Polk, and Floyd on the north; Campbell and Coweta on the east; and Heard on the south. Previously, in 1854, the term of the Carroll Superior Court was extended to two weeks each during March and September. One week was now devoted to civil and the other to criminal cases.

Just before the Civil War the Georgia Supreme Court was organized into five districts in which hearings were held. These were at Atlanta, Milledgeville, Athens, Macon, and Savannah. The Tallapoosa Circuit along with the Flint, Coweta, Blue Ridge, and Cherokee circuits composed the Third Supreme Court District, which met in Atlanta in March and August. Until 1860 only one native son from Carroll held any office other than a local one. This was Ezekiel Candler, who became Comptroller General of Georgia in 1849. However, in that year, Ahaz J. Boggess, who had served in the state senate in 1853–1854, was commissioned the surveyor general of Georgia, becoming the second native son to hold an office in any state or national administration.[10]

A number of developments occurred during the 1850s which marked the beginning of a more settled life than the people had known previously. A law of 1851 (although repealed three years later) recognized the need to conserve wild life by establishing in the county a seven-month hunting season for deer, between August 1 and March 1. During the same year, a Masonic Lodge was organized at Carrollton and a movement began to obtain a railroad connection to the Atlanta and West Point road just being completed. An effort was made later to establish a tri-weekly mail service with Newnan, the nearest point on that railroad. By 1860 tri-weekly service had been established with both Atlanta and Newnan, but weekly service continued with Franklin and with Weedowee, Alabama. The Franklin mail left Carrollton at 6:00 A.M. each Wednesday, arriving in Franklin at 6:00 P.M. The mail returned on Thursdays.[11]

The Carrollton Railroad Company was incorporated in 1852, but it was to be twenty years before a rail line was to reach Carrollton.[12] Much enthusiasm for a railroad was manifested throughout the remainder of the prewar era. Advertisers in the local paper in 1861 were attracting attention to their copy with such captions as "Look out for the Engine," "The Railroad is Coming," and "The Survey is Made." [13]

The second county courthouse, built in 1837, had become obsolete by 1850.[14] The minutes of the January term of the Inferior Court in 1852 stated that due to the inclemency of the weather it was necessary to hold court "at some place where they could have the benefit of fier [sic] & there being no means of procuring said comfort in the courthouse & therefore held said court in the Masonic Hall." [15] By the outbreak of the Civil War the old courthouse had been moved to the southeast corner of the Square and a new masonry structure had been completed in the center of the Square at a cost of $8,511.27 from a special tax levied for that purpose. In 1860 the county treasurer paid $672 for work in leveling the public square, filling up ditches, and providing guttering and lightning rods for the new building. Earlier, in 1854, the town limits were extended 800 yards in every direction from the courthouse in the public square, thus giving the town circular limits instead of the older rectangular form. The same law relieved citizens of the town from road duty beyond the town's limits.[16]

Carrollton's charter underwent other changes during this period. On March 3, 1856, an amendment gave the town commissioners power to pass all by-laws and ordinances, to choose a marshal, clerk, and treasurer, and to levy a tax "not exceeding fifty percent of the state tax on all persons and property." The town marshal acted as tax receiver and collector, and public fines were limited to twenty-five dollars. Two years later the commissioners were given authority to levy an extra tax on pin alleys, billiard tables, and "all other houses and establishments of amusement and pasttime that tend to deprave and corrupt the morals of the citizens." [17] Apparently the city fathers were to exercise their own judgment in determining the latter. The maximum fine was increased to fifty dollars and imprisonment up to ten days could be imposed by the new mayor's court.[18]

These advances in local government were somewhat sophisticated for a town of only twenty-five business houses, including the courthouse and jail.[19] In 1860 the town possessed a newspaper, the *Carrollton Advocate*. Earlier, two attempts had been made to establish a news organ. *The Southern Democrat* and the *Land of the South* were announced in the 1850s but no files of either of these papers have been discovered. The *Advocate* was destined for a short life. It issued only two volumes before it succumbed to the turbulent economic conditions of the war years. Published by James W. Anderson, Henry Asbury, and the Englishman, Dennis W. D. Bouley, it had its office "in the two-story building next to John T. Meador and Co.'s Dry Goods Establishment." The early editions of this paper contained announcements of Dr. George T. Connell and Dr. A. C. Hall (whose office was in the courthouse) who offered their professional services to the community. Lawyers included Walter Brook, R. L. Richards, George W. Austin, Archibald T. Burke, Augustus H. Black, Jesse C. Wootten, William W. and Henry F. Merrill, and Isaac N. Buyers. James M. Blalock, David Bowling, and Newton Ross were ordinary, clerk of court, and sheriff, respectively. William H. Acklen was clerk of the Inferior Court. A. L. Lett advertised his cabinet shop near the Methodist Church on Alabama Street. John and Newton Meador advertised fancy and staple dry goods, while the firm of Blalock and Martin advertised a stock of general merchandise. John Steele and Charles T. Hilton were grocers, and R. C. Young advertised masonry and rock work including "chimneys, Box Tombs, Marble and granite monuments." [20]

There survives a rather detailed description of Carrollton during the ten-year period following 1860, in which period the town had fewer than fifty dwellings. The description, given here with reference to mid-twentieth century landmarks, begins at a dwelling house on the south side of Newman Street where the A. J. Baskin store later stood. Next to this house, toward the Square, was a fifteen-by-thirty-foot apothecary's shop, followed by a row of three offices owned by William and Henry Merrill. These offices joined each other and faced the street with a single piazza fronting all three. Where the street entered the Square was Charles Hilton's grocery and barroom, which gave place in December, 1869, to a more modern structure built by Laban J. Smith and used also as a bar.

Entering the public square from Newman Street and turning south, one came first to the Buck Summerlin bar, and then to a vacant lot where Lovvorn's Jewelry Store stood in 1970. On the lot occupied by the modern Carrollton Hardware Company in the southeast corner of the Square was the old wooden courthouse, which had been moved from its original location and was used as a picture gallery. Later James Mullinix installed a workshop in this building. West from this corner, where the Western Auto Store was located in 1970, was a very small rectangular building in which Callie Timmons operated a shoe shop. At various times during this period the building was used as an office by Doctors Arnall, Reese, and Fitts. On the corner at Depot Street was a large frame building used by James M. Blalock as a dry goods store. On the opposite side of Depot Street, where the Bradley Building later was erected, stood the old Gillam Scoggins house, used about this time as a dry goods establishment by Zachariah P. Worthy and Son. Next to the Scoggins house, at about the middle of the block, was A. F. Starnes's bar and billiard room. Next to it was a one-room structure also used as a barroom by James M. Michael and later by Tom Steed. In the southwest corner of the Square was a two-story building whose upper rooms were rented by the Masonic lodge while the ground floor was used as a dry goods store. About the middle of the next block, moving north from this corner, was a grocery and barroom occupied by William D. Conyers, the backsliding former member of the Baptist congregation. Then on the corner at Alabama Street, later known as the Shaw Corner, stood a hotel operated by Andrew J. Daniel. Captain W. P. Kirkley was soon to build a house across Alabama Street from this hotel, on the spot where the First National Bank Building later was to stand.

In the northwest corner of the Square was a storehouse under construction to be used later by L. J. Smith and W. O. Robinson as a grocery and barroom and later still by James F. Pope. On the north corner before crossing Rome Street was Patterson G. Garrison's dry goods store and next was William Johnson's drug store built in 1854 in the northeast corner of the Square. This firm was still in operation on the same lot in 1970, being perhaps the oldest business firm in the county. Just south of the Johnson Drug Company, toward Newnan Street, was the Beall dry goods store, and then a building occupied by William C. New. Next was the dry goods store operated by a native of Vermont, John W. Stewart, later known as the firm of Stewart and Long. Finally was F. M. Williamson's little barroom which the post office was later to occupy. On the corner facing Newnan Street was a hotel known as the Carroll House operated by the Virginian, Thomas F. Wells. There was a total of thirty-two nonresidential structures in the town in 1860, of which seven were barrooms. There were approximately forty-two residences.

There was one residence on the Square and several others within a short distance. On Newnan Street was the Wells house, which stood at the intersection of College Street. At this time the house was occupied by Jethro Velvin, who operated a livery stable on the north side of Alabama Street where Lloyd Griffin's establishment stood in 1911 (in 1970 it was the Belk-Rhodes lot). Across College Street from the Velvin house was another dwelling, situated where the post office stood in 1970. On the corner of South and Newnan streets, where the brick First Baptist Church was erected in 1907, was another dwelling house. On the eastern end of Newnan Street was the house of the merchant, John F. Culpepper in which Sheriff Jim Webb later resided. Next was the house of the clerk of court, William H. Acklin, followed by the R. M. Fletcher farmhouse near the corner, a site later occupied by Dr. Maurice M. Hallum. The Fletcher farm extended along the south side of Newnan road. On the north side of this road, including what later became Cedar, Sims, and Stewart streets, were some old fields and a cow pasture.

On College Street Dr. New lived in a house later used as a Methodist parsonage. A widow, Mrs. Newton M. Fitts, the mother of Dr. Pryor W. Fitts, lived on the site later occupied by Lewis K. Smith. On the corner of Cedar and College streets lived the widow, Mrs. Joseph H. Broom (the mother of John A. F. Broom). After her death L. J. Smith occupied the house. Continuing north on College Street one came next to a house where Dr. Francis A. Morgan lived, just beyond which was a schoolhouse, known as the Masonic College. After that was a house occupied by Miss Elizabeth Curtis.

The first dwelling house on entering Rome Street from the Square was that of Patterson G. Garrison, in which Frank Weems later resided. Next was the house of J. M. Blalock, which was later occupied by Dr. William W. Fitts. Then came the house of John W. Stewart, across the street from which stood the house of Judge Beverly D. Thomasson. It was later occupied by Ossie Robinson. Dr. James H. Rogers lived in the next house on a lot later occupied by "Dock" New. Thomas Chandler's house and the Burke-Rodahan house stood apart from any street designations, but in the area northwest of the public square.

Only two or three dwellings stood on Alabama Street in the 1860s. Dr. George Connell lived some distance off the street on its north side where New's mill and shops later were located, and which in a more modern era became a parking lot. Another house stood where Kroger's store was situated in 1965, the house being one in which J. S. Travis later lived. The old jailhouse stood at the rear of the lot later occupied by Kaylor's store, near the 1965 bus station. To the west of it and facing east was a dwelling house. There was also a small house south of the old Methodist parsonage near the old cemetery, and west of the parsonage lived the widow Parr. The Methodist Church at this time was on the north side of Alabama Street, where the first cemetery was located. Farther down the street was a tanyard operated by John T. Hawkins. The tanyard pools nearby provided the first and most easily accessible swimming hole for Carrollton's youth.

Bowdon Road, later known as Maple Street, had only four dwellings in 1860. Augustus C. Reese, a New York–born schoolteacher, lived where the Presbyterian Church later was erected. A few yards west was a house soon to be occupied by Dr. William W. Fitts and later occupied by the editor, Edwin R. Sharpe. Appleton Mandeville lived on the hill on the west side of Maple Street in a house which was still standing in 1970. Across the street from the Mandeville house was the old residence of Benjamin M. Long. On this site in 1913 stood a large late-Victorian house belonging to H. Whit Long. (This house and all of its contents were destroyed by fire in December of that year, on the eve of the wedding of Long's daughter to Shirley C. Boykin.)

Near the Square on Depot Street was the house of the druggist and erstwhile South Carolinian, Dr. William Johnson. This house stood on the lot where the Lawler Hosiery Mill later was erected. Another house stood between this site and the corner of Center Street, although the latter street did not exist in 1860. In what later became the front yard of the Thomas Bradley house was a double-room house in which lived the sisters Abbie and Cynthia Wier, two arthritic spinsters. On the opposite side of the street lived Dr. Daniel B. Juhan and next to him was a house where later stood the Hamrick residence. An old shack stood where the front entrance of the Central of Georgia Depot later was erected, and across the street from this shack stood the Baptist Church on a site later crossed by the railroad tracks. Where the Charles H. Stewart mansion was built in 1911 stood a small house occupied by the Bracewell family. Next to it lived Eli Benson in a house later occupied by Judge Sampson W. Harris, Carroll's first contribution to the judiciary of the Superior Court. John T. Meador's house stood where the Wiley Stewart house later was erected. Living with him was a brother, Newton J. Meador. This lot in 1970 had been acquired for a public throughway connecting Rome and Dixie streets.

On the west side of Dixie Street was the New-Meadows-Smith house, which in 1860 was a sturdy one-story structure with a lean-to shed on the rear. Later this house was enlarged and it was standing as late as 1970. On the same side of Dixie Street, some 150 yards south of its juncture with Newnan Street, was the house of Hubbard Carter, a druggist. On the opposite side of the street was the home of the lawyer Henry F. Merrill, who represented the district in the state senate in 1859–1861; it later became the Shaw residence. Where the Silas P. Coalson family lived in the early part of the next century was the two-story dwelling of the family of Dr. Tanner. This house was later occupied by William W. Roop and was moved to Tanner Street where it stood in 1970. Still farther south, just below the point where the Central of Georgia tracks later were laid, was the old Shirey house. Dr. Hubbard Carter later acquired this lot and erected a two-story house there during the early part of the following century.[21]

As already related, the town limits in 1860 extended a half-mile from the public square. Outside these limits but within the periphery of the town stood two or three substantial plantation houses which remained untouched by progress and business expansion for more than a century. One of these was the Sanford Kingsbury house (originally the Grow house), which was the center of a large grain and livestock plantation lying along the Little Tallapoosa River. Later this plantation was famous for its racing horses. Another plantation house of pleasing design stood on a promontory on the northeast side of the town and just outside its limits. It stood on the west side of College Street then known as the Villa Rica Road. In 1860 this house was occupied by Henry Wooten, father-in-law of Benjamin M. Long. Later it was occupied by the Long, Gaston, and the William O. Perry families, in that order. This house, built about 1840, was demolished in 1963. Wooten in 1860 had a more elegant house constructed on the west side of Bowdon road where the Maple Street grammar school was erected in 1912. At this time the Wooten house was removed some one hundred yards northwest of its original location, and it was still in use in 1970.

A mile and a half west of the Square, on the Bowdon Road, was another plantation house with two Doric columns, the property of Thomas Bonner. The house stood on a knoll in front of what later became Mandeville Hall at West Georgia College. It became the first women's dormitory at the A&M school located in 1907 on the old Bonner-Sharp plantation. In 1916 it was moved some two hundred yards north of its original site on the front campus, where it stood in 1965 adjacent to Cobb Hall. Less elegant in style than the others was a story-and-a-half farmhouse owned by James Freeborn Garrison, brother-in-law of Thomas Bonner. The house, which stood on a high bluff overlooking Buffalo Creek, later became the Will Hay residence. This house was renovated and remodeled in the 1930s and demolished in 1969.

The houses described above were rare exceptions to the general style of rural dwellings in the county. Most farmers as well as a few residents of the towns and villages in 1860 still dwelt in log cabins. To be sure, some of these were undergoing transformation in the 1850s. This remodeling consisted of covering the outer logs with weatherboardings, or with the addition of rooms of frame construction to accommodate a growing family. Occasionally a single log cabin with an end chimney was supplemented by adding an identical room to the side with an open breezeway connecting the two. Thus the "double log cabin" was a symbol of some degree of affluence and stability.

Carroll County had by no means achieved the status of a plantation community on the eve of the Civil War. Archibald T. Burke expressed great misgivings in bringing his bride, Eugenia Du Bignon, to Carrollton in 1853. "I am sometimes fearful that you will not be pleased with the Society in the up Country," the young lawyer wrote to the Catholic daughter of a prominent Jekyll Island resident. "You will think it strange . . . to see white people living in Log Cabins . . . you will find all sorts of Society here except Aristocracy." [22] Eugenia's dowry included six slaves, but none of them were ever brought to Carrollton; they were hired instead to rice planters on the coast. Eugenia died of cancer in 1863. Her interment was delayed until a priest could arrive from Savannah. Her funeral was conducted at night and she was perhaps the first resident of the community ever to be accorded Catholic burial rites.

Only 10.5 percent of the county's population in 1850 were Negroes. Ten years later the Negro population had increased to 15.6 percent. The earlier imbalance between males and females had disappeared, but the characteristics of a frontier population had not completely disappeared. Carrollton was the county's only incorporated town in 1850, and it numbered only 250 people. Only slightly more than one hundred people in the county were engaged in industrial work outside the home. These industries included sawmills, grist mills, and a small textile manufactory on Snake Creek in the eastern part of the county. The total capital value of all these industries was only $54,300, and the annual value of the total production was $49,000. Home manufacturing, conducted largely by women, produced almost an equal value of goods.

Subsistence agriculture was the principal occupation of the people in the 1850s. The production of cotton in 1849 was limited to only 1,243 bales of 400 pounds each. At the same time the county produced 9,550 pounds of wool, 7,201 pounds of tobacco, 313,871 bushels of corn, and 62,000 bushels of small grain. In addition huge quantities of potatoes, beans, vegetables, and some upland rice were grown. There were over two thousand horses and mules, twelve hundred work oxen, and nearly eleven thousand other cattle, five thousand sheep, and twenty-six thousand hogs. All livestock grazed on the open range, except when farmers penned them for fattening preliminary to slaughtering.

Only about 17 percent of the farm lands were actually under cultivation. Land was still abundant and soil was relatively fertile and in its original state. Improved land could be bought for four to five dollars an acre, and the price of uncleared woodland was negligible.[23]

The tax on land was low, and the rate varied according to its assessed quality. First, second, and third class land, and "pine land" were the four categories used on tax returns. These categories were determined by the state of cultivation, by topographical features, and by the type of native growth which appeared on uncleared land. Oak and hickory land was thought to possess the highest quality. Taxes were so low, even on first-quality land, that owners often neglected their payment. In 1860, for example, 743 citizens were reported as delinquent in the payment of these taxes. Most delinquents owed less than a dollar, and the average amount of taxes owed by each delinquent was only $1.62. Uncleared land in any part of the county usually could be acquired for the amount of overdue taxes.[24]

Land ownership was relatively evenly distributed, most farmers owning only a family-sized farm. A typical holding was that of Moses Broom, whose 200 acres in the Fairplay district northeast of Carrollton was valued at $1,000. Being fifty-four years old in 1850, he owned no slaves but he had seven children, five of whom were able to do farm work. He possessed two milk cows and six other cattle, twenty-one sheep, eighteen hogs, and five work animals. He produced only three bales of cotton in 1849, but ample grain and food crops. Thomas Layton owned only 16 acres, one horse, a cow, three sheep, and nine hogs. He grew no cotton but made 100 bushels of corn. Typical of the more affluent farmers was James B. McDaniel, who was to represent the county in the legislature in 1863. With five slaves, eight work oxen, and one mule in 1849, he produced 11 bales of cotton, 700 bushels of corn, and 150 bushels of small grain on 200 acres of improved land. He held 385 additional acres for clearing and expansion; these he utilized as range for fifteen hogs and fourteen head of cattle.[25]

The very large landowners, of whom there were fewer than a dozen, apparently were holding land for speculative purposes. Samuel C. Candler of Villa Rica owned over 5,800 acres in Paulding and 2,000 acres in Carroll County, nearly all of which he returned as third quality. Candler, who also owned a "stock of trade" valued at $2,000 and town lots in Villa Rica valued at $500, paid a total tax in 1847 of only $26.99. Eliza Baxter owned 3,300 acres, most of which she returned as pine land, which bore the lowest assessment. John Robinson owned 3,000 acres. William Beall returned 3,400 acres, but most of his land was in Early County. John A. Jones of Villa Rica in 1847 was perhaps Carroll's largest landowner, although only a part-time resident of the county. His acreage totaled 5,900, distributed in fifteen Georgia counties. In addition, he returned for taxes six carriages and a number of town lots in Milledgeville, where he later served as state treasurer. Zadok Bonner, whose residence was at Laurel Hill, was perhaps the county's second largest landowner. Out of a total of 4,730 acres, 1,355 were in the vicinity of his residence. It was his proud boast that no one could settle within two miles of his house without his consent. He owned 680 acres in North Georgia, and the remainder of his land lay in Appling, Wayne, Irwin, and Wilkinson counties.[26] By 1860 there was a strong tendency for the larger landowners to put less capital in land and to invest more money in Negroes. The 1850s was a decade in which slave prices rose out of proportion to land values. However, Carroll never had more than 22.2 percent Negroes in its population, and even this figure was not reached until long after the Civil War.

As a result of these circumstances, land ownership in the county was never an accurate index to wealth, for slaves accounted for a disproportionate amount of the total personal property reported. The largest slaveowner in the county in 1860 was Elijah Dobbs, whose forty-five slaves apparently were employed on only 400 acres of improved land. Somewhat of a speculator in slaves, Dobbs's total wealth in this type of property amounted to nearly fifty thousand dollars, or ten times the value of his land. Henry P. Wooten's forty slaves were considerably out of proportion in value to that of his land, which consisted of only 348 acres, only 120 of which were in cultivation. The third largest slave owner was Zadok Bonner, who owned thirty-two slaves; his brother Thomas ranked fourth with twenty-four. Others whose slaves numbered between twenty and twenty-four were James McClure, William H. Daniel, Eli Benson, Jesse Roberts, and Samuel Hart. The average landholding of these five men was 463 acres, only about half of which was under cultivation. Forty-five Carroll farmers owned between ten and nineteen slaves. Eighty-seven others owned between five and ten, and 212 owned less than five. Of the last group there were ninety who owned only a single slave. The average slaveowner in the county might be said to possess one family of five slaves.[27]

If the traditional figure of twenty slaves is taken as the requirement for distinguishing planters from farmers, Carroll County possessed fewer than ten planters in 1860. There were only 355 slaveowners in the entire county, out of a total of more than ten thousand white people. It is significant to note that more than half of the county's 1,862 slaves were under fifteen years of age. Also, there were more than a hundred slaveholders whose names did not appear on the agricultural schedule. These possessed from one to twenty slaves each. Among the non-agricultural slaveowners was Nancy Curtis of Carrollton, who in 1860 advertised for sale "a likely negro woman" about thirty-five years old, an excellent cook and washerwoman—and her two boys, one five and the other three years old. Another was Arthur McMullan who advertised "a likely negro girl named Rachel about 15 years old," who had just lost a two-month-old infant. It is highly probable that in 1860 the county had less than a thousand slaves representing full hands engaged in agriculture.[28]

Only thirteen free Negroes were enumerated in the county in 1860, all of whom were mulattoes. This suggests a common practice of white masters, who were inclined to grant freedom to their illegitimate children born of slave mothers. The free Negro tended to live in town and to avoid the rigors of agricultural labor. There is no evidence that white men either feared or distrusted these black freedmen, as was the case in some Middle Georgia communities with a large slave population.

The largest concentration of Carroll's slaves was in the southeastern part of the county in a broad belt from Bowenville to Laurel Hill. Conversely, the northwestern portion of the county, from a point west of Villa Rica to Bowdon, was almost without a slave population. Only two Negroes, both of whom were free, lived in the town of Bowdon in 1860. A map showing the distribution of the rural Negro population of the county in 1930 reveals a pattern almost identical to that of 1860.[29]

Few people read a newspaper in the prewar period and the great political issue on the expansion of slavery into the Western territories did not appear to seriously concern them. Samuel C. Candler of Villa Rica was a member of the Democratic National Convention which met at Charleston in 1860. There, in accordance with the sentiment of many Carroll voters, he opposed the secessionists and supported the Douglas ticket. Lincoln's election in November of that year produced some misgivings among the leaders of the community and their sentiments must have spread to their less articulate neighbors. A mass meeting "to take some action regarding the impending crisis" was called for November 19, 1860. Subsequently a county convention was held early in January on the question of secession from the Union, a movement which already had made considerable headway in the older plantation belt of Middle Georgia. The Carroll convention decided not to exact specific pledges from its delegates to the state convention at Milledgeville, but "to bind them to the great essential of resistance." At the same time they were urged to adopt at Milledgeville such measures as "the consultation of wise men and the exigencies of the times may in their judgment demand." [30]

Two slates of three men each were presented for election. One slate contained the names of three small slaveowners, all of whom were farmers. The other slate named a lawyer, Augustus H. Black, who owned neither land nor slaves, a slaveless farmer, William J. Hemberee, and William H. Daniel, one of the five or six men in the county who might be termed a large cotton planter. It was the latter group which stood for secession. An attempt was made to prejudice non-slaveholders in favor of this slate by circulating a rumor that their opponents had stated that "no man not a slaveholder should be allowed to vote in the upcoming canvass." Despite this maneuver, the secessionist slate lost the election, but by only a small margin.[31]

The Unionist slate was composed of Allen Rowe, B. H. Wright, and B. W. Hargrove, who owned seven, ten, and seventeen slaves, respectively. All three were modest landowners. In their campaign for election they issued strong pro-South statements which confirmed the position of equal rights to slaveowners in all Western territories. However, at the convention in Milledgeville on January 19 they were among the eighty-nine Unionist delegates who cast their vote against secession. This vote doubtless reflected accurately the high sentiment for peace in Carroll County and the relative indifference of the people toward the central issue of slavery.[32]

In the meantime a few citizens of the county had placed themselves definitely on the side of the secessionists. Two of Carroll's representatives in the legislature had in December made bitter speeches condemning Lincoln and his principles. The thirty-nine-year-old lawyer, R. L. Richards, stated in the House of Representatives that there were "hundreds of men in Carroll County ready to cooperate . . . on the tented field for the vindication of the rights of the South." About the same time a meeting was held in the courthouse for the purpose of organizing the Minute Men of Carrollton. They perfected an infantry organization, which became the first company to offer its services in the war. They elected William E. Curtis captain, with Augustus H. Black, James W. Anderson, and Smith Bonner, lieutenants, and John B. Bailey, quartermaster. They called themselves the Carroll Guards and adopted the standard minnie rifles. Meetings of the company were subsequently held on the first Tuesday of each month. Robert B. Hammock, one of the privates, wrote a public announcement for the paper in which he denounced President Lincoln as a "vile traitor" and condemned his principles as unconstitutional and treasonable. He challenged the president-elect to a duel to be held at Harper's Ferry, Virginia, on February 22, which was Washington's birthday. The weapons, said he, would be "double barrel shot-guns each loaded with 18 buckshot."[33]

Carroll County lay at the southern extremity of a great region later known as Appalachia, which extends from New York state in a southwesterly direction through northwestern Georgia and northeastern Alabama. Although interspersed by fertile valleys, its general topography, climate, and soil decreed an economic life based largely on subsistence agriculture, rather than large-scale planting and the use of Negro slaves. This situation somewhat alienated the region from the main social, economic, and political currents of the Old South. As viewed on a map of the Confederacy, Appalachia appears as a giant dagger with its handle resting in the highly industrial Northeast, and its point plunging into the very heart of the Cotton Belt.

It is significant that Carroll's delegates at the secession convention cast their lot with those from the mountain counties of North Georgia, reiterating their faith in the Union. They were one with thousands of others in North Alabama, eastern Tennessee, western North Carolina, and western Virginia where slavery had not yet assumed an overriding influence in political and social life. These people did not feel violently concerned by the course of events that were slowly but surely changing the direction of Southern civilization. They were swept into the war somewhat against their better judgment and with no great enthusiasm for the conflict. Yet as the war between the sections became imminent and when the die was finally cast, the people of Carroll County in a large measure resolved their political differences. During four years of war they performed a valiant service to the Confederate cause.

V

War and Reconstruction, 1861–1872

*W*HEN Georgia seceded in 1861 it still was not certain that the South would fight a long war in support of its independence. However, the firing upon Fort Sumter in April ended all hopes for peaceful coexistence with the Union. Even before this event, Carroll's young men had begun to meet at country churches and at polling places in the various militia districts, where they organized companies, elected officers, and mastered the fundamentals of military drill. These activities took place in an atmosphere of public excitement and growing enthusiasm. A meeting was held on February 16 of the "Ready Rifle Volunteer Company" at County Line Church, in the eastern part of the county. After members of the company went through a drill session in the churchyard, they gathered with a large assembly of local people inside the church and listened to patriotic addresses.[1]

At the time of Fort Sumter's bombardment the college cadets at Bowdon constituted the most notable military organization in the county. These young men, 140 in number, expressed an immediate desire to volunteer en masse for Confederate service. They continued their studies only after the trustees voted to shorten the remainder of the academic year, which accordingly was ended on May 24. On this date all seniors and almost all lower classmen offered their services to the state. They elected President Charles A. McDaniel as their captain, and the college was suspended when most of the faculty and students marched off to war. The student soldiers were soon joined by local volunteers. In a few cases fathers enrolled in the company in order to be with their sons.

The cadets assembled at the college for the last time on July 27 to engage in a devotional service, after which they marched thirty-five miles to Newnan, the nearest point on a railroad. They became Company B of Cobb's Legion, whose rendezvous then was near Atlanta. By the end of the month they were in Richmond. One of the more famous units of the war, Cobb's Legion was involved in most of the important battles in Virginia. Organized by Colonel Thomas R. R. Cobb (later brigadier general) of Athens, the legion was composed of one battalion of infantry, one of cavalry, and a battery known as The Troup Artillery. Its first baptism of fire was at Cold Harbor and it was later engaged at Malvern Hill, Second Manassas, South Mountain, and Antietam. Later, in 1863, it participated in the Battle of Fredericksburg, where General Cobb was killed on Marye's Heights. In the spring of 1863 it participated in the Battle of Chancellorsville before going into Pennsylvania, where it fought at Gettysburg. Later still, it fought in the Wilderness campaign and at Spottsylvania Courthouse. It was engaged against Grant at Five Forks and Reams Station and was at the seige of Petersburg. Just before the end of the war it was sent into North Carolina to face Sherman, who had just completed his devastating march through their native Georgia. Cobb's Legion was finally surrendered at Goldsboro on April 26, 1865. Only eleven Bowdon cadets survived to the end, and most of these were wounded.[2]

Charles A. McDaniel did not remain long in Cobb's Legion. Soon promoted to the rank of colonel, he returned to Georgia where he formed, at Big Shanty near Marietta, the Forty-first Georgia Regiment which served in the Army of Tennessee. While leading a gallant charge at Perryville, Kentucky, the thirty-two-year-old McDaniel was fatally wounded, on October 7, 1862.[3] Had McDaniel survived to the end of the conflict he might have become the county's most illustrious warrior, for he was recognized as early as 1862 as one of the more promising regimental commanders. No other Carroll soldier held a rank as high as that of McDaniel at the time of his promotion to colonel.

John B. Beall, who attained the rank of colonel late in the conflict, had as interesting a war record as that of any other citizen of the county. Born in Tennessee in 1834, Beall moved with his parents to Carroll County where, in 1856, he enlisted in the First United

States Cavalry. He served at various frontier outposts in the West, including duty in Kansas and Nebraska. By 1860 he had obtained the rank of sergeant. When war began he offered his services to the Confederate cause and became captain of Company H (The Cotton Guards) of the Nineteenth Georgia Regiment. His company was composed of men primarily from Paulding County, but a few were from the northern portion of Carroll. The Nineteenth Georgia, originally the Second Regiment, Fourth Brigade, of the Georgia State Troops, was made up of men from Fulton, Campbell, Coweta, Heard, Carroll, Henry, Paulding, and Bartow counties. It was mustered into service at Camp McDonald in Cobb County, where a number of college boys from the Georgia Military Institute at Marietta were assigned to them as drillmasters.[4]

Company E of this regiment known as the Heard County Volunteers was under Captain Charles W. Mabry, who lived at Laurel Hill near Bowdon and who later was promoted to major. Mabry's brother, Henche Parham Mabry, was at the same time a colonel in a Texas cavalry regiment. Companies F and I of the Nineteenth Georgia were made up entirely of Carroll men. The former, commanded by Captain William E. Curtis, was known as the Carroll Guards, the first Carroll volunteer unit to be organized. Company I, known as the Gold Diggers, was composed largely of men from Villa Rica and was commanded by John T. Chambers. The Nineteenth Georgia Regiment, like Cobb's Legion, was soon ordered to Virginia, where it participated in the early campaigns of the war and suffered heavy casualties. After the Battle of Manassas, Captain Mabry's company, smitten by casualties and disease, had only fifteen men on active duty.[5]

Captain Curtis of Company F was promoted to colonel in March, 1862, and assigned to the command of the Forty-first Georgia Regiment belonging to the western army, thus succeeding Charles B. McDaniel. The former's successor to the command of Company F was Augustus H. Black, who later was killed at Seven Pines. Though not much over twenty-one years of age, young Black had already been admitted to the bar at Carrollton. Colonel Curtis survived the ordeal at Vicksburg but was captured and paroled there in July, 1863. He was later killed in a battle near Dalton in the Atlanta campaign of 1864.[6] Only thirty-six men of Company F out of an original 117, returned home after the war.[7]

After the Battle of Manassas, the Nineteenth Georgia Regiment was attached to Wade Hampton's Brigade and spent the winter at

Occoquan near the Potomac River. There the tedium of camp life was sometimes relieved by dances given by the young ladies of the vicinity. This was a social diversion to which most of the men were unaccustomed. "The boys from the cities and towns doubtless excelled in grace of movement to the strains of the spirit stirring violin," wrote one of the Carroll soldiers, "but we of the country prided ourselves on jumping as high and swinging partners as sturdily as any of them." Lacking immunity to all infectious diseases, rural soldiers from Carroll's farms suffered unusually heavy tolls from such diseases as measles and particularly from complications following this disease.[8]

John Beall was disabled at Mechanicsville on June 26, 1862, when a bullet broke his thigh bone. He spent several months at home in convalescence and did not again see active field service. Marrying soon after he returned to Carrollton, he became an enrolling officer, a collector of tithes, and a commander of the Home Guards. During the spring and summer of 1864, when Sherman was hammering at Georgia's northern passes and approaching close to Carroll's borders, four cavalry companies of Home Guards were organized in the county, and one in Heard County. These companies were made up of men outside the conscription age and also included a number of convalescing veterans. These five companies were formed into a battalion commanded by Beall, who now had the rank of major. There had already been two cavalry raids to the county during which several convalescing soldiers and a few others were captured. On one of these raids Federal soldiers encamped within the limits of Carrollton. The Home Guard battalion, called the "Tallapoosa Rangers," was largely without arms and equipment and ineffective against these raids. Beall had been ordered "to procure arms and ammunition at such points as he may find convenient" and to harass and destroy the enemy's foraging parties and communications.[9] Near Atlanta he found in an old cabin a wagonload of muskets which had been abandoned by Hood's ordinance train. With these he was able to arm most of his men. By this time, however, Hood had evacuated Atlanta and Sherman's legions had moved southward toward Savannah.[10]

Carroll County sent to the front a total of twenty-eight companies of all arms, in addition to hundreds of individuals who went as recruits to units originally made up in other counties. Occasionally some joined commands from other states. In addition to companies already mentioned, the more famous of Carroll's infantry units were

Company F of the Seventh Regiment of the Georgia Volunteer Infantry under Captain Archibald T. Burke; Company K of the Thirty-second Regiment, commanded by Captain William A. Walker; Company G, commanded by Washington Hembree and later Robert A. Wood; and Company H (known as the Wool Hat Boys) commanded by Captain Newton J. Ross, both of the Forty-first Regiment; and finally four companies of the Fifty-sixth Regiment—companies B, C, H, and I, whose commanders were James B. Martin, John A. Grice, Isaac M. Parrish, and John M. Cobb, respectively. Upon Parrish's death at Vicksburg in 1863, he was succeeded by Hugh M. McMullin. The commander of the Fifty-sixth Regiment after 1863 was Colonel John T. Slaughter of Villa Rica, who had risen from the rank of private in Company I. This famous regiment of the Army of Tennessee fought gallantly in the Mississippi campaign and remained with that army from Missionary Ridge to Dalton, Atlanta, Jonesboro, Franklin, and Nashville. In a single engagement, which occurred at Baker's Creek in Mississippi, Company I lost twenty-two men.[11]

The first Carroll boy to lose his life in the war was said to have been Corporal James C. ("Coon") Stamps, a member of Company F of the Seventh Georgia Regiment, who fell at Manassas on July 21, 1861. No complete casualty list of the County's Confederate soldiers has ever been compiled, but the number who were killed and who died of wounds and disease must have been considerable. Stories of unusual gallantry and heroism soon drifted homeward, a fact which helped to soften the news of heavy casualties. Typical of these acts of gallantry was that of James R. Leak, color sergeant for Company F of the Seventh Georgia. After being fatally wounded at Malvern Hill, young Leak fell forward and in a last dying effort he succeeded in planting the staff of the flag in the ground. The Milligan family alone sent five boys into Confederate service. Of these, Riley, age twenty, died at Richmond on May 25, 1862, of complications following a leg amputation at Yorktown. Seaborn Milligan was wounded at Manassas during the same year, as was his brother James, but both recovered. Thomas contracted measles and had to be discharged on account of the deafness which followed. Only Andrew survived without injury.[12]

Letters to bereaved families as well as words of cheer to soldiers in the field became part of the daily routine of homefolk. At a quarterly conference of the Carrollton Baptist Church in June, 1862, the moderator was asked "to appoint some Bro. to wright to each of our members that is in the Army so long as the War lasts." A few of these letters have been preserved, and they show more than a routine concern for the welfare of these men.[13]

The Paschal P. Grow family, which settled first at the Kingsbury place on the Little Tallapoosa River, had moved to Georgia from Vermont. They became ardent Southerners, and all three of the Grow sons went into Confederate service. Lewis and Paschal died in the fighting around Richmond, but Jacob survived only to die an early death soon after the war ended. Patrick Mandeville, the twenty-one-year-old son of New England–born parents, died of typhoid fever at Lynchburg in October, 1861, and his body was returned to Carrollton for burial.[14]

Charles L. Kingsbury, another son of a New England family, enlisted at the age of sixteen in Wheeler's Cavalry and served throughout the war, rising to the rank of captain. After the war, Kingsbury moved first to Rome and then to Atlanta, where he became a successful merchant. He died there in August, 1908. Private Joseph La-Fayette Cobb was another sixteen-year-old enlistee in Wheeler's Cavalry who served throughout the conflict. After the war he wrote a history of Carroll County, entered the practice of law in Atlanta, and died there on May 21, 1913.[15]

Ahaz J. Boggess, although forty-five years old, resigned his office of Surveyor General of Georgia and enlisted as a private in the Seventh Georgia Regiment. He rendered gallant service at the first battle of Manassas as aide to Colonel Lucius J. Gartrell. It was he who bore the dying Captain Archibald Burke from the field on that occasion. He cared for his wounded comrades until he was stricken with typhoid fever, from which he died on August 15, 1861. The state legislature made a special appropriation to his widow in the amount of what his salary would have been as surveyor general to the time of his death. Meetings held at Villa Rica, Carrollton, and at Farmville Academy gave public expression to the tragedy of his loss.[16] Boggess's body was brought back to Carrollton and entombed in the Methodist churchyard.

The death of Ahaz Boggess ended one of the most famous family careers in Carroll County's pioneer history. The early exploits of his illustrious father, Jiles S. Boggess, have already been noted. On leaving the county around 1845, Jiles was engaged briefly in running a stage between Augusta and Montgomery, and about 1846 he moved to Texas.[17] There at an advanced age he led Texas Rangers against the wild Comanche Indians of the Southwest. Upon the outbreak of the war, his son Jiles Boggess, Jr., became a colonel commanding a regiment in Ross's Brigade of Texas Cavalry. He participated in the battles around Atlanta and more particularly in the fight at Newnan in July, 1864. Ironically, these expeditions took him back to the scenes of his childhood. On one occasion he viewed his brother's grave and then marched past the old schoolhouse on the corner of Newnan and Dixie streets where, as a schoolboy, he had played soldier with wooden guns, fighting imaginary Indians and British Tories.[18]

Although one of the bloodiest battles of the war was fought at New Hope Church about twenty miles north of Villa Rica, and smaller actions occurred later between Newnan and Atlanta, there was no actual fighting on Carroll County soil, other than a skirmish at Moore's Bridge near Bowenville. However, the county was raided on four different occasions by Federal cavalry, which wrought considerable depredations to the countryside. All except one of these raids occurred in July, 1864, during the siege of Atlanta. The last occurred ten days after Lee's surrender. The first of these visits was by Lieutenant Colonel Fielder A. Jones who, with 600 cavalrymen, crossed the Chattahoochee at Philpot's Ferry after the main body of the command to which he was attached had been routed below Newnan during the latter part of July. He returned to his headquarters at Marietta over the Five Notch Road, arriving there on July 31. In the same skirmish near Newnan General Edward M. McCook was also defeated and took a circuitous route back to Marietta, riding through the lower part of Heard County to Weedowee, Buchanan, Draketown, and then through the northwest corner of Carroll County. On July 13, Major General George Stoneman was attacked in an attempt to cross the river into Carroll County at Moore's Bridge near Bowenville. Although driven off, he managed to burn the bridge. He turned south and succeeded in crossing the river near Franklin. Then riding northward he raided the eastern part of the county. Indicative of the nature of this raid are these comments which he wrote from his camp near Villa Rica on July 15: "We got plenty of forage for the horses, beef, blackberries and some bacon for the men. . . . It is impossible to move without every step we take being known, women as well as men acting as scouts and messengers. I have sent to the rear about 40 prisoners." [19] Stoneman was later captured near Macon by the First and Second Georgia regiments. Company E of the former was composed of Carroll County boys under Captain Oliver P. Shuford, an erstwhile North Carolinian who had been a merchant in Carrollton for a short period before the war.[20]

Again on July 10, General Lovell H. Rousseau, with five federal cavalry regiments comprising 2,500 men and two pieces of artillery, left Decatur, Alabama, on a raid which took him south to Talladega, Opelika, and West Point. Here he turned north through Troup, Heard and Carroll counties on July 20–21, and reached Marietta on the following day. Approaching Carrollton by the old Franklin road, his arrival in the town on July 21 took the people completely by surprise.

The last raid occurred a few days after Lee's surrender and was the most devastating of all. It was part of the famous raid of General James H. Wilson, which began on March 22 from northern Alabama and encompassed a broad area through central Alabama to Macon, Georgia. General John T. Croxton, with his entire brigade, was sent by Wilson in April to make a raid to Tuscaloosa. In this vicinity he fought several skirmishes, then destroyed and pillaged along a route of 250 miles to Macon, where he joined Wilson on April 30. During this entire period Croxton's exact location and the condition of his command were unknown to his superior officer, who frantically sought news of him. It later was learned that Croxton had crossed the Coosa River near Talladega and entered Georgia west of Bowdon, marching through Carrollton, Newnan, and Zebulon. On the night of April 26 he camped two miles west of Carrollton.[21] His brigade subsisted of supplies which its members seized from civilians along this route.

The nature of these seizures is revealed in the experience related by John H. Word of Bowdon. Word had been in the Confederate Army until his capture at South Mountain in September, 1862, after which his leg was amputated. In prison camp he contracted smallpox, was struck by lightning, and then had to undergo a second amputation without anesthesia. Paroled, he returned to Bowdon in 1863 where he opened a general store. Despite Word's parole and his physical disabilities, his store and its contents were seized by Croxton's men and the veteran was left penniless.[22] Among the plantations raided at Carrollton was that of Thomas Bonner on the Bowdon road, near which the brigade had camped. For reasons which are not clear, Croxton's men set fire to buildings on the north section of the public square and with a cordon of guards prevented citizens from extinguishing the flames.[23] Wilson's raid, one of the most

86

famous of the war, was climaxed by the capture of Jefferson Davis at Irwinville on May 10, 1865.

During the latter part of the war, the Confederacy resorted to taxes-in-kind of one-tenth of a farmer's produce to support its military operations. Patterson G. Garrison became war tax assessor for the county after he resigned his commission in the army early in 1864. John B. Beall, who became collector of tithes, reported that the people at first responded with enthusiasm to the payment of these taxes, but later collections became unusually difficult.[24] Being a region of subsistence agriculture, the county had never produced a large surplus for market. By 1864, nothing was produced beyond family requirements and much of this was seized by raiding Federal cavalrymen or consumed by public animals stationed in the vicinity. At times corn had to be obtained from a distance of "40 to 100 miles" and wagon transportation was scarce and expensive. The wheat crop for 1864 was severely damaged by late frost and this increased the food shortage. Since less than 10 percent of the white families owned slaves in 1862, the people were largely dependent upon their own labor for subsistence.[25]

This labor supply was severely curtailed by the army draft. In 1864 the county had 2,400 soldiers in the field, representing thirteen fully organized companies. This unusually large drain upon its producing classes resulted in 2,313 women and children of the county being placed on the state's indigent list. Approximately four and a half bushes of corn were provided for the relief of each soldier's family. Such small aid in most instances had to be supplemented by local relief. An unencumbered single man sometimes rendered "gratutitous assistance and partial support to . . . five or six families." A number of women, some of whom were widowed by the war, were driven to desperation. They frequently appeared at the tithe depot to demand a share of the corn collected for army use.

The problem of subsistence was aggravated by the fact that the county's supply of work animals was seriously depleted both from Union and Confederate seizures to replace cavalry horses and to supply transportation.[26] The situation was so serious that the local collector of tithes, in April, 1864, asked the Bureau of Conscription at Richmond to exempt the county from the operation of the conscription law of that year.[27]

Although its large percentage of small farmers made it difficult for the community to supply both men and food, this situation proved an advantage in making the transition to reconstruction conditions after 1865. Farmers were not seriously burdened by the disorganization of labor through emancipation. After the Thirteenth Amendment the county had less than two thousand freedmen, of whom only a small minority were adult males.

When hostilities ended, a small group of Federal soldiers were sent to Carrollton to issue paroles and to administer the oath of allegiance. Later a group of seven soldiers was stationed in Carrollton to supervise the 1868 election held under the new reconstruction act of the previous year. The election was conducted in the former barroom of Tom Steed, located near the southwest corner of the public square. No full Freedman's Bureau agent was on duty at Carrollton during the period from 1865 to August, 1867. Its work was conducted largely by specially appointed notaries public who could qualify under the test oath. The loyal Unionist William F. Merrill was the federally appointed notary in Carrollton.[28]

For purposes of administration of bureau affairs, the state was divided into ten subdistricts, Carroll becoming part of the Atlanta subdistrict under Captain F. Mosebach. Lieutenant William F. Martins was an assistant to Commissioner Mosebach with an office at Newnan; the counties under his jurisdiction were Coweta, Carroll, Heard, and Haralson. In June, 1867, Edwin Belcher, a native of Augusta, opened a suboffice at Carrollton for the jurisdiction of Carroll and Haralson counties, but it remained in operation only until August 10, when Belcher was ordered to close the office and to ship its furniture to Forsyth. During his short administration he had fifty-five barrels of corn meal sent to Haralson County from government stores in Atlanta, and 550 pounds of bacon were sent to Carrollton.[29] This food apparently was supplied to destitute Negroes, although the bureau was known to provide food without discrimination to all people in need.

The work of the Freedman's Bureau not only included such public welfare activities as supplying food and clothing to destitute people, but it supervised the work contracts of freedmen. It also served such probate functions as normally would have been provided by the county Ordinary. Typical of these was the disposition of four orphan Negro children who had been bound as apprentices to James F. Garrison. Around the end of October, 1867, Garrison had made plans to move to Texas and wanted to take the apprentices with him. The case was referred to the bureau official in Atlanta, who saw no reason to prevent Garrison from departing with the Negroes. However, on December 16, a similar case arose in Heard County when

Reuben Philpot planned to move to Florida and to take with him a fourteen-year-old Negro girl who had been "bound to him against her wish." The Heard County Ordinary gave him permission to proceed to Florida with the girl. When the case was appealed to General Sibley, head of bureau affairs in Georgia, he ordered Philpot not to remove the child from the county.[30]

Military reconstruction in Georgia had ended by 1872, when all Federal troops left the state and the Democrats regained full control. However, occupation troops did not leave some parts of the South until 1877, and there was always the threat that they might be returned to Georgia. This situation gave the Republican party the role of watchdog over political affairs in both local and state government.

A sizable Republican organization was formed in Carroll County after the end of Reconstruction. A group calling themselves Union Republicans met in the courthouse in May, 1872, and adopted resolutions endorsing the administration of President Grant and calling for his election to a second term. William H. McDaniel was chairman of this group and Michael Goodson was secretary.[31] The Democrats held their mass meeting on June 1 and appointed Moses R. Russell, Laban J. Smith, Samuel C. Candler, and Robert H. Springer as delegates to the state convention in Atlanta. This meeting passed resolutions condemning the usurpation of power by federal authorities and the corruption in Grant's administration. They called for the restoration of local self-government and the subordination of the military authority. They condemned "all the centralizing tendencies of the Federal government." [32]

Democrats in the county outnumbered Republicans at this time by only two to one. They charged the Republicans with favoring "mixed schools, mixed families, mixed congregations, mixed guests at hotels and on public conveyances." The main burden of the argument against Republicans was that they favored social equality of the races. Such charges were followed by countercharges. An outbreak of lawless disorder occurred on the public square at Carrollton on Wednesday, June 26. This affair presented a crisis in municipal government and led to an indictment against Richard Lyle and others on a charge of inciting a riot.[33]

In the election for representatives in the state legislature in 1872, Benjamin M. Long, the Republican candidate, received 952 votes to win over Democrat Samuel C. Candler, who received 887 votes. In the gubernatorial election, however, the county gave the Democratic candidate, James M. Smith, a total of 1,191 votes to 657 for the Republican candidate. It was evident that Long won his election largely because of his personal popularity at Carrollton, which was never a Republican stronghold. The results of the presidential election of 1872 provide another index to the number of Carroll County Republicans in this period, as well as to their location. Out of 1,263 votes cast, 403 were for the Republican candidate, General Grant, over the Democratic candidate, Horace Greeley. Eighty-six percent of the Republican voters lived in the northern part of the county. Half of the votes from the Villa Rica precinct were Republican. The Turkey Creek precinct just west of Villa Rica was almost solidly Republican. On the other hand, in the southeastern part of the county, where the largest concentration of Negroes lived, the precincts were almost solidly Democratic.[34]

Carrollton's city charter underwent amendment in August, 1872, when the limits of the town were extended "one mile in every direction from the court house on the public square," but three years later these limits were reduced to 1,000 yards. The government of the municipality was vested in a mayor and four councilmen, and the tax rate was not to exceed "two fifths of one percent of the returned or corrected value of the property." The first official municipal election in Carrollton was held on October 24, 1872, when Eli Benson became the first mayor. His authority now replaced that of the old town commissioners.[35]

Even before the Civil War the old Inferior Court, established in Georgia in 1789, had lost some of its former jurisdiction. The Constitution of 1868 abolished this court and conferred much of its remaining powers on the county Ordinary, which office had been established in 1852. The first county criminal court was established in 1872. Three years later its jurisdiction was enlarged to include matters of contract not less than one hundred nor more than three hundred dollars; and in all matters of torts, from fifty to three hundred dollars. The judge and the solicitor, each appointed by the governor, were compensated on a fee basis.[36]

Even after the extension of her limits in 1872, Carrollton had a population of only five hundred people, yet it was the largest town in the old "Creek Strip" west of the Chattahoochee. Franklin had been incorporated only a year before. Tallapoosa, the first seat of Haralson County, was only a dozen years old at this time. Carrollton presented anything but a thriving appearance. The grand jury reported the streets in deplorable condition. Alabama Street, on which

the old log jail and the early Methodist church still stood, was a positive hazard. A nocturnal church-goer had recently fallen into one of
its gullies and was badly injured. The grand jury noted an insufficient number of "horse racks" in the town and complained of animals
running loose on the streets as well as on the Square.[37] The public
square was littered with horse stalls. Damage to shade trees along the
sidewalks, caused by animals biting off the bark, soon caused these
feeding stalls to be shifted to the rear of the buildings. Thus began
the era of the "wagon yard," the precursor of the auto parking lot of
a later day.

As yet no single masonry mercantile or office building existed in
the town, but early in 1873, Patterson G. Garrison began the construction of a two-story brick building with a basement and a slate
roof at the north corner of Rome Street. Later known as the Mandeville Building, this structure stood in 1970 as the oldest building on
the Square. A lot 25 by 75 feet on the northwest corner of the Square
was sold by Garrison at this time for only $600. As yet the town had
no hook and ladder company and no organized means of controlling
fires. Brick construction was urged as a means of diminishing fire
hazards and reducing insurance rates.[38]

The *Carroll County Times* in its first edition in 1872 announced
the plans of Edwin W. (Watt) Wells "to put up a Livery and Sale
Stable which Carrollton has been needing for some time," and it also
noted that the town was "weeping" for a good journeyman tailor.
Ernest G. Kramer had just moved to Carrollton where he opened a
store in the Edgeworth Building. A salesman for Eureka and Wando
Company, he was the county's first fertilizer merchant and cotton-
buyer. Laban J. Smith was selling wines and liquors and John W.
Merrill operated a dry goods business. Leon Mandeville and Dr.
Daniel B. Juhan were selling drugs and confectioneries. William
Beall was the town's photographer. James Mullinix was a boot and
shoemaker. Thomas C. Barnes was a gunsmith, while Frank A.
Robinson advertised his skill as a carpenter and joiner. There were
seventeen doctors in the county, four dentists, and fifteen lawyers.
However, many lawyers were frequently without clients. To help
keep their wits on edge they organized in 1872 a debating society,
called the Carrollton Law Club, wherein they proposed to discuss
legal and constitutional questions. Their debates were often on less
sophisticated subjects, however. Typical of these was an argument to
determine if a husband could be justified in murdering another man
for debauching his wife.[39]

The new city government soon was to take cognizance of the town's many needs. It appointed Jerry D. Jordan as city surveyor. He began laying off new town lots and ascertaining the location of streets and alleys in the original plan of the town. A street commission soon was appointed which authorized the laying off of new streets "parallel to those already in existence and then cutting these at right angles by cross streets." Old streets were widened. For example, eight feet were added to each side of Depot Street. In order to give the town a more pleasant air, a city ordinance forbade any further cutting of shade trees on the public square or along its sidewalks. The mutilation or defacing of any public building or church was forbidden. No gaming tables, billiards, or ten pin alleys were allowed. No person was permitted "to fire a gun, pistol, cracker, squibs, etc. calculated to damage any person or property or to frighten a horse within the corporate limits." Kite-flying and the use of sling shots were also prohibited. Yet the sale of whiskey was still tolerated. It was not until 1875 that a law enacted by the legislature began to regulate the sale of liquor. This law, applying to Carroll and thirteen other North Georgia counties, limited its sale to quantities of not less than one gallon. This law was designed only to put an end to barrooms.[40]

The county's agriculture suffered serious decline during the war. The white population for 1870 was only 10,116; this was approximately the same figure as that for 1860. However, the Negro population declined 29 percent during the ten-year period, to a total of 1,346. Although there was no perceptible shift of the Negro away from the southeastern third of the county, there was a tendency for him to move away from the farms. Under freedom he was quick to exercise his right to move into town, to own a dog and a gun, and to enjoy whatever leisure he could find. Neither of the county's two municipalities had any recorded slave population in 1860 but ten years later there were 291 Negroes in Carrollton and 31 in Bowdon. In Carrollton two segregated Negro communities developed, one each in the northeastern and northwestern sections of the town. These were called Dogtown and Sticktown, respectively. The latter term was derived from the flimsy and temporary structure of the houses in which the blacks then lived.

There were approximately five thousand fewer acres under cultivation in 1870 than there had been at the beginning of the war. The number of horses, mules, and oxen had seriously declined, there being 1,246 fewer work animals of all descriptions. Thirteen years after the war, in 1878, John Handley was still using a heavy-set bay horse which he rode throughout the war in Shuford's company of the First Georgia Cavalry. As late as 1881, a citizen estimated that there were "1,000 horses in the county that ought to be shot to keep their owners from idling away time on first Tuesday trading on them." [41]

There was a decline also in the number of all types of livestock as well as in general agricultural production. There were 1,901 fewer sheep, 7,523 fewer hogs and 616 fewer milk cows. Corn production had decreased by 126,000 bushels and small grains in like proportion. Garden vegetables maintained their prewar level of production, and food supplies in 1870 were enhanced by the annual production of approximately 17,000 gallons of sorghum syrup, a commodity unknown in the county ten years earlier. Only 1,964 bales of cotton were produced in 1869 as compared to 3,982 ten years earlier. Less than 600 bales were marketed in Carrollton in 1871. Indeed, the county was so devoid of outward signs of economic rejuvenation that the editor of the *Griffin News* in 1872 referred to the region as "the land of possums and persimmons." Cotton was then selling at nineteen cents, corn and peas at a dollar per bushel, and eggs at fifteen cents a dozen. The use of commercial guano had been introduced into Georgia in the 1850s, but none was reported in Carroll County until 1871, when Wesley Smith of Sand Hill applied one ton on thirteen acres of cotton and reported that the experiment was a success. He claimed a net income of fifty dollars per acre.[42]

Although agriculture did not quickly regain its prewar position, urban trades and manufacturing were moving forward slowly. In 1870 there were 168 people employed in manufacturing as compared to 77 ten years earlier. The total value of goods produced was $211,037, an increase of more than 42 percent. These manufacturing establishments were small and numerous, and they were barely outside the category of home manufacturing. The total number of establishments numbered ninety-one, including sawmills, grist mills, wagon, tool, and furniture manufacturing. Each establishment employed an average of less than two laborers. The largest labor force in any single enterprise was twenty people. Steam was beginning to replace water power and there were eighty-two steam engines in the county in 1870.[43]

Despite these developments in manufacturing, the total annual output of homemade goods declined from $12,923 to $9,412 in the ten-year period following 1860. The labor of women in their homes, largely in the manufacture of textiles, was being shifted to the factory.[44] This decline in home manufacturing and the concomitant increase in factory production was a trend that continued to gain momentum. The loom and the spinning wheel continued to be used on some farms until well into the following century, but home manufacturing had all but disappeared by 1920.

VI

Postwar Recovery, 1872–1893

THE community's economic doldrums following Reconstruction were brought to an end by success in securing rail connections to Carrollton. As already noted, these efforts began in 1852 when the Carrollton Rail Company was chartered. This corporation was supplanted two years later by the Savannah, Griffin, and North Alabama Railroad Company, to which the older corporation had transferred its rights and franchises. The new charter called for the construction of a road from Griffin through Newnan and Carrollton to the Alabama line "at any point in Carroll County." The new company included thirteen additional members, some of whom were from adjoining counties.[1] The organization attempted to raise $750,000 in stock, one-third of which was to be subscribed by citizens of Carroll County. Subscriptions lagged because the exact western terminus of the road was left undetermined, and various communities were competing for the route. This situation, however, stimulated great speculation in land.

The original survey routed the road directly from Newnan to Carrollton, but a subsequent survey indicated that the road should cross the Chattahoochee at a point lower down the river near Dorris' Mill, on Whooping Creek. Apparently this plan was to have the line bypass Carrollton and to run through Bowdon to Jacksonville or Oxford, Alabama. The contract for grading the latter route was actually let on July 28, 1860, without yet determining its exact western terminus. At this point Carrollton citizens employed Professor John M. Richardson to locate a route which would pass through Carrollton. This he did, claiming that it was a shorter and more practicable line than the one by Dorris' Mill.[2]

Carrollton citizens threatened legal action against those who sought the construction of the other route, pointing out that both the charter and subscription contracts had stipulated that the route should include Carrollton. The editor of the *Carrollton Advocate,* in ridiculing the letting of the contract for the Dorris' Mill route, stated that the road would "haul 56 bales of cotton a season and 11 passengers." The controversy created some bitterness, even invoking the old ghosts of the county's early cattle-rustling days.[3] Only the outbreak of the Civil War brought the controversy to an end. It also ended temporarily the railroad enterprise.

The popularity of the Dorris' Mill route apparently stemmed from the fact that certain people had speculated heavily in land lying along that proposed right-of-way. Among these speculators was Andrew J. White, president of the road, who began to dispose of his land in 1874 after the railroad was completed to Carrollton. Included in his holdings was the land on which the New Lebanon Church later was erected, which he donated to that Baptist congregation. White later acquired land in Carrollton near the railroad depot, but his speculative ventures ended in bankruptcy. The last of his holdings in the county was sold at a sheriff's sale in 1889.[4]

Construction on the road was not resumed until 1870. In the following year the eastern end was completed to Newnan. In the meantime, a group of Carrollton citizens composed of Patterson G. Garrison, Benjamin M. Long, John W. Stewart, and William W. Fitts had prevailed upon the authorities to build the road through Carrollton instead of Lowell. In 1872 the local editor reported that many who had left Carrollton "to go to the railroad" were now returning, and there was a noticeable increase in property values in the town. People continued to speculate while engineers located the site for the depot which was finally placed "near the Baptist Church . . . on South Street, just beyond the residence of W. O. Robinson and on the same side of the street . . . between it and the residence of Mr. John Stewart."[5]

During 1873, while grading the road west of the Chattahoochee River, workmen encountered a huge layer of rock under the surface just east of the future site of Whitesburg. At this point the road grade called for an excavation to a depth of 50 feet along 500 yards of the right-of-way. Some thirty workmen, using mules, wheelbarrows, and simple tools, were employed for several months at this task, during which the site became a rock quarry, but more significantly, it became temporarily the western terminus of the railroad. This accident of nature caused a town to spring up on the spot almost overnight. By September a post office named "Whitesburg" (in honor of Andrew J. White) was established there with Jeremiah McMullen as postmaster. Within a short time several business houses were constructed and the population of the new town reached almost a thousand people. The community was almost as large as Carrollton, which it threatened to outgrow.[6]

Thus Whitesburg became the first rail center in Carroll County. Trade there became immediately profitable. Guano from Savannah, as well as other freight, was shipped to this point and distributed by wagons over a large area of western Georgia. William H. Baker, a Carrollton livery-stable owner, operated a lucrative stage business from Whitesburg to Carrollton, and to Bowdon. Several local companies were engaged in cutting cross-ties for the railroad. By May, 1873, the town boasted thirteen business houses, a steam sawmill, a planing mill, restaurant, hotel, and three barrooms. The hotel, operated by Andrew Marine, was said to serve the best meals in the South, for variety, richness, and fine cooking.[7]

The citizens boasted that the town had no city council and "no petty marshals to foam and curse among us, and frequently rid honest countrymen of their hard earnings." However, with a predominance of construction workers and three barrooms, the town frequently was disturbed by outbreaks of rowdyism.[8] As a result, Whitesburg was incorporated in 1874, its limits extending a distance of a half-mile in every direction from the depot.[9]

The first train from Whitesburg did not enter Carrollton until 1874, and the westward extension of the road to Alabama was never made, probably because the Georgia Pacific Railroad (later called the Southern) was completed through Villa Rica and Bremen in 1882, thus promising a practicable rail connection with central Alabama. In 1881 the Rome and Carrollton Railroad Company was chartered to form a connection with Chattanooga. In 1887 its name was changed to the Chattanooga, Rome and Columbus. Track-laying began on the Cedartown division of this road in August, 1885, and the last spike was driven at Carrollton on June 19, 1888, when only a short gap above Rome remained unfinished. A celebration of this feat was held at the newly-constructed Carrollton depot in July;

more than a hundred guests from northern points on the road were welcomed by Mayor Oscar Reese. They were served "with refreshments both liquid and solid" and then were taken over the city in carriages and buggies.[10]

The 140-mile road line had been built in just seven months with the use of state convicts leased by the contractors. A long line of these prisoners, chained together, passed through Carrollton in June, 1888, on their way to Columbus. This train of convicts, including their wagons and equipment, was almost a mile long.[11]

It was planned at one time to continue this road from Carrollton to Columbus, passing through Franklin, LaGrange, and Chipley. The grading of a road, called the North and South Railroad, had been completed from LaGrange to Chipley in 1885. Citizens of Franklin who had subscribed $20,000 for a branch line from Newnan, now were urged to put this money in the new road to insure its passage through Heard County. In the meantime a group of businessmen in West Point organized the Chattahoochee Navigation Company for the opening of the river for navigation from Columbus to Franklin. This group now advised Franklin citizens to use caution in their determination to build a railroad, or they might lose the opportunity to have their town become the head of navigation on the Chattahoochee. Indeed, steamboats had long been running between Franklin and West Point, but because of rapids in the stream, none had appeared above Franklin until 1884. At that time, W. E. Cantrell and F. F. Dupree placed a six-horsepower steam engine on a flatboat to bring guano as far south as Aderholt's ferry from the point on the Chattahoochee eight miles northwest of Atlanta, where the Georgia Pacific Railroad crossed that river. It was the high cost of delivering guano to Carroll's farmers that provided much of the impetus for railroad building.[12]

Caught between the various contending factions, Franklin was destined to lose its opportunity both for a railroad and navigation system. In 1894 Heard County completed a $12,000 bridge over the river at Franklin; the bridge was the only transportation improvement in that community until the advent of automobiles and paved roads.[13]

The Chattanooga, Rome, and Columbus road was bought by the Savannah and Western in 1890. After this company went into receivership as a result of the depression of 1893, the road was returned to its original owners in the following year. Three years later it was again sold under foreclosure proceedings, then reorganized under the name of the Chattanooga, Rome, and Southern Railroad Company. It was acquired by the Central of Georgia in 1901, thus giving that company a complete line from Griffin to Chattanooga.

The Bowdon community displayed persistence and self-reliance in its determination to have a railroad. The Waco and Bowdon Railroad Company was formed in 1890, with Henry Lanier as president and general manager, but this road never materialized. Bowdon's noted spirit of enterprise finally achieved the completion of a branch line to a point on the Central of Georgia road a few miles north of Carrollton. This branch line of twelve miles, called the Bowdon Railroad, began operation on Thanksgiving Day, 1910.[14]

The railroads did more to quicken the economic tempo of Carroll County than any other event during that century. By 1890 there were four passenger schedules daily, two in and two out of Carrollton. It was possible to leave Carrollton at 5:00 A.M. and change at Bremen to the Georgia Pacific for Atlanta, where one could spend the day and return to Carrollton at 8:00 P.M. Farmers now were able to use more guano and to produce more cotton, and Carrollton soon became the cotton market for a wide area. A visitor in 1871 noted that there was no new construction in the town but only decay and deterioration. Two years later however, when the railroad was assured, the population of the town and the number of stores had more than doubled.

In making a decision to establish a newspaper at Carrollton, Edwin R. Sharpe noted that the county, although thickly populated, "had never been cut down and butchered up, as had Middle Georgia, by the curse of slave labor," and that it also was "a White Man's Country," with timber, minerals, and fine waterpower sites to attract industry.[15] Sharpe, together with W. H. Meigs, began the publication of the *Carroll County Times* in January, 1872, just a year before Patterson G. Garrison constructed the first brick store building on the public square.[16] Sharpe's newspaper played a leading role in imparting to his adopted community a confidence in its future growth and prosperity.

Despite Sharpe's editorial activities, the community did not develop rapidly until after the depression of the 1870s. In this decade vacant lots on the public square sold for less than $100 and vacant land within the cooporate limits of the town could be bought for $13 an acre. Horse racks still littered the Square and a few razor-backed hogs could be seen roaming the streets. Mulberry trees in front of Thomas A. Mabry's store provided a favorite spot for town loafers.

To protect the frame store buildings from fire, the city in 1879 employed William S. Tanner as night watchman at a salary of ten dollars a month.

One note of progress appeared late in the 1870 decade when John H. Russell installed the first telephone in the town, connecting his store with his residence.[17] Others soon followed. In February, 1890, Leon P. Mandeville and Henry Lanier built a telephone line from Warren M. Meadow's store to the railroad depot. They set to work to obtain fifteen subscribers, which was the minimum needed for establishing an exchange. Two years later a telephone line was laid from Carrollton to Bowdon. At this time the Carrollton Telephone Company, with a maximum capitalization of $10,000, was chartered by Ernest G. Kramer, W. D. Taylor, Thomas Bradley, John A. F. Broom, and W. E. Jenkins.

By 1890 the Carrollton Light and Power Company was chartered to provide the town with electric lights generated by a stream-driven dynamo, a new and exciting venture in private enterprise. The original company was succeeded by the Carrollton Electric Corporation three years later.[18]

The building boom began in the middle of the previous decade with the construction of two-story brick buildings on the square, for which purpose a brickyard near the tannery on Alabama Street was operated. By 1890 each of the four corners of the square had been equipped with a public well, and a fifth well had been added on Newnan Street. Private residences also underwent additions and improvements in keeping with the Victorian style of the period. The *Free Press* of 1889 reported that Mandeville Hill on Maple Street was to be the location of several new residences. The Kingsbury family had returned from Atlanta, if only briefly, to occupy the elegant plantation house at Oak Lawn which had been vacant for many years.[19]

Many new business firms were in existence by the end of the 1880 decade. Among these was the Carrollton Brick Company, and a coal company operated by Joseph Croft and Joseph A. McCord. William S. Tanner and Company was advertising watches and jewelry. A. S. Sparks announced the establishment of a "hardware and house furnishing business . . . something needed in every county site. . . ." The Jesse Blalock building at the southeast corner of the Square was being fitted for a book and stationery store. William C. and Dock F. New had ordered machinery for making window blinds, adding this activity to their blacksmith and wagon shops. They were also erecting a steam grist and flour mill in a two-story brick structure in front of their blacksmith shop. The front part of this building housed a dynamo for generating electric lights.[20]

The Whitesburg firm of Brooks and Aycock had moved to Carrollton, where they purchased one and a half acres west of the junction of Alabama and Maple streets for the location of a planing mill. Four cotton warehouses at the end of 1889 showed a total annual business of nearly 15,000 bales. Askew, Bradley and Company had begun the town's first department store, supplying groceries, furniture, and clothing. They also offered for sale "coffins ready furnished, cheaper than you can make them." [21]

Early in 1888, Clifton Mandeville, Ernest G. Kramer, and others applied for a charter for a building and loan association which, however, was not granted until 1891. At a public meeting held in August, it was suggested that this group combine their efforts with others to establish a bank instead. They also began a movement to obtain a cotton factory and a guano plant, naming William W. Roop as chairman of a citizens committee to pursue these objectives. Subsequently the organization of the Merchants and Planters Bank was completed in September, 1888, with Ernest G. Kramer, president; Clifton Mandeville, vice-president; and Henry Lanier, cashier.[22]

At a meeting held later in September, committees were named to increase the total capitalization of the bank to $25,000. Other committees were named specifically for the cotton and guano factories, hotel, public park, and opera house. By 1890 a second bank, known as the Carrollton Bank, was organized and opened in January of the following year. Stock was subscribed for a new hotel to be built "in the wagon yard near the Presbyterian Church." This two-story frame structure, 80 by 120 feet, having forty rooms and costing nearly $15,000 was completed in March, 1891. The grand opening was marked by a banquet followed by an all-night ball with music furnished by the Cedartown band. The north end of the wagon yard along Alabama Street was equipped with individual feeding stalls, not only for the accommodation of animals belonging to hotel guests, but to humor farmers who came to town to trade.[23] Carrollton at this time had approximately fifty business houses, many of them of brick construction. The town's taxable property was assessed at approximately a half-million dollars, having almost doubled during the preceding four years. A total of 18,000 bales of cotton was marketed during the season of 1889–1891.[24]

Along with these evidences of growth, there appeared an acute awareness of the town's unattractive appearance. Someone complained in September, 1876 that "all the buckets [were missing from] all the wells at all corners of the square." Others mentioned the "unsightly and dilapidated structures on Depot Street," which was the town's most used thoroughfare. Carrollton's sidewalks were full of gullies, with weeds and briars growing along the pathways. One compared them in appearance to Indian trails and complained that they soiled the ladies' dresses. He suggested that stepping-stones be laid at street crossings, which was done. What was described as "the new cemetery," laid out in 1880 on the west side of Alabama Street, was badly in need of cleaning. There were frequent outbreaks of night riots in those sections of the town where the Negro population was concentrated, and the noise from these was particularly disturbing to women and children. The county grand jury in October, 1891, took note of a complaint by citizens of "the filth of the jail being emptied on the lot near the Methodist Church," and they recommended the removal of the courthouse from the center of the public square. A new building "costing not less than $30,000 nor more than $50,000" was proposed. The cornerstone of this building at Newnan and Dixie streets was laid in May, 1893. [25]

Destructive fires in the center of the town occurred in the early 1890s. The first of these fires occurred around Christmas, 1892, when four wooden storehouses and a Negro dwelling burned on the southwest section of the Square. The fire threatened to spread to the entire business section. The Askew and Bradley buildings next to the Long corner were barely saved by the heroic efforts of citizens who organized a bucket brigade. The fire seriously threatened brick buildings on the south side of Alabama Street. One building was saved only by placing wet blankets on the roof. [26]

In April, 1893, an even more destructive fire broke out on the south side of Newnan Street, where the wooden buildings were located close to each other. The fire, which started about twelve o'clock at night in the office of Dr. M. D. Watkins, destroyed fifteen buildings. Ten of these were on the south side of the street, beginning at Williamson's store on the corner and moving eastward to an old trunk factory. It then spread across the street to consume five other buildings between Jasper Pope's brick storehouse and the new Methodist Church, which also caught fire. The blaze was extinguished with some difficulty. [27]

Earlier, in 1889, the city council had passed Carrollton's first zoning ordinance when it specified that no structures of combustible material could be erected "from the square to the first alley running off Newnan, Rome, Depot and Alabama streets." However, the ordinance did not apply to buildings already erected in this area As a result of this ordinance, the burned-out areas were restored with masonry buildings, and this type of construction was soon adopted elsewhere in the business area.[28]

Because of the absence of immediate waterpower sites, Carrollton was late in developing large-scale industry. The earliest manufacturing community to develop in the county was on Snake Creek, some two and half miles north of the future site of Whitesburg. A textile mill with 500 spindles was operating there as early as 1846, by Thomas, William, John, and Kit Bowen. Their yarn was sold to individuals to be woven on home looms. Three years later a post office appeared under the name of Bowenville, with William Bowen as postmaster. After the original structure burned in 1850, the Bowenville Manufacturing Company obtained a new charter. The incorporators, John, William, Thomas, and Christopher Bowen, now produced osnaburgs in addition to cotton yarn, and their charter permitted them to peddle their products in Carroll and adjoining counties.[29] Soon after the Civil War, a new corporation known as the Carroll Manufacturing Company was organized by William Amis, John M. Moyers, William P. Chilton, and Jet S. Miller, as successors to the Bowenville Company. Occupying a new masonry structure, they had as their purpose the manufacture of both wool and cotton yarn and the processing of it into cloth, and also to manufacture meal, flour, lumber products, shoes, leather, "and machinery of any description." At the same time Kellog and Company established a paper mill nearby. Both of these enterprises lagged, and in 1878 they were sold at a sheriff's sale, bringing only a little more than $3,000. The paper mill later was acquired by U. B. Wilkinson of Newnan, who spent over $50,000 in its reconstruction. In 1889 it was employing twenty workers and producing twelve tons of wrapping paper each week.[30]

The textile mill was acquired by Arthur Hutcheson, Robert McBride, and Joseph Hayden of Palmetto, and Thomas Bramblett of Boston. Capitalized at $93,000 under a charter of 1882, the Mill operated fourteen cards and 2,000 spindles in the manufacture of warp and bunch yarn. In the following year the factory began making cloth. The paper mill burned in 1892 and the Hutcheson charter was amended in the following year to authorize "the manufacture of paper from wood pulp" and to purchase land and real estate. Thus at this site was established one of the earliest pulp mills in western Georgia. It was more than half a century before this new industry became fully developed in the Southeast. At the time of Arthur Hutcheson's death, on April 5, 1895, the company was in a thriving condition, owning 1,300 acres of pulp and timber land. It operated a textile mill of 5,000 spindles, in addition to two pulp mills, a paper manufactory, a grist mill, and a sawmill. All of these lay within a mile's length along Snake Creek. All the machinery was powered by water from a single dam. Operating day and night and employing a total of 240 workmen, it was perhaps the first electrically lighted industrial establishment in the county.[31]

After the completion of the railroad through Whitesburg, this town became the first shipping point for the Bowenville factory, and later a station and a post office were established at Banning, the nearest rail point from Bowenville. With the coming of improved roads, Bowenville, Banning, and Whitesburg were merged into a single community.

When the railroad was extended to Carrollton in 1874, Whitesburg's growth abruptly ended, but the town did not disappear as some had predicted. The community was sustained not only by a number of small industries in the vicinity but by the large and thriving agricultural population in the eastern part of the county. Jethro Jones owned 1,300 fertile acres near Whitesburg and produced annually from 125 to 150 bales of cotton in addition to huge quantities of corn.[32] His plantation was perhaps the largest in the county during this period.

A newspaper called the *Whitesburg Advance* began publication in 1890 under the editorship of James L. Almon. In September of the following year its office was moved to Newnan, where it continued for a brief period under the management of W. R. Smith, Jr. After it was discontinued, it was replaced by *The Whitesburg Monitor,* which also had a brief life during 1895. It was about this time that a movement developed to change the name of the town to Atselma in recognition of its location on a proposed new railroad from Atlanta to Selma, Alabama. However, this road never materialized and Whitesburg remained a rural village.[33]

Many of Whitesburg's citizens began to move away after its original boom of the 1870s. The high quality of those who remained, however, is indicated by various facts in the community's subsequent history. The town produced Dr. Marvin Parks, who became the second president of The Woman's College of Georgia and later the

state superintendent of schools. One of the early principals of the
academy at Whitesburg was George W. Griner whose son, General
George W. Griner, Jr., achieved fame in World War II. Whitesburg
had an attractive group of young people in this period and it was
a favorite courting-ground for many of Carrollton's young men.
"Whitesburg had the honor Friday night to entertain several of
Carrollton's young society men," wrote the local editor in March,
1890. He named Thomas Merrill, Thomas New, and Ben Crider.
"They wore lavender overcoats, patent leather boots, black silk
handkerchiefs, and pleasant smiles," he concluded.[34] Many Carrollton
men married Whitesburg girls.

While Whitesburg was being sustained by a wagon trade from a
large agricultural area, Villa Rica also took on new growth from
agricultural developments. By 1890, it had become the second largest
incorporated town in the county. It was a shipping point for a large
area in the northern part of the county after the Georgia Pacific Railroad was constructed through that point. Its mining industries secured greater financial backing during the postwar period and they
underwent new developments.

During the 1870s there was considerable surface mining in the
area, giving individual farmers off-season employment. In May,
1876, one Villa Rica merchant alone, Samuel C. Candler, bought five
hundred pennyweights of gold from his customers. The Clopton
Gold Mines were yielding $100 per day. The Pine Mountain Mine
near the Douglas line was operated by Tom Mable and T. M. Hamilton, who were installing pumps to get water to the top of the hill.
Copper ore was also discovered there during this period. The Reid
Copper Mine ten miles north of Carrollton produced copper ore
assaying 12½ percent.[35] A gold vein three feet wide was discovered at
Oak Mountain four miles east of Carrollton in 1878 and a stamp mill
was erected on the site, but later abandoned.

By 1893 the Clopton, Henry Grady, Jack Jones, and Watkins
mines all were being sought by Northern capitalists. The last was
being worked by a St. Louis Company. One Brooklyn woman, Jennie
Stone, was said to own $100,000 worth of mineral lands in the area,
acquired through the death of her uncle. The Copton Mines later
were acquired by Pennsylvania capitalists, who erected a four-story
processing mill employing twenty hands. The Villa Rica Gold Mining Company erected a new stamp mill which, in 1893, was running
forty tons of ore each day, and yielding a highly profitable return
on the capital investment. These stamp mills pounded the rocks

until pulverized and then the gold was secured in various ways.

This improved technology was a radical departure from the earlier methods. The first mining was the simple panning method which was said to require only "a mule, a fool, and a pool." Later a simple device called a rocker was hollowed from logs. Improved rockers which appeared still later were called "long toms." Resembling a child's cradle, these were used to wash large quantities of dirt. The gravel was shoveled into a perforated plate and carried forward over the sloping floor. Under continuous rocking the heavier gold was caught in the riffles at the bottom of the rocker, the riffles being pieces of wood which broke the water's current and provided a place where the gold settled and could be easily spotted. Mercury was often placed in the riffles to amalgamate the gold. The gold was originally placed in goose quills for marketing, but later small vials were used.

Reflecting the mining interests in this community was the *Villa Rica Gold Leaf,* which began publication in the 1880s, followed later by the *Villa Rica Record* whose editor, Oscar Groce, began the publication of a paper at Waco in 1890 called *The Waco Wide Awake.* The third paper in Villa Rica was the *Villa Rica News,* which suspended publication for a time after 1895. By that date the increased depth and scarcity of ore in the vicinity made mining unprofitable except by methods employing even more advanced techniques.[36]

In 1890 Villa Rica had approximately a thousand inhabitants, three hundred of whom still resided in the old town. The new town possessed fifteen stores, two hotels, a Masonic lodge, three churches, a large ginnery, and an oil mill. It shipped out an estimated five thousand bales of cotton in 1889. In that year a group of Villa Rica citizens attempted to get legislative approval for the creation of a new county with Villa Rica as the county seat. The proposed new county would include Villa Rica, Temple, and Fairplay in Carroll County and parts of Douglas, Paulding, and Haralson counties. This area was thickly populated and its limits lay within 20 miles of Villa Rica.[37]

One of the more prominent families in Villa Rica, the Candlers, was already recognized as among the more illustrious families of Georgia. The head of this family, Samuel Charles Candler, had come to the community around 1830 and had settled in a frontier cabin, working at times in the gold mines at six dollars a month. In 1833 he married Martha Beall, who had barely reached her fourteenth birthday. His opposition to secession in 1860 and his support of the Douglas ticket were by no means a political liability after the war. In 1865 he represented his county in the General Assembly.

Most of Samuel C. Candler's eleven children became outstanding leaders in various fields. Asa Griggs Candler was perhaps the best known of his sons. As a youth he wanted to become a physician and for a time studied medicine under private tutors. This training led him to a successful career as a druggist in Atlanta, to which place he moved in 1873. In 1887 he bought the formula for an elixir known as coca cola, the processing of which he improved and later developed into the giant Coca Cola Company. In 1890 he sold his prosperous wholesale drug business and devoted his full energies and enterprise to the manufacture and sale of Coca Cola. He sold this business in 1919 for $25 million and then entered real estate and other ventures in Atlanta, where he was highly successful. One of the better-known philanthropists and civic leaders in the South, he became the principal donor to Emory University. His influence and financial support were instrumental in transforming that small rural college into an urban university of national significance.

Other members of the Candler family of Villa Rica included Warren Aiken Candler, who became a bishop in the Methodist Church; Ezekiel S., a brother of Samuel C., who was Comptroller General of Georgia from 1849 to 1854; John S., who was an associate justice of the Georgia Supreme Court from 1902 to 1906; Milton A., who represented his district in the United States Congress; and finally William B. Candler and Samuel C., Jr., who remained in Villa Rica to become successful in various enterprises. William B. engaged in merchandising, banking, and manufacturing. Ezekiel, another son of Samuel C. Candler, moved to Mississippi where his son became a member of Congress from that state. A nephew, Allen D. Candler, became governor of Georgia in 1898.

Although the Baptist and Presbyterian denominations were represented among them, most of the Candlers were Methodists. No other family looms so large in the history of the North Georgia Methodist Conference. When the question of Methodist unification was debated in the 1930s, Bishop Warren Candler was one of the bitterest foes of the unification movement. At the same time his youngest brother, John S. Candler, delivered a resounding speech in favor of the movement on the floor of the convention.[38]

Villa Rica lies in a valley some sixteen miles northeast of Carrollton. About the same distance to the southwest of the county seat, where the old McIntosh trail crosses a high ridge, is the town of Roopville. Beautifully located at the highest altitude in the county, this community was surrounded by rich uplands and well-watered alluvial bottoms which produced large quantities of cotton and corn. Since early settlers avoided such rock-laden ridge land upon which Roopville was situated, the town was slow to develop. Martin Roop, born in South Carolina in 1810, came in 1855 from Coweta County to this vicinity, where he raised nine children. Soon after the Civil War a double log schoolhouse surrounded by a rail fence was built on the ridge and one of the Roop boys was engaged as the teacher. A little later John K. Roop opened a store there and also built the first dwelling in the immediate vicinity. By 1880 Baptist and Methodist churches were established. A post office appeared in 1882 with Thomas M. Roop as postmaster, thus giving the community its permanent name. Two years later the village boasted three stores, several neat dwellings, a sawmill, "and other machinery." [39] Zedrick T. ("Dock") Freel began a blacksmith shop there in 1881 and he added woodworking machinery a few years later. The town continued to grow throughout the remainder of the century. By 1893 it had an additional general store, two drug stores, a shoe shop, gin, sawmill, planing mill, grist and wheat mill, and a flourishing school known as the Henry Grady Institute. It had a population of approximately 150 people. John K. Roop was the largest property owner. In common with his neighbors he produced on the farm everything which the household required. [40]

Located at the intersection of four roads, Roopville enjoyed an early wagon trade which extended into the northern part of Heard County. A short distance to the south was the community of Lineville, which had its beginning in the 1880s when a group known as the Lineville Reading Club was organized there. By 1892 the community had a gin, saw mill, store, and school. "We would . . . like to have some professional men in our vicinity such as a minister, lawyer, doctor and some one to call colonel," wrote a resident in March, 1892. At that time a mail office was established, with William B. Huff as postmaster.

About four miles to the southwest, on the edge of Heard County, Joseph and Ed Walker built a corn mill on Pink Creek. Later, in 1889, they transferred the property to Sim H. Dorough, who added a steam cotton gin. [41] In 1886 a post office was established at the Dorough residence known as Glenloch, a Scotch phrase meaning "lake-in-the-glen." About the same time Benjamin F. Banks erected a schoolhouse at a crossroads some two miles east of the Dorough residence, which he called Farmville School. The steam ginnery was removed to this location which became the final center of the Glenloch community. By 1905 it had two stores, a new double-story schoolhouse, a blacksmith shop, and a Baptist church.[42] It was somewhat in this manner that numerous small communities developed throughout the area in the 1880s and 1890s.

The scarcity of post offices immediately following the war was a result of the difficulty of obtaining postmasters who could qualify under the test oath in use during the Reconstruction period. This oath excluded most ex-Confederates from such positions. Before the Civil War a total of twenty-three post offices had been established in the county but only thirteen of these were in existence when the war began. Only two were established in the ten-year period following the outbreak of the war. Both appeared in 1870, the first of which was Loyal, a few miles west of Carrollton, with Wiles G. Robinson as postmaster. The name "Loyal" suggests that the postmaster who presided over these mails had been a Unionist during the war.

Between 1871 and 1880, thirteen new post offices were created. During the twenty-year period to the end of the century, a total of forty-nine additional offices were created in the county. Since rural free delivery of mails was begun soon after the turn of the century, only seven new offices were created after 1900, these being Jet and Katherine which were west of Mt. Zion; Reavesville, south of Bowdon; and Still, Bowdon Junction, and Genola, all three of which were near Carrollton. The last was established at the district agricultural school on October 22, 1915.

Several passenger stations sprang up along the railroad line, all of which have since disappeared. In one or two instances the original name of these stations has been supplanted by that of a post office established near the site. The early train schedule showed the station of McCartyville north of Whitesburg and also the station of Atkinson, where Clem later was located. The Clem post office was established in 1885 and in the following year a special building was constructed for this purpose.[43] As yet there was no storehouse or depot at Clem. However, the community had two Baptist churches, a Methodist church, and a small chapel for the Lutherans who lived there. Mandeville in 1892 had a post office as well as a depot whose agent was Daniel Creel. Two general stores there were operated by H. T. Lambert and W. C. Shelnutt, the latter serving also as postmaster.[44]

Prior to 1882 there was no community at Temple, the site being known as Ringer's Cross Roads. By the time the railroad reached that point, Dr. Richard L. Rowe and J. P. Griffin had built a store for general merchandising. The town was surveyed in 1882 and the lots sold to the highest bidder. By 1890 Temple had a population of approximately 250. The firm of Barge and Sewell had just constructed a new store 20 by 80 feet with concrete walls and a brick front. In 1890 the town was making plans to light its principal streets.[45]

The numerous petty post offices which peppered the early local maps have a peculiar historical significance. More often than not they represented early rural centers where there was a general store, a grist mill, a ginhouse, or perhaps a voting place near which resided the local justice of the peace. These small communities often bore colorful names, although frequently they took the name of their first postmaster. Lairdsborough at the site of the Bonner Gold Mine at Laurel Hill was presided over by Andrew J. Laird. The first official at Emily, northeast of Clem, was Emily McClendon. Joel P. Yates was the first postmaster at Joel, situated south of Bowdon. The post office of Lang near Hulett was established in 1887 with Benjamin F. Lang as postmaster. Caleb Sprewell was the original postmaster at Sprewell. Andrew J. Gulledge, George A. Bonner, William T. Harman, James J. Stogner, Herman J. Reaves, and Victoria Hines (Victory), all gave their names to post offices over which they presided.

Some of these early place names defy interpretation. However, they suggest a variety of influences—literary, biblical, aesthetic, and historical. There were Buckingham, Ithaca, Kansas, Corbett, and Lowell; Mount Zion, Abilene, Moses, and Temple; Lilac, Mistletow Bower, and Coraxi, and names of such local significance as Tall Pine, Flint Hill, Copper Hill, Buffalo, Gold Village, Central Point, Billow, and Still. The last suggests the period when the manufacture of whiskey was unregulated by law. Billow was located near Simonton's Mill on the Little Tallapoosa River west of Carrollton. Within a radius of one mile there were thirty-seven families and a total population of 147, nearly half of whom were adults. A dam to provide power for a grist mill was constructed there by one Hibler at a very early date and was known later as Epsey's Mill. This mill was in existence in 1830, when some of its earliest customers were Creek Indians.

Located in rural shops and stores and sometimes in dwellings or in an out-building, these rural post offices were far from remunerative to those who operated them. Paid on a fee system, the postmaster's annual remuneration often was less than $20. These annual receipts not only indicate the size of the communities which they served, but they reflect their growth as well. The total cancellations at Lowell in 1879, for example, amounted to only $6.20, but by 1901 it had increased to $30.53. Clem's first annual postal receipts, in 1887, amounted to $33.66, and this figure had grown to $147.90 by the end of the century. Roopville increased from $10.37 in 1883 to $139 in 1901. During the same period Temple's receipts increased from $115.77 to over four hundred dollars. The total annual receipts of the Carrollton post office did not reach $3,000 until after 1900.

Mail was delivered to rural stations once or twice a week by men who had contracted with postal authorities for this service. One of the general contractors during the 1890s was Henry Roop of Carrollton, who sublet individual contracts. Some of the subcontractors were Negroes who drove oxcarts or traveled by mule-back. It was not uncommon to find undelivered letters lost by the roadside. Mail which originated on one of these routes was usually delivered to the local distribution point without postage charges, as were county newspapers originating at Carrollton. In 1879 the editor of the *Carroll County Times* complained that some postmasters to which his papers were sent for distribution were permitting these papers to be taken out and read by the entire community before the actual subscribers received them. Since this practice resulted in the occasional loss or mutilation of a paper before it reached the subscriber, the *Times* thought it wise to send an extra copy to these post offices "for the benefit of loafers and loungers." [46]

By 1890 Carroll County had a population of slightly over 22,000, of whom only 2,888 lived in the six incorporated towns. These were Carrollton, Villa Rica, Bowdon, Whitesburg, Temple, and Roopville.

Bowdon with a population of 354 was third in size. It had shown a remarkable capacity for survival despite its remoteness. In the 1870s a regular tri-weekly hack service was established there which delivered passengers and freight to the railroad at Carrollton.[47] Bowdon's trade area included much of the western part of the county and it extended into Alabama. Bowdon College had resumed operation in 1867, and was one of five institutions in the state where Confederate veterans could receive tuition and subsistence from state funds. It reopened as a college for men only, but in 1872, when most of the veterans had departed, women were again enrolled. In 1880 it had only 117 students, but six years later registrations totaled 169, nearly 40 per cent of whom were women. Major John M. Richardson, although still suffering from severe wounds he had received at the Battle of Winchester in 1864, had returned as president. Many of his old students now reentered college.[48]

The town of Bowdon suffered a disastrous fire in February, 1887, when five stores in the heart of the town were destroyed. Except for gallant action by the bucket brigade, the entire business section would have perished. The town was slow to recover from this catastrophe. Five years later a visitor noted "the sleepy appearance and primitive style" of the place but lauded the hospitality of the people. By 1900 Bowdon had five general stores, two drug stores, three groceries, and a combination furniture and undertaking establishment. Despite their setbacks, Bowdon's citizens continued to sustain their college. Even during the depression of the early 1890s, a new two-story college building was planned. Constructed of brick, it was completed in 1900 under the leadership of William D. Lovvorn, who had moved to Bowdon from Alabama in 1878. In a quarter of a century he is said to have made a total contribution of $100,000 to the college.[49]

Sixteen miles north of Bowdon, on the Tallapoosa River near the Alabama line, was the town of Tallapoosa. It was located in the extreme northwestern corner of what was originally Carroll County. While the settlement was one of the first within the original limits of the county, it did not begin to thrive until 1884 when the Georgia Pacific Railroad, connecting Atlanta with Birmingham, laid its tracks about three-fourths of a mile south of the town. Here the new town of Tallapoosa was born. It had grown to 400 people by 1887, at which time it became a boom town under the aegis of the Georgia-Alabama Investment and Development Company. Incorporated under Alabama laws and with a paid-in capital of $4.5 million, this company was headed by Benjamin F. Butler, a nationally known Massachusetts politician, with Robert L. Spencer of Connecticut as promoter. The company conducted offices in New York, Boston, Philadelphia, and Chicago, as well as in Tallapoosa. Characteristic of the gilded age, the company's published brochures promised to double one's investment in six months.[50]

The corporation acquired 8,000 "city-lots" covering more than 2,000 acres in and adjacent to Tallapoosa. It also possessed 2,458 acres of "valuable mineral land" in the vicinity, and it held stock in the Georgia, Tennessee and Illinois Railroad, which was a prospective builder of a north-south rail line to intersect with the Georgia Pacific Railroad at Tallapoosa. It also owned an iron furnace and a glass works in the town for the manufacture of "Flint Glass Flasks and Prescription Ware." The avowed purpose of the company was to develop its large interests at Tallapoosa and to build there a sprawling and prosperous manufacturing city, as well as to make it a popular resort center.[51]

For a time efforts to make Tallapoosa a second Birmingham seemed to promise some success. Its brochure, circulated throughout the United States, not only claimed that the town was located in a section rich in iron ore, but it also was in a rich gold-bearing region. The name, Tallapoosa, it claimed, meant "Golden River" in the language of the Cherokees. The town possessed an excellent climate for winter and summer, good mineral water, and abundant agricultural resources. One of the town's four hostels was the Lithia Springs Hotel, completed in 1892 at a cost of $100,000. It was a frame structure containing a large dining room and ballroom, 130 bedrooms, steam heat, electric lights, and an elevator. At that time the town boasted a water works system, glass works, foundry and machine shops, cabinet, lumber and sash mills, a chemical manufacturing plant, a wagon factory, brick plant, an overall and hosiery mill, and a number of other small enterprises. The Camille Gold Mine, situated two miles south of the city, was equipped with modern stamp mills. The Farmers and Miners Bank was capitalized at $100,000. There were two newspapers.

In 1892, Tallapoosa claimed a population of nearly 3,000 people, "two-thirds of whom had moved there from northern states." The town was embellished with many neat and newly painted houses, built in a modified Gothic style. It boasted "no rough or objectionable elements," no saloons, and "no unreasonable laws to oppress the working man." A New England-style clambake was held there in April, 1890, which probably was the first occasion of this nature ever held in the South.[52]

The Tallapoosa enterprise was widely advertised in national newspapers. The *Boston Post* and the *Hartford Times,* each in an editorial, compared its rapid growth to that of Birmingham. Henry W. Grady in the *Atlanta Constitution* said that there seemed to be nothing of the fictitious boom about Tallapoosa. "It rests on a solid basis and is having a solid growth," he concluded.[53]

Tallapoosa's rapid growth did not rest on a sound economic basis, however. By the fall of 1892 the Georgia-Alabama Investment Company, and the Farmers and Miners Bank which it controlled, were in the hands of receivers. The company was an early victim of the depression of 1893, which proved to be the most severe panic in the history of the United States up to that time. During the next four years, thousands of business firms throughout the country, including banks and railroads, went into receivership. Armies of unemployed tramped about looking for jobs. Expansion of railroads and the production of industry and agriculture had gone far beyond the country's consumption capacity. Money borrowed on over-evaluated property could not now be repaid, and there was a general collapse of the financial structure.

Carroll County felt this depression in both its commercial and agricultural life, although such a depression was not fatal to an agricultural economy. The price of cotton had ranged from nine to eleven cents between 1877 and 1892, when the price fell to less than nine cents. In the following year it drooped still further. Corn was seventy-five cents and meal was eighty cents a bushel. The year 1893 was not only a year of low prices but also one of short crops as well. Farmers who could pay their taxes and live from a subsistence agricultural program were little affected. As a result, large cotton planters suffered more than small farmers. William D. Lovvorn of Bowdon sold eight bales of cotton for money to pay his 1893 taxes, but he was still short of his tax bill by fifty dollars.[54]

In the years from 1865 to the depression of 1893 many Carroll County families moved to other states, largely to Alabama, Mississippi, and Texas. The state receiving the largest number of these families was Alabama, although Texas was not far behind. Alabama was the new home of Benjamin M. Long. In his adopted state he became the leading Republican party organizer in Walker County and later became the nominee for governor of Alabama on the Republican ticket. Thomas Bonner sold his farm just west of Carrollton soon after the Civil War and moved to Alabama, settling in Clay County near Ashland, where he died in 1881. William B. W. D. Huff sold his farm at Lineville to F. M. Black in the early 1890s and moved for a short period to north Alabama near Cullman.[55]

Unlike the earlier migration to Texas, the postwar migration to this state often was accomplished by traveling at reduced rates on an "immigrant train," composed of freight cars equipped to carry several families and all their belongings, including food for consumption while en route. The train stopped on a side-track at intervals to permit cooking on an open campfire. Such journeys to Texas were taken by numerous Carroll families in the 1880s and the 1890s. These families seldom moved singly to new homes in the West but nearly always to communities where former neighbors or their own relatives had already settled.[56] Sometimes a group of former neighbors and relatives settled simultaneously in the same Texas community. This pattern of Western settlement is aptly illustrated in the history of Rusk County, Texas, and in the history of counties adjoining it. This general area was a popular destination for Carroll families who moved westward after the Civil War. As early as 1847 Jiles S. Boggess moved to this area, where members of his son's family (Ahaz J. Boggess) followed him. Caleb Jackson Garrison, son of James F. and Abigail Bonner Garrison, moved to this Texas community in 1851; Caleb became a merchant, planter, and lawyer, and he represented his county in the Texas Senate. His second marriage was to the widow of Jiles Boggess. In 1866 the remainder of the James F. Garrison family moved from Carroll to Rusk County in a forty-six-day journey by covered wagon. In 1874 Patterson G. and Mary Ann Curtis Garrison left Carrollton for Rusk County. In January, 1880, Andrew J. Garrison resigned from the city council and departed for Cleburne, Texas.

Perhaps the first of Carroll's native sons to achieve distinction in academic life and scholarship was George Pierce Garrison, a son of Patterson G. Garrison. Born in Carrollton in 1853, the younger Garrison attended the Carrollton Masonic Institute and later entered Sewanee College in Tennessee. He taught school in Rusk County for five years and then attended the University of Edinburgh, from 1879 to 1881. He received a Ph.D. degree from the University of Chicago in 1896. Earlier he had risen to the chairmanship of the Department of History at the University of Texas, where he became a noted author of books on the history of Texas and the Southwest. Garrison Hall, the seat of the History Department on the campus of the university, was named as a memorial to this famous historian.[57]

Not all of these transplanted Georgians found Texas and the Southwest to their liking. Samuel E. Grow, who moved to Hillsboro in 1880, remained less than two years in Texas. On returning to Carrollton he claimed that he had witnessed more funerals there than in five years in Carroll County. William Mobley, writing from McDade, reported three men lynched and three killed in gunfights during Christmas of 1884. There was a tradition in Carroll that all who left the county would eventually return, if only for a brief visit. The columns of the local paper provide ample testimony to this tradition. Jiles Boggess III (son of Ahaz) who had moved from Texas to Modesto, California, returned to Carrollton for a visit in the summer of 1883. The *Carroll County Times* noted in June, 1888, that one of the younger Garrison boys visited Carrollton on his way to Henderson, Texas, from the University of Virginia where he had studied law.[58] In December, 1883, several wagonloads of these Texas immigrants returned together, including the family of J. K. Rooker, his two sons-in-law, and a widowed sister with two children. One of these claimed that he had drunk no good water since leaving Carroll County. Emaciated and disillusioned, he was seeking the restoration of both his health and his spirit in his native Georgia hills.[59]

VII

Social Life in the Postwar Period, 1870–1900

IN the last decade of the nineteenth century, life in Carroll County still bore many fundamental differences from that of the old cotton belt of Middle Georgia. Plantation agriculture in the older area produced a somewhat stratified society, but there was little evidence of this process west of the Chattahoochee. Here there were fewer Negroes, fewer tenant farmers, and a greater reliance upon subsistence agriculture than in the traditional cotton belt. Among many observers who noted this difference was the editor of the *Macon Telegraph*. After a visit to Carrollton in 1889 he wrote that the town was "magnificently located in the center of a white man's country" and its people were "sturdy, hard-working, tillers of the soil." The area was "divided up into small farms, often not exceeding fifty acres in extent, and rarely reaching 200 acres," he wrote.[1]

The rural pattern of life was everywhere predominant. Even in the county seat nearly every resident had a milk cow, a flock of poultry, and a kitchen garden. In the late fall they observed hog-killing time with as much enthusiasm as full-time farmers. John W. Stewart operated a farm just off South Street, which had on it one of the finest vineyards in the county. The more affluent families had a horse and buggy, although ox carts were common until well into the next century. When rural families left home for an overnight visit they often were seen with their milk cow tied to the back of the wagon, followed by a hound dog. Horseback riding was still a common mode of travel only for the more affluent members of the community, and horse-racing was a popular sport.[2] The Oak Lawn Driving Club, chartered in 1890 by the Kingsburys and several others, was among the earliest social organizations in the county.[3]

Bicycles were just coming into vogue in the 1890s. R. Lee Sharpe and Humber Cheney were early bicycle enthusiasts and they formed a club to encourage this sport. On a bicycle trip from Carrollton to Villa Rica in 1892, Sharpe reported encountering several people who had not seen such a conveyance before. These early bicycles had a front wheel more than four feet in diameter to which pedals were attached. The rider sat above this wheel some sixty inches from the ground. The rear wheel, which held the tail, was so small as often to become hidden from view by the ruts and gullies which traversed the road bed. These strange contraptions, like the automobile of the next decade, often frightened horses and caused hard feelings. Once on a bicycle trip to West Point, Lee Sharpe arrived at Franklin just at nightfall. He reported seeing many Negroes fleeing to their cabins as he pedaled down the road. The next day the Negroes reported having seen the devil with a long tail going toward Franklin in the twilight.[4]

Carrollton was said to be the horse-trading center for western Georgia.[5] Since the county's organization, "First Tuesday" had been the traditional trading day on which hotels and restaurants did a thriving business. The day was marked by large gatherings in the wagon yards, where farmers indulged their wits, not only in every form of trade and barter, but in swapping yarns as well. Spectators were known to follow their favorite trader from one stall to the other to observe his techniques. One farmer in August, 1877, was said to have ridden a thirty-dollar mule into the "bone orchard," and by nightfall, after eight transactions, he had parleyed this mule into a horse worth seventy-five dollars and a hundred dollars in cash.[6]

Other amusements and social diversions possessed a distinct rural flavor. Wild game was still plentiful and its pursuit was a sport enjoyed by the old and the young. As late as 1880 Haralson County was the scene of numerous deer-hunting expeditions.[7] A fox hunt along Shadinger's Ridge in January, 1878, was participated in by thirty-nine men and as many dogs. Jesse Wood, living five miles north of Carrollton, killed fifteen wild turkeys during the season of 1873, and such sport continued into the 1890s.[8] An occasional bald eagle and a wild catamount could still be found. Quail sold on the streets of Carrollton for five cents each, and the trade was brisk. As late as 1890 the Little Tallapoosa swamps near Simonton's Mill were said to be full of wildcats, and that stream abounded in carp and speckled catfish. Rattlesnakes and highland moccasins also were plentiful.[9] Fur-bearing animals, including beaver, muskrat, otter, and mink, might still be trapped and their furs marketed to add a little cash to the farmer's income. J. H. Garner of the Villa Rica community was said to be the champion trapper in the county. Albert F. Sharp's store on Rome Street was the principal market for animal skins and furs.[10]

Hunters used old fashioned muzzle-loaders until about 1880, when the new breech-loading gun was introduced. Its brass shells could be reloaded with powder and re-fused for indefinite use. In 1876 a hunting group formed a club which purchased several of these new weapons. A shooting gallery was set up on Newnan Street where men gathered to improve their marksmanship. For several years an annual contest determined the "champion shootist." [11]

Christmas celebrations took various forms, many of which had little religious significance. Perhaps the most sophisticated mode of observing the occasion was a community Christmas tree, a custom which began after the war. Such an occasion held at each of two of the Carrollton churches in 1886 was typical. The assembled crowd sang Christmas carols around a tree loaded with presents. The Methodists were said to have assembled gifts "estimated as worth $250," and it was claimed that the Baptists outdid their rivals in this matter.[12] At Whitesburg a similar occasion was held in the two principal churches. Santa Claus delivered the presents, said the report, "with as much rural dignity as the varigated costume which he labored on the inside of could afford. . . ." The remainder of the day the men amused themselves with egg-nog, egg-flips, and Tom-and-Jerry. Notwithstanding all this, wrote an observer, "there were young men enough whose mental equilibrium remained unshaken to join the young ladies in the accustomed tea parties." At night young men serenaded houses with three familiar tunes, "Obediah," "The Miller's Blue Dog," and "Sandy's Mill." [13]

In some of the more rural communities these celebrations became extremely spirited and sometimes were accompanied with rowdy behavior. At Turkey Creek the young men turned out for an evening serenade "with guns, bells, bugles, horns, shells and [with] every other imaginable instrument [they] tramped from house to house at breakneck speed and awoke everyone in the district." [14] The boys at Roopville enjoyed "a lighted kerosene ball throwing" on the school campus. Christmas at Bowdon in 1892 was said to have been characterized by "an overflow of blind tiger tanglefoot," even some members of the church were said to "take license to get drunk and curse." [15]

Dancing was indulged in only by the more sophisticated. In the early 1870s, the courthouse at Carrollton was the scene of a number of Christmas dances. Dancing in this period was called "swinging the calico" and "pulling freight," which suggests that the more dignified Austrian waltz had not yet been introduced to Carrollton's younger set.[16] However, in 1889, one Professor Bush announced the opening of a dancing school at Croft's Hall, where he promised to teach all the latest dances and guaranteed perfect satisfaction to "a class of Ladies, Misses, and Masters." [17]

Religious groups usually condemned dancing in any form, and this type of social activity was unpopular in many rural communities. After a Sunday school picnic at Old Camp Methodist Church in May, 1880, a group of young people collected at Simonton's Mill to spend the remainder of the afternoon enjoying the coolness of a beautiful grove near the millpond. Neighbors got the impression that the miller, Gaines W. Lovvorn, had given a dance in his millhouse, and they were greatly offended. Apparently feeling that both his reputation and his business would suffer, the miller sent a hurried explanation to the local paper. There was no dancing in the millhouse, he explained. "One set was danced on the bridge but I did not consider I had any authority whatever to stop them from dancing there," he wrote.[18]

Entertainment at parties and social gatherings of young people usually consisted of playing games. Parlor games most common were Stealing Partners, Fishing for Love, Old Sister Phoebe, Rain and Hail, and Cold Stormy Weather.[19] Weddings generally were held at the bride's house and they were simple affairs. However, a wedding held in Carrollton on October 25, 1889, uniting John Redwine and Etta Roop (daughter of the Reverend William W. Roop), must have been somewhat typical of the more decorous home weddings of that period. Held in the evening at the residence of the bride's parents where about fifty guests were assembled, the ceremony was followed by an elegant supper. "The presents were numerous and costly," wrote the editor of the *Free Press* in a column which listed in detail a total of thirty-eight presents and their donors. These included "a $10.00 bill by Mr. and Mrs. Henry O. Roop, a $10 gold piece by Appleton Mandeville, a Smyrna rug by Mr. and Mrs. J. A. McCord . . . and a silver butter dish by Sanford T. Kingsbury. . . ." [20]

In that age of limited transportation, an occasional road show visited the larger towns situated along the rail lines. One of these which appeared in Carrollton in March, 1876, was described as "a one-horse affair, a regular penny catcher." The exhibitor claimed to have an Egyptian mummy, the daughter of a pharoah. "Those who examined it claimed it was nothing but a patched up skeleton," said one.[21] In 1889, James Moore, an erstwhile barkeeper, had opened an opera house fitted with special chairs. This establishment attracted such itinerant stars as "Boseo, the Prince of Magicians," who opened an engagement in March, 1890.[22]

For many years it had been a custom in various communities to have an annual barbecue after "laying by" the crops, at which time there was a lull in farming activities. Such a custom was begun before the war by Captain Sharp and continued by his sons Hiram and George. At one of these affairs held at Sharp's schoolhouse, five miles north of Carrollton, on August 1, 1872, an estimated twelve hundred people were present.[23]

This was also the day of music conventions, frequent and well-attended meetings of Masonic groups, agricultural clubs, literary and debating societies, and sewing clubs. Log-rollings, corn-shuckings, and quilting parties were common.

Just west of Carrollton in the vicinity of what later became the campus of West Georgia College was a community called West End which had its origin in a literary club formed in 1891 at the Bluford A. Sharp residence. In addition to a literary club, the community boasted of "two flourishing stores," a schoolhouse, and a Sunday school at Old Camp Methodist Church. Charles P. and James H. Turner were engaged in the nursery business there in 1891. Near their establishment at the forks of the Bowdon and Tyus roads, where Croxton's raiders had camped one fateful night in April, 1865, was now a favorite campground for gypsies.[24]

A number of rural social clubs known as granges were organized after the Civil War and they provided one of the earliest formal means of social diversion for rural people. They were short-lived, but reunions of Confederate veterans soon filled the social void left by their demise. The veterans' reunion got under way during the 1880s, and throughout the succeeding four decades these annual affairs provided a happy variation from the drab routine of agricultural life. The first reunion of Company F, Cobb's Legion, was held at Fairplay courtground in August, 1884, where Captain W. F. S. Powell led the company off to war twenty-three years earlier. During the same year, Captain Walker's company held a reunion at the Goshen Masonic lodge south of Roopville and invited Captain James R. Thomasson's company, "the County Line Rangers," to join them.[25] In the following year, the first reunion of Company K, Thirty-fourth Georgia Regiment, was held at old Salem Church where the company had been organized at the beginning of the war. The Kingsbury farm was the scene of the reunion of companies B and L of the Tenth Georgia Cavalry on June 16, 1891.[26]

The 1886 reunion of Company K of the Thirty-fourth Georgia Regiment, held at Roopville, was typical of these occasions. Any person in the community who was interested in attending was invited to do so, provided that he bring a basket dinner. In the morning a company drill was held, commanded by the senior surviving officer. After this there was a prayer, and then addresses by Judge Sampson W. Harris, Frank S. Loftin, and E. A. Walder. After a sumptuous dinner, there was music by the company musicians and any others who might care to join them. At the 1889 meeting of Company K, held at Caney Head Church near Rockalo, only twenty survivors were present, including two officers, Lieutenant J. A. Hollingsworth and Orderly Sergeant Joseph Atkinson. Yet there was a large crowd in attendance. "Not a single member of the rough and uncouth class who usually thrust themselves upon such gatherings was to be seen," wrote an observer.[27]

The only regimental reunion ever organized at Carrollton was that of the Seventh Georgia Regiment, held at Chandler's Park (later the City Park) on July 20, 1889. Made up of companies from Carroll, Cobb, Coweta, DeKalb, Fulton, and Paulding counties, this regiment had one of the largest and best-organized veterans associations in the South. Despite the fact that it had served from Manassas to Appomattox and had fought with Longstreet's Corps in the bloody battle of Chickamauga, there were three hundred survivors in 1889.[28] Ten thousand people crowded into Chandler's Park for a public barbecue to which all citizens in Carrollton had been asked to contribute. The town had just organized a brass band which, resplendent in new uniforms, was ready for the occasion.[29] But the moving elegance of the principal speaker, Governor John B. Gordon, must have aroused the wrath of Jupiter Pluvius. As he closed his address and dinner was announced, the heavens opened one of the heaviest downpours of the summer. The governor was hurried off to a nearby shelter where he partook of barbecue, but the spread dinner consisting of meat, bread, pies, pickles, and cakes was snatched by guests running for cover. A lucky few who had brought their umbrellas stood by and devoured. Others got under the table and ate what they could. "Those gowns of snowy white which but a few moments ago enveloped the fair forms of our lovely daughters hung like bathing suits, dripping, dank and dragglings," wrote an eye-witness. "The skirts [were] bespotted with mud . . . and bodies blotched with varigated stains of dyestuffs, rinsed by the rain from the many-colored ribbons [and the] flowers and feathers that erstwhile adorned their summer hats." [30] Thus ended in near disaster the most ambitious public occasion the people of Carrollton had ever planned.

Modern baseball made its debut in the community during the 1870s, at which time the game was played only in the more sophisticated circles. The old antebellum game of town ball now became a misnomer, for it came to be played only in the rural countryside where it continued until well into the following century. Town ball was usually played with a sphere of India rubber wrapped with stocking yarn and sometimes covered with genuine buckskin. The bats consisted of wide paddles similar to "battling sticks" used in the home laundry of clothing. Two players chose sides, and there was no limit to the number of players on each team. One of the two who chose the teams spat on one side of the paddle and before throwing it into the air would ask the other to call "wet or dry." If he called the fall correctly he would get first choice of a teammate. In the same manner the offensive team of the first inning was chosen. In the process of the game, a ball caught on the bounce was an "out." Every player was a fielder, there being no basemen. A runner was put out by tapping or by hitting him with a thrown ball while he was off the bases.[31] Agility in dodging such balls was a fundamental skill in this game. The game might run on interminably.

Baseball demanded more refined techniques and greater skill than town ball, and it came to be played by two teams of only nine men each. This encouraged practice, drill, and the careful selection of the most skilled performers. One of the earliest baseball games of record in Carrollton took place in May, 1877, between two local clubs called the Russian Bears and the Athletes. The game was witnessed by a large crowd and resulted in a 46 to 24 victory of the Athletes over the Bears. However, the Bears won the next two games of a three-game series, the score in the final game being 23 to 12.[32]

By 1884 matches were being played between organized teams representing different communities. In July of that year a team from Hogansville challenged the Carrollton team in a game played in Newnan in which the Carrollton team won 40 to 24.[33] Games were also played that season against teams from Newnan and Villa Rica. The second victory over Villa Rica was played on a Wednesday at a field located near the depot, and all businesses in the town suspended for the occasion. At the close of the eighth inning the score stood 15 to 16, but the game ended with an 18 to 19 victory for Carrollton. Olin Johnson was accorded a hero's honors when he brought in two runs in the last half of the ninth inning.[34] Occasionally these games ended in a bloody fight, as was the case at Villa Rica in August, 1890. Bats were swung and blood flowed freely, causing the participants to be fined in Mayor Hodnett's court for disorderly conduct in public.[35]

Disorderly conduct, even violence and murder, were not unusual for Carroll County in the 1880s and 1890s. Attendance upon Superior Court trials and viewing an occasional public hanging were acceptable social diversions for men, although women were always among the spectators. The most sensational murder in the community's annals occurred in Heard County near the Carroll line in 1884. This crime involved John Smith, a notorious character who lived south of Roopville. Smith's career as a desperado began in 1876, when he was twenty-three. He and a cousin, John Craven, became involved in a Christmas brawl at the house of Green Huckeba, at Blue Shin in Heard County. Smith's companion, Craven, was stabbed to death by Robert Huckeba, an act later adjudged as justifiable homicide.[36] A feud between the Huckeba family and their relations on one hand, and the Craven and Smith families on the other, increased in intensity over the ensuing years. Smith was said to have killed a number of men during this period and he became a terror to his community.[37] In January, 1884, the family feud erupted in a second brawl. Encountering Robert Huckeba in the woods near Black Jack Mountain, John Smith dismounted from his horse and fired several shots at him without warning. However, none of the shots was fatal.[38] A year later Smith, his brother An, and A. S. King came to Samuel Barker's farmhouse near the Carroll-Head line. With drawn pistol, Smith cursed Barker and his wife, struck the former a blow, and then shot him to death in the presence of three eye-witnesses. The crime was called "the most willful and cold-blooded murder that ever disgraced the annals of local history." [39]

For several days Smith was hunted by a posse of several hundred men, and finally he was captured three miles south of Roopville on a ruse organized by Sheriff James Hewitt and his deputy, John Skipper. Secreted for a brief period at the home of John Roop, he later was brought to the Carrollton jail. Because of Smith's numerous and prominent connections in Heard County, where he was indicted, it was difficult to obtain a qualified jury to try him. However, after a trial lasting three days, in January, 1886, he was sentenced to be hanged.[40]

Smith's execution did not take place until June of the following year. In the meantime desperate efforts were made to have his sentence commuted, and once Governor John B. Gordon granted him a brief respite from death. While languishing in jail, he was married to Mit Levens, who had been threatened with prosecution on a charge involving the illegality of their former relationship. Smith had been married on two previous occasions and was the father of two children. The significant aspect of his execution was its bizarre character as a public spectacle. "A good many Carrolltonians speak of going down to the John Smith hanging at Franklin today," wrote the editor of the *Free Press* on June 17. Later the paper carried several columns captioned "Heard's Terror John W. Smith Hangs in Presence of 3,000 People." [41]

The *Free Press* did not omit a single gruesome detail of the execution, including events immediately preceding and following it. Before taking Smith from the jail to the gallows, which had been erected a half-mile away, Sheriff John Lipscomb had placed a hangman's noose around the condemned man's neck. "The crowd rushed through the town, through the woods, down the hill like a sweeping mighty avalanche," wrote an eye-witness. During the divine service preceding the execution, men and boys climbed trees with shouts and laughter. In his remarks to the crowd, the weeping prisoner proclaimed his innocence. In a somewhat contradictory statement, he attributed his conviction to lies and his own downfall to whiskey. He pleaded with the sheriff not to proceed with the execution. The sheriff bade him good-by three times before springing the trap. The rope was afterward torn into thousands of pieces by souvenir seekers. Smith's body was brought under guard to Roopville where it was interred in the James D. Green cemetery, two miles north of that village.[42]

Public executions in this period apparently offered no deterrent to crimes of violence and murder. The 1890 decade was perhaps the most lawless in Carroll's postwar history. In 1893 alone, a year of depression and emerging Populist politics, two people were cut to death in fights, two others were shot in brawls, and a few robberies were committed. Three murder cases were tried in the new courthouse during the first year of its use. "The day is not far distant when Carroll County can furnish some Rube Barrows, Jesse James [*sic*] and brutish outlaws," said one.[43]

An almost universal idea prevailed in this period that all crime was somehow the result of intoxicating liquor. As already noted, prohibition had its beginning in the county just before the Civil War when its sale was forbidden in the vicinity of Bowdon College. After the slaves were freed, drunken Negroes were thought to be a special menace to white women. During the 1870s and 1880s numerous communities throughout the state obtained special legislation outlawing liquor and saloons within a restricted area. Such an act was passed in February, 1876, which prohibited the sale of whiskey within the corporate limit of Carrollton, Whitesburg, Villa Rica, and Bowdon.[44] Apparently thinking that the law applied only to wholesale dealers, the mayor and council at Carrollton then placed a license fee of a thousand dollars on retailers of whiskey in any amount under one gallon. As a result, all barrooms were closed on the first of March. One barkeeper, James Moore, paid the fee on March 10 and reopened his establishment.[45]

After some equivocation, the state law was interpreted in such a way that Moore's grog shop was again closed on April 14, thus becoming the last of Carrollton's barrooms. In the period which followed, whiskey dealers sprang up on the outskirts of the town where they did a lively business.[46] In 1877 the sale of liquor was prohibited in certain other communities, including a four-mile radius around Villa Rica, Old Bethel, and Pleasant Grove churches in the Sixth District.[47] A legislative act of 1885 made prohibition possible by a countywide local option vote, after which the entire county became officially dry. However, actual distillation was not forbidden in the county until 1893, after which illicit manufacture became widespread throughout the area. Certain communities, notably in the extreme western and in the eastern part of the county, appeared to harbor a great majority of these illegal operations. These were called "blockade stills" and "blind tigers."[48] One man reported three of these stills operating within a mile of his house.

To ameliorate such a situation, church-going people and religious leaders carried on a steady crusade for temperance. "Pistol toting and whiskey drinking are twin children of darkness, [and are] off-springs of evil, and no clean, brave, law abiding person will tolerate them," was the general theme of these crusades.[49] In eulogizing Henry Huff who, in February, 1891, was lying ill at his home in the Providence community south of Roopville, a neighbor reported: "Henry is a good boy he never drinks no whiskey, smokes nor chews no tobacco, never cursed an oath in his life, and is a good true Methodist." [50]

Indeed the Methodists, particularly those following the episco-pal form of organization, appear to have been far more decorous in their official attitude and behavior toward these matters than were many other religious groups. Churches with a congregational form of organization, particularly the Primitive Baptists, were least likely to object to strong liquor. Even their clergymen were sometimes known to possess this vice to an intemperate degree.

The non-doctrinal aspects of Methodist worship in this period had little resemblance to the formal and sophisticated air which they bore in the following century. The Reverend John Boykin McGehee was a presiding elder of the LaGrange District of which Carroll's Methodist Episcopal churches (South) were a part, having been de-tached from the Rome District soon after the Civil War. On his first tour of Carroll County, made by horseback, McGehee conducted a quarterly meeting at Bonner's Gold Mine. Here he described "two lovely women" who became infused with what he termed "the old time religion" and forthwith they engaged in an exercise called "the holy dance" which he said was not forbidden by Methodist discipline. At a meeting in Villa Rica a short time later he converted to Metho-dism Samuel C. Candler, then sixty years of age, together with his wife, who was a former Baptist. He betrayed genuine pride in his report of this accomplishment.[51]

The Methodist Church at Carrollton became a station in 1875 when the Rev. J. W. Stipe was its pastor. The church was without a musical instrument until three years later, when Lula Thomasson and Carrie Skinner secured enough subscriptions to acquire an organ. Not to be outdone, the Baptists also acquired an organ.[52] In 1876 the Baptists moved from their Depot Street site into a new frame church building on the corner of Newnan and Dixie streets (in 1907 this building was replaced by a permanent brick struc-ture).[53] This achievement apparently stimulated the Methodists to similar action. In 1881 they acquired the lot on Newnan Street "just east of Robinson's stable" for the site of a new building to replace their original house of worship on Alabama Street. At the same time the pastor of the Colored Methodist Church, Archie Samuels, who was a skilled craftsman, built a small structure for his flock on Newnan Street "beyond the Culpepper place." Later this congregation acquired the old Methodist property on Alabama Street.[54]

The energy and zeal back of the movement for a new Methodist building was supplied by the Reverend James Wideman Lee. He began this movement in April, 1879, securing an initial fifteen hundred dollars. His original plan was to erect a building costing about two thousand dollars on the recently abandoned jail lot on Alabama Street near the Square, which the owners offered to sell at cost. However, the enthusiastic response to Lee's appeals resulted in the completion of a more costly structure at what then seemed to be the most desirable location in Carrollton. This was a lot near the Square at the corner of Tanner and Newnan streets. This structure served the Methodists until 1904, when a masonry building replaced it. The older building was removed to Hulett.[55]

Lee moved to Dalton in December, 1880, before the new building was completed. He was one of the better known and resourceful ministers in the North Georgia Conference during this period. His greatest claim to historical recognition perhaps is the fact that he was the father of Ivy Ledbetter Lee who, after graduating from Princeton in 1898, became the advisor in public relations to John D. Rockefeller, Bethlehem Steel Corporation, and other large industrial interests. For a period he was a member of Rockefeller's personal advisory staff. Ivy Lee is said to have persuaded his famous employer to inaugurate various philantrophic enterprises, partly as a means of giving him a better public image and to direct the attention of Rockefeller's critics away from his controversial business methods.[56]

The Methodist churches in Carroll County in 1885 numbered nineteen, although ten of these were not affiliated with the Southern branch of that church. The "Northern Methodists" (the Methodist Episcopal Church) had organizations at Bowdon, Mt. Zion, Corinth, Bethel, Ebenezer, and Friendship, while there were Methodist Protestant churches at Carrollton, Antioch, Bowdon, Smith's Chapel, and Harmony. One of the more notable Methodist Congregational churches was Goshen, near Roopville. There was a total of thirty-three Baptist churches in the county, ten of which were of the

Primitive Baptist group. Presbyterian churches had been established only at Carrollton, Bowenville and Villa Rica. There were four Christian churches in the county, and a Lutheran Church called Beth Eden had been established near Clem. Carrollton at this time had a Methodist Episcopal Church (South) and a Methodist Protestant Church, and also a Presbyterian Church and a Missionary Baptist Church.[57]

The Baptists were now the most numerous group, both in Carrollton and throughout the county. For a brief period during the Civil War the Carrollton Baptist Church was a member of the Arbacoochee Association centering in eastern Alabama, near the Carroll line. During this period S. G. Jenkins and George D. Tumlin served as pastors. The Carrollton Baptist Association was formed in October, 1874, at a meeting held in the Masonic Institute. At that time there were seventeen churches in the association, representing a membership of 1,363.[58] By 1877 the number had grown to twenty-one churches, only fifteen of which were within Carroll County. These were at Carrollton, Bowdon, Whitesburg, Indian Creek, Eden, Bethesda, Pleasant Grove, New Lebanon, Mount Olive, Mount Pleasant, Cross Plains, Macedonia, Bethel, and Abilene. Four of the total were in Douglas County, and one each was in Heard and Coweta counties. The total financial support given to the association at this time was less than a hundred dollars. Yellow Dirt in Heard County, Oak Grove, and Pleasant View were added in 1877. The Yellow Dirt congregation wavered between the Missionary and the Primitive affiliation and finally withdrew from the Carrollton Association.[59]

By 1890 the Carrollton Association had grown to thirty-four churches, including at least one church in all counties adjoining Carroll except Paulding. The membership in each church ranged from twenty-three to one hundred. Cross Plains had 104 members; Bethesda, 131; Pleasant View, 132; Bowdon, 188; and Carrollton, 274.[60] It became necessary at this time to divide the association into three districts.

The Baptists were also most numerous among Negro churchmen, although their churches were not members of the Carrollton Association. The majority of the Negro members of the Carrollton Baptist Church did not move their membership until 1873. At this time however, at least two Negroes, Howard Wells and Lizzie Stilman, continued their membership in the original church. It is not known at what date the Carroll County churches became completely segregated. As late as 1869 there were sixteen Negro members of the old Concord Methodist Church and one of these, Larkin Walker, was a local minister.[61] The colored Baptist Church of Carrollton was officially established in 1894 when a corporate charter was granted.

The record of the Baptists' finances indicates that they were slow to recover from the Civil War, and it may be assumed that other churches in the area had a similar experience. In 1877, when J. A. Wynn was pastor, the Carrollton Baptist Church had a membership of 157 and nothing was given that year either to home or to foreign missions. When William W. Roop succeeded Wynn as pastor in 1879 there was some improvement in finances. By the time that Isaac P. Cheney took over ten years later, the annual contribution to missions reached $196.00 and membership had grown to 274.

An unfortunate schism appeared among the Carrollton Baptists during the latter part of the 1890s. A controversy which developed over J. C. Wingo's retention as pastor resulted in the withdrawal of a number of persons from the congregation and the organization of the Central Baptist Church (later known as the Tabernacle).[62] This church was organized in December, 1899, with an original membership of thirteen. William W. Roop was elected pastor of the new congregation, which position he held until 1907. During these years worship was conducted in a building on the east side of Tanner Street.[63] More conservative in outlook than the group from which they had seceded, the "Central Baptists" made a strong appeal to members of their faith who moved to Carrollton from surrounding rural areas. As the town expanded from the inflow of rural people, the new church grew both in membership and in financial resources and it ultimately became the largest religious group in the county.

The earliest Presbyterian Church established in the general area of old Carroll was organized at Providence in the southeastern corner of Heard County in November, 1831. Discontinued in 1836, it was replaced by a church at Franklin, which continued until 1843. In the following year appeared the third church of this denomination in Heard County, at Brainard, located in the southwest corner of the county. This church was dissolved in 1882. In the meantime, on December 18, 1841, the Carrollton Presbyterian Church was organized with Paschal Grow and Horace Smith as ruling elders, and six other charter members.[64] By 1845 it had added six new members, and in 1860 its membership was only sixteen. Three years before the Civil War the Villa Rica Presbyterian Church was founded. The only other church of this denomination in the county during the nineteenth century was at Bowenville, and it existed from 1873 to 1878.[65] The founder of the Carrollton and Villa Rica churches was the Reverend Benjamin Dupre, who lived at Powder Springs on the road leading to Villa Rica and Carrollton, where he often visited and held services

At the time of Carroll County's organization, this area was part of the Hopewell Presbytery, which embraced all of the northern half of Georgia west of the Ocmulgee River, including the Cherokee country.[66] In 1833 this presbytery was divided along the original northern boundary of Carroll County. The southern division, of which Carroll County was now a part, was known first as Good Hope, then later as the Flint River Presbytery. Although its official southern limits extended to the Florida line, all of its twenty-five churches were located north of Columbus. The Georgia Presbytery at this time embraced the older section of the state east of the line of the Ocmulgee River. In 1866 the Atlanta Presbytery was formed. It included the northern third of the Flint River Presbytery. The new presbytery began at the old Cherokee-Creek boundary along the northern border of Carroll County but extended northward to include the area around Atlanta and Decatur, and southward to West Point. Its eastern boundary was the Ocmulgee River.[67]

The Carrollton Presbyterian Church remained small in membership throughout the remainder of the nineteenth century, but it appeared to enforce rigidly its Calvinistic discipline. Recalcitrant members were prodded into regular church attendance and reproached for "neglect of the various ways of grace and too great conformity to the world." In February, 1880, "Bro. A. J. Laird" was called up on the charge of dancing at his own house. Before the Presbyterians constructed a church building they held their services in the Methodist Church, and at other places. One of their earliest sessions, in August, 1871, was at "the Oak Ridge Sabbath School House." [68] The Presbyterian church structure built by Thomas W. Dimmock in 1875 cost only sixteen hundred dollars, a large part of which was contributed by members of other denominations. There were sixty-eight members in 1875.[69]

William Dimmock was the county's most notable Presbyterian of the early period. Born in Bedfordshire, England, in 1820, he arrived in Carrollton after the Civil War and became an elder in the local church. Becoming interested in Sunday school work, he later dedicated his life to the establishment of Sunday schools of whatever denomination the people in any particular community might choose. He was engaged in this work from 1867 until his death, after which he was succeeded by his son, Thomas Dimmock. He was interested not only in organizing new Sunday schools but in improving existing ones. Meetings were held in such places as school houses, brush arbors, and in one instance a former saloon, and in another an opera house. Many of these enterprises developed later into churches.

It was in connection with this work that Dimmock was licensed first as an exhorter; later, in 1872, he was ordained to the full ministry. He promoted the organization of the Carroll County Sunday School Association in 1876.[70] In August, 1884, delegates from five counties adjacent to Carroll met at Villa Rica and organized the first district Sunday School Association in Georgia, which continued to the end of the century. At the annual convention held at Temple in July, 1896, Carroll was divided into seven Sunday school districts. One convention was held annually in each of these districts in addition to the annual county convention.[71]

At the time of Dimmock's death, on March 19, 1880, he had served for many years as the pastor of the Carrollton and Villa Rica Presbyterian churches. His will stipulated the minute details of his burial vault and his funeral service, including the hymns to be sung and the text to be used. He requested that Methodist and Baptist ministers participate in the function. He was described as an humble, dedicated, and unselfish individual, and it was said that all who knew him were grateful for this privilege. He was succeeded to the pastorship by the Reverend James Stacy of Newnan, who held services at Carrollton on the fourth Sunday of each month.[72]

The religious organization which had the smallest membership in Carrollton during this period was Saint Margaret's Episcopal Church. Saint Margaret's was begun as a mission in 1892. The wife of Thomas B. Slade was the principal founder. A chapel was constructed through popular subscription during the following year, the Slade family making the largest single contribution. Standing on the corner of West Avenue and White Street, the small Gothic frame structure was consecrated on July 15, 1893. It remained an unorganized mission until 1910 and it did not have a resident priest until the early 1950s, when the Reverend Dewey Gable, Jr., became its rector. At this time a new church building was constructed on Newnan Street. The original building on Adamson Avenue was moved to the campus of West Georgia College.[73]

The Lutherans also were a small religious group. Clustered around a community one mile west of Clem, where they erected a chapel called Beth Eden, were several families of German origin, including the families of Arthur Swygert, Olin Blandenberg, the Aderholds, and the Kempsons. The pastor of this church in 1885 was J. A. Julian, who was succeeded in the following year by G. E. Lavender. As late as 1917, David Adam Sox (originally Sachs) was making an effort to keep the Lutheran group together. In that year the last Lutheran service in the county was held in the Christian Church on Newnan Street.

Sox served as pastor for several Lutheran congregations in western Georgia and eastern Alabama, including missions at Haralson, Senoia, and Clem, and at Fruithurst and Muscadine in Alabama. The work of organizing these congregations was originally undertaken by Reverend E. C. Conk. These early Lutheran mission workers, including Sox, were members of the Tennessee Synod, a conservative group which was part of the United Synod of the South. In 1918, about the time of the disappearance of the Lutheran church at Clem, the various Lutheran groups merged to form the United Lutheran Church in America (which in 1962 became the Lutheran Church in America). This reorganization procedure may have contributed to the demise of the Lutheran Church in Carroll County. Other factors were the World War I prejudice against Americans of German birth and the advent of national prohibition, which destroyed the economy of many wine-making families of German origin, particularly those living at Fruithurst and Muscadine.[74]

Members of the Jewish faith were conspicuously absent from the records of the county throughout the entire nineteenth century. Living principally in the larger towns and cities, they shunned agricultural occupations, for Jews were often subject to discrimination in rural communities. A Jewish youth, Jake Mount, was clerking at a store at Trickum (Lowell) in 1876 when he was intimidated and left the community. He offended his neighbors when he attempted courtship with one of the local girls.[75]

Only fifty-one people in Carroll County in 1880 were either foreign-born or of foreign-born parents, but this figure had declined considerably by 1890. Almost half of this group were Irish, among whom were Michael Powers, Bluford Sharp, John Ferrell, and James Robinson. The remainder were English, German, Swedish, and Scotch, in that order.[76] The Irish, most of whom were of

Catholic background, did not have a church of their faith nearer than Atlanta until the early 1890s, when one was established in Haralson County. The Irish were farmers, although there was an occasional well-digger and stonemason among them. Many of them remained apart from any church. In time, some became affiliated with the dominant religious group of the community in which they lived.

The people who remained unchurched were by no means conspicuous because of this fact. At no time in the nineteenth century were more than 40 percent of the people of the county members of any religious group.[77] Ministers were the smallest professional group in 1880, the census of that year enumerating only thirteen in the county. Their average age was forty-three years, higher than that of any other professional category. Milton Cooper, the oldest, was seventy-five; the youngest, John W. Quillian, was twenty-five.

The number of medical practitioners was almost double that of the ministry. There were twenty-four in 1880 whose ages ranged from twenty-two to sixty-five. In this period a doctor could be found in almost every rural community able to sustain a store and a blacksmith shop. In 1881 there were nine "registered practitioners" in Carrollton alone, four in Villa Rica, and three in Whitesburg. Eight others lived in various rural communities. Of these twenty-four physicians, two were admitted to practice by license only, and the remainder were admitted upon presenting to the county clerk a diploma from a medical school. Medical colleges of that day were numerous and of poor quality. Institutions represented by the county's physicians in 1881 were the Reform Medical College of Macon, the Savannah Medical College, the Augusta Medical College, the Atlanta Medical College, the Southern Medical and Botanical College (Macon), and the Nashville Medical College.[78] The course of study in these institutions rarely required more than a year to complete, and there was no internship. The diploma, a few basic drugs, and a willing patient were all that was needed to begin practice. One doctor told the story of a professional associate who practiced in the county with a license originally issued to an Alabamian. Another story has been related of one who presented to the county clerk a paper napkin on which were printed some Chinese words. Claiming that it was a diploma from a Chinese medical school, he was promptly registered.[79] Some medical colleges actually sold diplomas without requiring attendance at classes. In other instances only a token period of study was required. In 1892 Dr. William Cohen Brock spent six weeks at the New York Polyclinic Institute and returned with two diplomas, one covering "diseases of the rectum," and the other covering "female disorders."

One of the better-trained physicians of this period was Dr. J. D. Walker who, before studying at the Atlanta Medical College, earned an academic degree from Mercer University. After two years of practice, somewhat equivalent to an internship, he went to New York for a six-months' course and later studied in Germany. Roy Harris, son of Sampson W. Harris, graduated in 1890 with distinguished honors from the Jefferson Medical College at Philadelphia. W. S. Lyle, son of William Allen Lyle, graduated summa cum laude at Augusta in 1893.[80]

Without doubt there were a number of persons engaged in the practice of medicine who were dedicated men of science, yet there must have been numerous others who looked upon this occupation merely as a convenient source of livelihood. Such appears to have been the case of J. P. Houston, who began his career as a blacksmith in Carrollton soon after the Civil War. He then entered the ministry for a short period, preaching at Tallapoosa. In 1884 he took a short course at one of the medical colleges in Atlanta and then began practice in Cleburne County, Alabama. Isaac P. Cheney reversed this process. He began his career as a physician, but in 1889 he became chaplain of the Georgia House of Representatives from which office he was called to the pastorate of the Carrollton Baptist Church.[81]

Whether one followed a medical career as a means of livelihood or from nobler impulses and dedication, he was not likely to earn more than a modest income. During the 1870s Dr. Isaac Cheney supplemented his income from the practice of medicine by engaging in farming. Dr. James D. Green operated a tanyard at his house two miles north of Roopville. Dr. Frances Marion Brock operated a mercantile establishment at Roopville while waiting for professional calls. Dr. Eugene Thomasson taught school at Bank's schoolhouse (Glenloch) while practicing medicine in that community. Dr. W. J. Hallum, who died of typhoid fever in 1894 at the age of thirty-seven, was able to leave his wife and three children only two thousand dollars from a life insurance policy.[82]

Home remedies and patent medicines were widely used by those who became ill. Turpentine, calomel, and castor oil were the most popular cure-alls. Neither the public nor the medical fraternity seemed to be aware of the lethal possibilities of calomel, a potential mercurial poison. Turpentine was used for the greatest variety of ills—backache, muscular pains, cuts, bruises, pneumonia, colds, and tuberculosis. For some of these ills it was taken internally, and the kidneys paid a heavy toll. Its general popularity stemmed from the fact that it had all the characteristics of an ideal medicine of that period. It was cheap, it smelled strong, it tasted bad, and "it burned like hell." Up to 1911, when Federal narcotics laws became effective, it was possible to buy laudanum, opium, and paregoric from drug shelves without a prescription. Doctors frequently solved their therapeutic riddles by administering one or more of these narcotics.[83]

The common penchant for patent medicines caused many practicing physicians to become apothecaries of a sort and to engage in the manufacture of medicines. The Carrollton drug firm of Hamrick, Crider and Company in 1888 advertised Woolford's Sanitary Lotion as a cure for "Itch, Mange, and Scratches of every kind in 30 minutes." This firm also offered to sell for one dollar "Dr. King's New Discovery" which, it was claimed, would "give relief to consumptives." [84] Reputed cures for cancer were many and varied. Medicine shows often visited the larger communities, sometimes for a week's stand. One of these was the Wizard Oil Medicine Show, which advertised its performance by exhibiting a large tapeworm at the Fitts Drug Store. These shows entertained the people with free performances, after which their prime purpose was to make everyone in the audience feel that he had some deadly disease. They usually succeeded and did a brisk business in the sale of worthless concoctions. The package bore high-sounding labels and spurious testimonials. It was not until 1908 that a federal food and drug law took note of these matters, but even then it did not bring about effective regulation.

Around the turn of the century two corporations were chartered in Carrollton for the manufacture of patent medicines. One of these, the C. W. C. Medicine Company, had a paid-in capital stock of $25,000. The Hitchcock Medicine Company had a paid-in capitalization of $30,000. The charter permitted the company to engage in the "manufacture, compounding, and selling at wholesale and retail, all kinds of drugs, medicine, ointments, extracts, toilets . . . commonly known as drugs. . . ." [85]

If practicing physicians were not gainfully employed, it was not because the people of the community were enjoying unusually good health. Dr. Luna J. Aderhold's books for the year ending September 1, 1885, showed that he had written 3,113 prescriptions for nearly twelve hundred patients, and he had attended forty-nine births.[86] Because of competition from numerous midwives, the standard delivery fee seldom exceeded three dollars, including travel of several miles by buggy or horseback to the patient's bedside. Physicians in this period also pulled teeth at a cost to the patient of twenty-five cents. Competing for this work were a few itinerant tooth-pullers. One of these wore around his neck, as a badge of his occupation, a long necklace made from teeth which he had extracted.

There were 253 deaths reported in Carroll County during 1889. Slightly more than half of these were children under five years of age.[87] Diarrhea took the highest toll, with tuberculosis, pneumonia, and diptheria next in that order. Reported in the summer of 1886 was an unusually large number of "deaths from flux [which was] raging among children and Negroes." There were few cases of typhoid fever for the six years previous to 1883, at which time the disease became epidemic and raged for several years. It began in the early part of the summer and took many lives. There were also numerous cases of malaria.[88] The number of deaths from childbirth was equal to the number who succumbed to cancer, as it was then being diagnosed. A woman's life was indeed hazardous. Old tombstones throughout the county tell this tragic story. William W. and Lucy Awtrey Merrill were parents of sixteen children. Hiram Sharp died in 1877 at the age of 51, but he had already outlived two of his three wives.[89] Jordan Wood of Roopville lived to the age of sixty-two, but he had been married twice and fathered sixteen children. John Bonner, who was married three times, fathered twenty-three children, seventeen of whom survived him. It was little wonder that the enterprising physician desiring to improve both his skill and his income sought a specialty in "female diseases."

The female members of the community were likely to suffer from a wider variety of organic disorders, but the males were the principal victims of accidents. These appear to have been far more numerous in this period than in a later era of automobiles, although not so fatal. Accidents with runaway horses were frequent and they were the most dreaded. Cotton gins, sawmills, and other types of machinery were crude and unprotected against the occurence of accidents. Gin saws often took off arms and fingers, but sawmills were equally hazardous. Boiler explosions were frequent and usually catastrophic in their results. Because there was a strong frontier tradition favoring child labor, accidents bore heavily upon youthful workers. Typical of such accidents was that which caused the death of the fourteen-year-old son of Martin Taylor, in 1894. While he was working the press at Owen's gin near Stripling's Chapel, his coat became caught in a revolving shaft. He was thrown many times against the floor and his body was badly mangled.[90] Perhaps because there were no compensation and liability laws to protect workers, there were also no crusades for installing safety measures, either in the form of improved and protected machinery or in the routine of a worker's movements.

While safety measures did not concern the public mind during this era, there were popular, sporadic crusades against certain vices. These crusades commanded much attention. In the early 1890s the *Free Press* conducted an editorial offensive against cigarette smoking, although cigarette smokers were rare indeed in that age. Tobacco-chewing and snuffing were by far the more popular forms of tobacco consumption. Pipe and cigar smoking were next in order, but only the more affluent addicts could afford the latter. Cigarette smokers were called "cigarette fiends" and the habit was associated with "worminess" and related disorders. "A cigarette fiend was taken ill the other day and died in three hours," ran a story in the local paper. Physicians attributed his death wholly to excessive smoking. "Death and Insanity Lurk in Paper-Wrapped Cigarettes," ran a headline in February, 1892.[91] This crusade against cigarettes was by no means a local one. A state law in 1891 forbade the sale of cigarettes to minors, but no curbs were placed on the sale of other forms of tobacco.

Such crusades were typical of the 1890 decade. Campaigns were launched against liquor, railroad monopoly, and corruption in politics and business. These activities were paralleled by an expanding interest in public education, prison reform, and economic democracy. In isolated rural areas such as Carroll County, education was looked upon as the key to social and economic well-being. It would provide farm youth with urban skills and thus free him from a life of rural toil.

VIII

Postwar Political Developments

THE homogeneous character of a frontier people delayed the development of class conflicts until well into the 1880s. Conflicts originating in a developing class consciousness of a rural people began to take form in the community's political life by 1890. The long period of agricultural depression following the war was also one characterized by railroad expansion, industrial development, the growth of the towns, and relative urban prosperity. Many farmers now sensed a degree of economic exploitation by urban interests.

Culminating in the Populist movement of the 1890s, this rural-urban schism in Carroll County can be traced to local conflicts over the repeal of the frontier law providing for free-range livestock. The open range tradition came under the opposition of organized pressure from railroads, urban progressiveness, and large-scale farming interests.

The old frontier practice of branding and marking livestock for identification on the open range was still in use as late as 1890, and Carrollton was headquarters for drovers from a large section of western Georgia and eastern Alabama. Animals of inferior quality were purchased from farmers at low prices and driven seventy miles to the Atlanta market.[1] A combination of inferior quality and low prices made the shipment of these animals by rail impracticable.

A movement to amend the open-range law, which permitted free grazing, was begun in 1873. This became a local political issue of major importance and remained so until the fence law became countywide in the early 1890s. Railroad stockholders in Georgia claimed that their companies paid annually $70,000 in damages for animals killed on railroad tracks and for injuries which passengers sustained in such accidents. The *Carroll County Times* very early joined the movement to force farmers to fence their animals. Since the existing law made it necessary to fence only the arable lands, the *Times* emphasized the fact that cultivated fields in some areas now exceeded the total acreage of wild land.[2] It also called attention to the scarcity and high cost of fence rails.

Farmers whose stock had access to large areas of wild land belonging to others were not eager to have the law changed. A large group of small farmers and tenants derived a particular advantage from the open range. Those living in the towns and villages and in the more highly developed farming areas, who generally were favorable to enclosing all livestock, now found themselves in opposition to the small farmer, rural element. Members of both factions often displayed strong convictions. John Shadinger was so opposed to changing the law that he constructed a 10-foot stone fence several hundred yards in length to partly enclose a field in front of his house on Shadinger's Ridge. It remained until 1934 as a monument, not only to Shadinger's conservative faith, but also to his skill as a stone mason.[3]

John Bonner of the Laurel Hill community also was among the conservatives on this issue, although apparently for novel reasons. He represented the county in the legislature in 1882–1884 as the farmer's candidate. Being the owner of "1200 acres of good land," he must have felt it politically expedient to write that "the poor man's stock is welcome to graze on it." He also expressed an aversion to the use of guano delivered by railroads at high freight rates. He claimed that he could make 1,200 pounds of cotton to the acre without it. Bonner also believed that the public school system then being advocated by many urban groups was not in the best interests of rural people. "Neither am I in favor of certain books," he wrote. "I think the legislature ought to let us have a three months school and let us send any time in the year that we can spare our children." [4]

Carrollton, being the most urban community in the county, was the first to enact local regulations against roving livestock. In 1877 its city council required owners of buildings to erect enclosures to keep hogs from sleeping under them. Ten years later an ordinance made it unlawful for "any cow, steer, bull, calf, heifer, hog, pig, goat, sheep, or any other animal of similar description" to run at large within the limits of the town.

In the meantime, in 1872, an enabling act of the state legislature permitted counties to hold local elections to determine whether cultivated land should remain fenced. If the vote was in the negative, then the legal land boundaries would be considered "the same as a lawful fence." Livestock trespassing on cultivated lands could then be impounded as when previously they had broken through a tangible fence made of rails, wire, ditches, or one formed by a navigable stream. This would force owners to pen their livestock. The law received a local option amendment in 1880 to provide for separate action by militia districts. A petition of only fifteen freeholders and certain other requirements could initiate such a precinct referendum.[5]

An ambiguous provision of this law led to widespread misinterpretation. When a countywide referendum was held, voters were required to indicate their choice either for "fence" or "no fence," the latter meaning that all existing fences around arable lands would come down. If voting on local option by militia districts, however, the choice was between "fence" and "stock law." The latter choice meant that fences around arable lands could be removed and the animals themselves would be placed in enclosures. Because of this ambiguity much confusion resulted in the marking of ballots.[6]

Three communities petitioned for a referendum on the matter in 1885, at which time the 642nd (Villa Rica) and the 1122nd (Fairplay) militia districts voted on the new stock law which, if approved, would become effective in March, 1886. Villa Rica failed to approve it by only two votes. It was claimed that defeat of the measure was a result of confusion on the part of voters on how to mark ballots. The Fairplay district gave a substantial vote favoring a change in the old law. They would no longer require the fencing of cultivated fields, but instead, livestock would have to be penned or pastured inside enclosures.[7]

An increasing interest in the movement appeared in 1887 when several additional districts conducted a referendum on the question. In advocating a change in the law, I. N. Richardson of Hickory Level emphasized the growing scarcity of labor and timber for fencing. "Thirty or forty years ago when the range in this county was good our smallest interest then was our farms," he wrote. "But at this age our smallest interest is our stock. . . . We can better afford to fence our stock which can be done at least one-sixth cheaper than we can fence our farms." A farmer living at neighboring Sand Hill complained of "razor back hogs hammering over his fences and long horned, long haired cattle walking the lanes." He suggested that the fencing of animals would result in improved breeds.

By April the new law had been approved in six militia districts, namely, Carrollton (714th), Villa Rica (642nd), Fairplay (1122nd), Kansas (1152nd), Turkey Creek (1240th), Bowdon (1111th), County Line (1297th), and Temple (649th). Roopville district (713th) approved it in September, at which time Cross Plains (729th) rejected it by a vote of 73 to 41. In a countywide vote held in July, however, there was a margin of 595 votes against its application throughout the county. In a similar election held in Haralson County two years later it was rejected by an even larger majority.[8] Thus the areas which chose to remain under open range were in the extreme northwestern and the extreme southeastern portions of the county. These were areas of relatively low population density.

In many areas the provisions of the new stock law were not rigidly enforced. Despite the requirement that stock be enclosed, animals were turned out in the fall after the crops were harvested. They found substantial grazing on the canebreaks of the swamps, the rough grass not yet killed by the frost, and the unharvested remnants of cornfields. This practice prevented farmers from sowing fall grain. The trampling of stock on wet clay soils also caused clods to form which wrought serious damage to the land. The system of adopting the law by militia districts placed a heavy burden on farmers who had to build fences around the entire district to keep livestock from open range communities within bounds. Otherwise, such stock found in restricted areas could be impounded by landowners in these closed range areas. Such a fence was constructed in 1889 south of Roopville along the length of the Heard County line, and also between the Roopville and the Lowell districts. Gates had to be constructed on the roadways crossing the boundaries of the units. Since the Lowell district remained under open range, its citizens were saddled with the burden of constructing the fence, in the absence of which they ran the risk of being charged with owning trespassing animals.[9]

In May, 1890, Smithfield (1006th) in the northwest corner of the county voted for the stock law by only a ten-vote majority. Three months later Flint Corner (1436th), which lay adjacent to Smithfield, voted it in by a majority of three votes. In a second countywide referendum held in July, 1890, the county again refused to make the law general in its application. Allegiance to local control in these matters is demonstrated by the fact that many voters who had approved the law for their own communities in a local referendum refused to cast a favorable vote in a countywide canvass.[10]

The southeastern corner of the county nearest the Heard and Coweta lines was the last area to give a favorable vote on the new law. Here the Chattahoochee River formed a legal fence between them and Coweta County on the east, which earlier had adopted the closed range. However, Heard County on the south remained an open range county. These facts eliminated much of the need for erecting and maintaining expensive district line fences. Indeed, it was the cost of building fences along district lines which often provided the margin of victory for the proponents of the new law. The Lowell district (1163rd) was among the last to vote favorably on the issue. In an election in that precinct in 1891 the vote was 80 to 83 against the closed range. However, a dispute resulted over charges of illegal voting and subsequent adjudication by the Ordinary gave a victory for the proponents of the new law.[11] It is significant to note that the voting on the stock law seldom produced clear-cut victories. A change of five votes would have altered the results in most of the voting by militia districts.

As already noted, the general result of the fence law issue was to create a schism between small farmers in isolated areas and those living in the more densely populated areas. This was the precursor of some of the most spirited political battles which the county had experienced since the days of the Pony Club. Central to these issues was the class consciousness of farmers and their exploitation, both real and fancied, by business and industrial interests. By the early 1890s these issues were focused in the Populist movement, which threatened to end the dominance of the Democratic party, to revitalize the Republican party, and to enhance the Negro vote.

Rural consciousness received great impetus in the formation of local agricultural groups soon after the war. Known as the Granger movement, the original purpose of these groups was to ameliorate the social drabness of rural life. But when farmers got together they invariably discussed politics. Meeting in rural churches and schoolhouses, the grange became a medium through which farmers could strike back at railroads and other monopolies associated with urban life.

One of the earliest granges organized in the county was the Bog-

gess Grange at Whitesburg in 1873.[12] Another club was organized at
Billow near Simonton's Mill in 1877 with twenty members. Two
years later the meeting place of this organization was moved to Carrollton, where assemblies were held on the first Saturday of each
month. A typical rural chapter was the Keystone Grange whose
activities centered around several committees. Those entitled Ceres,
Pomona, and Flora (grains, fruits, and flowers) were headed by
women. The Keystone Grange, like most of the others, debated the
merits of guano, and after a spirited discussion of this subject, the
audience rejected the arguments sustaining the merits of this product imported by railroads at a high cost. An annual picnic held in
August featured a prominent speaker.

The Granger movement had greatly declined by 1880, at which
time it was deemed logical to consolidate chapters at Farmville,
Eureka, Union, Keystone, and Smith's Chapel.[13]

During the 1880s farmers entered a new organization known as
the Farmers Alliance, which sought to bring about needed social,
political, and economic reforms through the Democratic party. The
Alliance did not become active in the county until August, 1887,
when chapters were organized at Cross Plains and at Clem. At this
time cotton prices were suffering as a result of the expansion of
cotton-growing in Texas and the Southwest, and other factors. In
fact, all farm products suffered from low prices. Watermelons in this
period sold on the streets of Carrollton at twenty cents a dozen.

The principal topic of Alliance discussion, like that of the grange,
was the high cost of fertilizer.[14] County membership in the Farmers
Alliance grew rapidly, reaching over two thousand by 1889. There
were 125 members in the Rotherwood community alone, and 70 at
Clem. John K. Roop of the Carrollton chapter was elected vice-
president of the State Alliance at its annual meeting held in Fort
Valley. By February, 1890, the number of local chapters in the county had grown to forty. All rural communities as well as the towns
were represented in the list. A few chapters bore names which defy
geographic identification: Bob Toombs, Wilkes, Richards, Five
Points, Bay Springs, Midway, and Enterprise. The Carrollton Alliance held its meetings in Liberty Hall, a small auditorium over Charley Williamson's store, situated west of the Presbyterian Church on
Maple Street.[15]

The Alliance's principal weapon for striking down monopolies
and cutting the cost of manufactured goods was the cooperative
movement. Among the cooperative ventures proposed for the county

was a guano plant, a ginnery, and a coffin factory. Local merchants were not enthusiastic about cooperatives. John B. Beall, in ridiculing the idea of a coffin factory, produced figures to show that most of these items already were being produced by rural carpenters. However, the Carroll County Alliance established what is said to have been the first cooperative retail store in Georgia, which opened on September 1, 1888. Having a paid-in capitalization of $6,500, the Carroll Co-operative Company had its business establishment at the southeast corner of the public square with John K. Roop as business manager.[16] A similar establishment was organized at Bowdon in 1890, as well as a cooperative ginnery near that place. Three years later an Alliance warehouse was chartered for the storage of cotton and other commodities. Built near the railroad, this building later was rented out by the directors and used as a private cotton warehouse.

By 1895 Alliance activities in the county had perceptibly declined and two years later little evidence of the organization remained. In that year the Alliance cooperative store, now called the Alliance Mercantile Company, was bought by Edwin P. Stone and converted into a private enterprise. Eventually this site was acquired by the Carrollton Hardware Company.[17]

Alliance activities came to an end largely as a result of the injection of controversial political issues such as the fence law in local and countywide meetings. Some members became apprehensive over the question of loyalty to the Democratic party. By 1891 many Alliance leaders were convinced that farmers could not affect control over the Democratic party and they sought to form their own political organization. The Populist party was the result.[18] Since populism was tailored to the vote of all farmers including the Negro, the main argument of opponents to the movement was that a splintering of the Democrats would enable the Negro to hold the balance of power and thus to dominate the outcome of elections. By the early 1890s a new agricultural depression increased the militancy of the Populists, frightening conservative interests.

The Populist threat to white supremacy was more generally feared than its threat to business interests. The strength of the Republican party in the county waned considerably after the "Home Rule Constitution" of 1877 and the end of federal occupation troops in the South. In the county elections of that year both parties nominated candidates for all county offices. The Democrats were returned to office by a three to one majority, which was slightly higher than the ratio of whites to Negroes in the county's population.[19]

Negroes voted in the county from 1868 until their temporary disfranchisement forty years later, although their appearance at the polls in significant numbers often was sporadic. The unofficial white primary in use in this period reduced the size and effectiveness of the Negro vote only so long as white men stood firmly behind the Democratic organization. Between 1877 and 1886 various methods were used to select delegates to state conventions of political parties, all of which were designed to control the Negro's vote. These included mass meetings in the county courthouse and the appointment of delegates by county executive committees and by conventions of militia districts. (There were fourteen militia districts in the county in 1877, and seventeen in 1890.)

Few delegates were chosen by popular vote. At a Democratic mass meeting at the courthouse on July 4, 1876, however, it was decided "henceforth that nominations for county officers and the state legislature be made by primary elections" and a plurality vote was declared sufficient to nominate. To the executive committee was left the details of running these elections. Nominations for the legislature and for county officers were held on separate days, as were general elections for filling these offices. At a similar mass meeting two years later the question of extending the primary to all elections became a burning issue. The little courthouse in the center of the public square was filled to overflowing and decisions were taken by *viva voce*. Contrary to custom, the meeting did not begin by electing an executive committee, and because of poor management it ended in wild confusion.[20]

Governor John B. Gordon, in his gubernatorial canvass in 1886, denounced the mass meeting as a means of naming delegates to state conventions where the governor and other state officials were to be nominated. He called for primaries in which the wishes of all the people could be known. Despite this sentiment by a popular Democratic leader, the county in 1886 reverted to the mass meeting for nominating candidates for the legislature. Little interest, however, was shown in this procedure. Only twenty-two people showed up at the meeting. These chose from among their number a slate of delegates to the senatorial convention to be held at Franklin, where J. W. Burns and Lindsley Holland were nominated as candidates for the lower house of the legislature. Denouncing this procedure as "bossism," the *Free Press* stated: "Shall 22 men dictate to the 3000 Democrats of Carroll County, who to vote for? Down with the fraud." [21]

By 1890 the candidates for public office who had declared themselves to be Alliance men had almost complete control of state and county offices. Edwin R. Sharpe and George W. Harper, staunch Alliance men, were sent to the legislature. Charles L. Moses, a thirty-four-year-old farmer and schoolteacher of Coweta County, was a strong Alliance man who won the nomination for Congress, but only after the sixty-fifth ballot. Of the 221 members of the General Assembly in 1890, only fifty were not avowed Alliance men. The failure of this Alliance majority to pursue a "farmer's program" within the Democratic party caused considerable disaffection of its rural members. Typical of its conservative actions was that of Representative George W. Harper, a Carroll Alliance man, who made the key speech in the Alliance legislative caucus in Atlanta. Harper favored the nomination for the United States Senate of the businessman's candidate, John B. Gordon, who subsequently was elected. Other actions of the so-called Alliance legislature proved equally disappointing to farmers seeking to strike at representatives of business monopoly.[22]

The schism among the Democrats of the county later was revealed on the issue of building a new courthouse. The old building in the center of the public square was characterized as small, poorly lighted, ill-arranged, and in need of expensive repairs. Various grand juries had recommended a new building at a location removed from the traffic noise on the Square. Many Alliance men were unfavorable to the idea because construction would have to be financed from a bond issue which they opposed. One Alliance man cited the fact that a new courthouse would not benefit the farmers whose justice courts were held in old shops, abandoned tenant houses, and school buildings throughout the county. One expressed the idea that "the politics of the county [were] run by a handfull of men" anyway, and the old building could easily accommodate the number. In 1891 the county commissioners finally adopted a resolution to construct on a new site a larger courthouse "not exceeding in cost $20,000." Completed two years later at a cost of $35,000, the structure stood at the corner of Newnan and Dixie streets, on the old academy lot. (Destroyed by fire in 1928, it was later replaced by the county's fifth courthouse.)[23]

As the year 1891 advanced, there was growing sentiment for the organization of a third party to oppose the Democrats. The Buck Creek chapter of the Alliance, led by George W. Harper, went on record as standing firmly with the Democratic party. Harper became that party's leading defender in the county. Alliance chapters at Bay Springs, Villa Rica, and the Second District followed his lead. They threatened not to pay additional Alliance dues if the county Alliance adopted the principles of the National Populist Party which had been organized in Cincinnati in May. The national organization was criticized mainly because it made no distinction between white and black members. Despite this, however, a Carroll County Populist party was organized, with I. H. P. Beck of Bowdon and John J. Holloway of Clem as two of its early leaders.[24] Holloway remained longest in the Populist movement and became an outstanding member of that party's inner councils.

In October, 1893, the Populists held a mass meeting and named a list of candidates for county offices to oppose the Democratic slate. The Populist candidates included William Gaulding, W. T. Morris, William S. and Bennett W. Bonner, Tom Muse, J. W. H. Russell, George F. Spence, David R. Martin, Thomas O. Houston, John J. Holloway, William D. Lovvorn, and Richard Wynn. The Populists now represented a solid front against the Democrats, who were themselves divided because some of their candidates who had been declared nominated had received only a plurality vote.

Sensing a split in the white man's voting potential, a group of Negro Republicans now held a mass meeting in Howard Wells's blacksmith shop and proceeded to organize. Their leaders included Wells, Lige Long, J. G. Rains, Bob Sewell, and H. Mallin. In the November presidential election the Democratic vote exceeded the combined vote of the Populists and the Republicans by approximately two to one. Such a victory surprised most Democrats and they rejoiced at Cleveland's victory. In the county election held in the following January, the Democrats also won all offices. Lacking Republican candidates for county office, that party's strength in this election is not recorded. However, the Populist vote was 28 per cent of the total.[25]

The Populist movement was essentially a liberal agrarian one, aimed not only against business interests and railroads in particular, but against existing political rings, lawyer-dominated legislatures, and other symbols of power and affluence. Thomas E. Watson became the leader of the movement in Georgia. His following consisted largely of small farmers, tenants, mill workers, and people of moderate economic status who had never stood high in the councils of the Democratic party. Felix Cobb expressed the prevailing sentiment developed by the Populist movement in describing "the leading people" of his community during this period. "There are

148

no leading people," he said. "Every man in Carroll County thinks he's as good as anyone else if not a damned sight better." [26]

Both Democrats and Populists sought the Negro's vote as well as that of the white tenant farmer. During the period of Reconstruction the county had been remarkably free of subversive activity aimed at reducing or eliminating the Negro's vote. No Ku Klux Klan influence was ever reported in the county, although in the late 1860s there were serious outbreaks of night riding by these groups in Haralson and other counties in western Georgia. Early in 1893, however, a group known locally as White Cappers appeared in the Bowdon and New Mexico districts. A group of these, about twenty in number, made a raid on the home of one Britt in the New Mexico District in March, 1893. They administered a whipping to Mrs. White, described as "a notorious character," and also to Sam Bowen, Sam Eason, and the elderly Britt. This incident apparently was inspired by a number of complex factors, including court testimony by the Britts in a whiskey revenue case involving some prominent people of his district. Back of the outbreak was also a faint odor of Populist politics. Seventeen of the night riders were sentenced to prison and later pardoned by Governor William J. Northen upon the recommendation of Judge Sampson W. Harris, backed by a strong petition from leading citizens of the county.[27]

Much political factionalism centered on the office of county sheriff, whose incumbent was James M. Hewitt, a former city marshal of Carrollton and a staunch Democratic insider. Through Populist influence on the grand jury, an investigation of the books and accounts of various county officers was launched in 1894. This resulted in charges of irregularity in the clerk's office and also in the sheriff's office. Paid on a fee system, the sheriff was reluctant to release his records and never produced all of them. Edwin Sharpe of the *Free Press* accused Sheriff Hewitt of larceny after trust in connection with money deposited with him by Grant Gilley in lieu of personal security on his bond. Hewitt encountered Sharpe in the post office and attacked him with a policeman's club, whereupon he was fined in city court on misdemeanor charges.[28]

This disaffection was also reflected in the employment of ministers, particularly of those churches in which the congregation exercised the power of appointment. It was even more evident in the employment of schoolteachers. An example was the employment of Joseph F. Durrett, a Populist, to teach at Emily in 1892. He was to receive the regular county funds plus one hundred dollars to be paid by the school's patrons. One of the latter, Willis D. Jones, a Democrat, threatened to withdraw his own children from the school and those of his Democratic partisans if Durrett did not change his politics. Subsequently Jones and the J. H. and J. G. Hollands withdrew their children. Because they had contracted to pay tuition, the amount of their subscription was given to the local justice of the peace for collection. This led to a series of scurrilous charges against the Populist teacher and countercharges by his friends, all appearing in the local paper.[29]

The year 1894 was a significant one in the political history of the county. The Democrats in a mass meeting passed resolutions to have primary elections in each of the seventeen militia districts to determine the gubernatorial candidate. The candidate receiving the largest number of votes would then, through authorized friends in the county, name delegates to the state convention. These delegates were apportioned according to the county's representation in the lower house of the legislature, each county receiving a number of delegates double its representation. This system was enacted into law in 1917. It remained in effect throughout the state for the next forty-five years.

The years 1893 to 1896 marked the peak of Populist activity. For a brief period in 1894–1895 the local Populists published a news sheet entitled *The Carroll Populist*. Their party organization was strengthened in 1894 by a five-man committee in each militia precinct. The county executive committee was then made up of the seventeen chairman of the precinct committees. Populists held their own primaries and party conventions somewhat in the same fashion as the Democrats and endorsed the state and national platforms of the Populist party.[30] The Democratic primary for state officers was held on May 26 and for county officers on September 8. The latter was the largest Democratic primary ever polled in the county up to that time. Many Populists voted clandestinely in this primary, centering their opposition on Sheriff Hewitt, who subsequently was defeated.[31] The Populists in a cagey maneuver deferred their own primary for county officers until after the general election for state officers in October. In this election they turned out in full strength. With their Republican allies, most of whom were Negroes, they voted for the Populist gubernatorial candidate, James K. Hines, who carried the county by 472 votes over William Y. Atkinson. This margin was approximately the number of Republican voters in the county. The Populist candidate for state senator, W. F. Morris, also won over Edwin Sharpe. The latter, however, won the election in Heard and Troup counties and became senator of the Thirty-seventh District. Only the Democratic candidates for seats in the lower house were successful, but by very small majorities. These were W. H. Malone of Villa Rica and William W. Fitts of Carrollton, who were victorious over John R. Spence and Jesse A. Murrah. The Democrats claimed that the Republicans had voted illegally for the Populist ticket because the Republican State Convention had not given its endorsement to the Populists.[32]

"We have met the enemy and we are theirs," wrote a disappointed Democrat after the 1894 election. He claimed that the Negroes who voted solidly for the Populists had held the margin of victory. "Several wagon loads [of Negroes] were hauled up to the Kansas district Tuesday night where barbecue was given them," he charged. He explained that the Democratic defeat was due not only to the Negro's vote, but to the poor turnout of the Democrats, the better organization of the Populists, and the friction of the Democrats caused by their irregular primaries. He called the defeat "a blessing in disguise, for the Democrats will not let it happen again." [33]

A close analysis of the Populist vote in this election indicates that their strength lay mainly in the more rural precincts. Although the vote was close in Villa Rica and Whitesburg, both precincts returned Populists majorities. Democratic majorities were recorded in Carrollton, Bowdon, and Roopville. The remaining precincts, all of which were solidly rural, returned large Populist majorities. Two maps in the section following page 52 show that the geographic pattern of the voting returns bore close similarities to that produced by the earlier voting on the law to require the enclosure of livestock.

In the election for congressman held on November 7, Charles L. Moses, the Democratic nominee, won the county by a majority of three hundred votes, but Villa Rica and eight rural districts gave majorities to his Populist opponent. In the meantime, on October 13, the Populists nominated their slate of county officers for the January election which included Joseph F. Durrett, W. L. Kinney, J. F. Jackson, J. M. Thurman, Thomas O. Houston, Bennett W. Bonner, and N. D. Elrod. As had been predicted, the results of this election were in direct contrast to those of the state election held in the preceding fall. The Democrats won by a landslide.[34] While a heavy snowfall on election day undoubtedly decreased the voting in the rural areas where Populist strength was greatest, the principal reason for their defeat was that the Republicans who supported them in October had now switched their loyalty to the Democrats. This fact seemed to confirm the fears of many that a divided white vote, such as was being manifested, would enable the Negroes to hold the balance of power in political contests.[35]

Sensing the advantages which the situation offered them, a group of white Republicans began efforts to strengthen the county organization of their party early in 1895. William D. Lovvorn of Bowdon and George W. Merrill of Carrollton were the leaders in this movement. Some of the older Republicans, such as Benjamin M. Long, had earlier renounced membership in that party. Lovvorn believed that many of these could be brought back into the organization and that control of the local party could be wrested from the Negroes. He believed only such a development would save the party. He affirmed his position on the Negro's right to vote and to have it counted, but he emphasized the basic conservative principles for which the party stood.

The Negro Republicans, led by Robert ("Bob") F. Sewell, chairman of the county executive committee, and schoolteacher J. G. Rains, secretary, met at the courthouse on March 2 and denounced the efforts to organize a white-dominated Republican party in the county. They passed resolutions not to endorse for office any man who belonged to such a group. One week later the white Republicans met and appeared to be divided on the course to pursue. Zachary T. Allen of Villa Rica was among those who discouraged the alienation of Negro Republicans. The group passed resolutions endorsing the national party and its platform and stated that "we are not a separate party but only the white wing of the party, and will induce all men who believe in our principles to become members." They did not perfect a county organization, but they did assign a committeeman to work up interest in each militia district. Thus the Republican party seemed as hopelessly split by the "lily white" element as were the white Democrats by Populist agitation.[36]

At a meeting called by the white Republicans early in February, 1896, the Negroes turned out in force and dominated the proceedings. They succeeded in naming a majority of Negro delegates to the district convention at West Point.[37] The Negro-white schism in the party was never healed before the registration law of 1908 eliminated the Negro from political activity.

Although the city of Carrollton was by no means free from these political cross-currents, it was the only community in the county which possessed at this time a working majority of old-line Democrats. City government was simple and inexpensive. The principal officials in 1877 were a mayor, clerk, tax collector, four councilmen, and a city marshal. The highest paid official was the marshal, J. G. Tanner, who received $240 annually. Mayor L. G. Pirkle's annual salary was $100. The clerk received $40 and the tax collector $25. The councilmen each drew $20 a year. The total taxable property of the Tenth District, which included Carrollton, was less than $700,000.[38]

At this time no well-organized method of extinguishing fires existed either at Carrollton or elsewhere in the county. In 1872 an attempt was made at Carrollton to form a hook and ladder company with a bucket brigade, but the project lagged. Twenty years later efforts were made to secure donations from businessmen to buy the simplest fire fighting equipment and to obtain for members of the fire company exemption from the street tax. A legislative act two years earlier had empowered city authorities to collect additional taxes for this purpose and for street lighting, but apparently no such taxes had been levied.[39]

Carrollton's public square was lighted in 1884 when oil lamps were erected. In 1891 the city council purchased a privately owned electric plant for public use but failed to submit the question to the voters. Two years later the Carrollton Electric Company was chartered. At the same time the city was authorized to hold an election on the question of issuing bonds to provide a system of water works. Because of the depression of this period, all of those projects lagged.[40]

In 1891 the corporate limits of the town were extended to 1,000 yards in every direction from the public square. Two years later a new subdivision was opened on the east side of Bowdon Road. This involved the extension of South Street and the opening of Longview Street to the old Franklin Road. This area originally had been the Stallings farm, which was now acquired by Charles H. and E. C. Stewart, Clifton Mandeville, Charles B. Simonton, and Arthur D. Harmon. The new development was called Oakland. This community now was known as West End in which appeared the homes of Charles B. Simonton, Arthur D. Harmon, and E. A. Reagin. The area on Alabama Street beyond the limits of the town was known as Jersey City.[41] These communities had their own schools and their own community life, somewhat apart from that of Carrollton.

No discussion of political life in this period would be complete without a detailed reference to the career of William Charles Adamson (1854–1929), whose preceptor was Judge Sampson Watkins Harris (1832–1912). The latter arrived in Carrollton from West Point in 1873 and began legal practice. The son of an Alabama congressman, Harris had spent much of his youth in Washington where his family resided before the Civil War. Adamson came to Carrollton in 1876 from Bowdon, where he had just graduated from Bowdon College. He studied law under Harris while the latter was serving as solicitor of the Coweta Circuit. Harris was elected judge of the circuit by the legislature of 1880. He remained in this position until his resignation in 1903, after which he became adjutant general of Georgia.[42]

When the old inferior court was abolished in 1868 most of its former jurisdiction had already been transferred to other agencies. However, in 1872 a county court was established with Beverly Thomasson as judge. Appointed by the governor, Thomasson was responsible for all county business formerly discharged by the justices of the inferior court. His court also had jurisdiction in cases of contracts and torts not exceeding a hundred dollars. However, this new court was abolished after five years when its jurisdiction was divided between the justice courts and the Superior Court.[43] In 1884 the City Court of Carrollton was created with countywide jurisdiction. Its first judge, appointed by the governor, was William Charles Adamson. At the same time a board of commissioners of roads and revenue was created which now discharged all county business formerly managed by the county court. With the end of Adamson's first term as judge, in 1889, his court was discontinued, being largely a casualty of the Farmers Alliance and incipient Populist politics. (Its opponents objected to the annual cost of $1,500 to operate it.) Finally, in October, 1891, a legislative act enabled counties with populations of 15,000 and over to provide a city court after a grand jury recommendation. A new city court for Carrollton was organized two years later with William F. Brown as presiding judge. This court survived a move to abolish it in 1918, and was still functioning in 1970.[44]

Always strongly opposed to the Populist movement, Adamson became a Democratic presidential elector in 1892, served for several years as the city attorney, and in 1897 he entered the 55th Congress. He defeated Charles L. Moses of Coweta County, who in 1892 had been elected to that office as an Alliance man. Adamson was succeeded in Congress in 1917 by William C. Wright, who had been born in Carroll County and in 1886 was associated with Sidney Holderness in the practice of law at Whitesburg. Wright later moved to Newnan, and Holderness came to Carrollton. The former served in Congress until his death in 1933.[45]

While in Congress, Adamson was chairman of the Committee on Labor. He was instrumental in obtaining passage of the Adamson Eight Hour Law and in the organizing of the new Department of Labor. He was skeptical of Woodrow Wilson's nomination in 1912, characterizing him to his Carrollton friends as "just another damned schoolteacher." However, he became one of the president's admirers and a staunch supporter of his policies. Upon Adamson's retirement from Congress, President Wilson appointed him to the United States Customs Court, where he remained until his retirement in 1928, just one year before his death.[46] For more than thirty years people of Carroll County took pride in the brilliant career of "Judge Adamson." He knew a host of Carroll people by their first names and he possessed a rare combination of dignity, a sense of humor, and a grassroots philosophy. To many rural citizens he was the only symbol they ever had of the power and might of the government at Washington. In 1970 he remained the only citizen of the county who had served his district in the United States Congress.

IX

Educational Developments after the Civil War

DURING the early period of Reconstruction all of the schools in the county, with one or two exceptions, were one-teacher private schools. Classes were held in churches, log houses, and abandoned dwellings. In 1868 a school at Carrollton, later known as the Old Seminary, was operated on College Street with Mollie Thomasson as its only teacher.

Some progress was noted in 1871 when a county board of education, comprising thirteen members, was created. This board forthwith established thirteen "sub-school districts," one for each militia district. At this time the total educational fund for the county was $2,421.50, but the full amount was not provided until near the end of 1874. School funds came from the state, the county poll tax, and private tuition. The highest salary accorded a county teacher in 1873 was $76.32, paid to J. C. McGarity.[1]

A county teacher's association was organized in 1872.[2] Five years later a total of 2,974 pupils were enrolled in the county, of whom only 202 were Negroes. The average daily attendance at fifty-seven white and five black schools was only slightly in excess of fifteen hundred. Thus each school had an average registration of forty-eight pupils and an average attendance of less than twenty-five. At this time the county received from all sources for school purposes only $3,315.36, including tuition as well as state funds.[3]

By 1880 there was a total of eighty public schools, of which ten

Above, Carrollton Seminary, built in 1853, later the Carroll Masonic Institute, became the Carrollton Public School in 1887. *Right,* the Thomas Bonner House on the campus of West Georgia College.

Above, Bowdon College, founded in 1856, received much support from the small town of Bowdon until it finally closed in 1936. *Below,* Governor Joseph M. Brown attends the A&M School commencement in June, 1911. Standing on the bottom step is Congressman William C. Adamson; on the sixth, left to right, are Judge Walter Milligan, Mrs. Brown, and Mrs. Adamson. Governor Brown is behind Mrs. Brown, and Judge George P. Munro is between Mrs. Brown and Mrs. Adamson.

Above, the 1910 A&M School football team, one of the region's earliest. *Below,* the A&M baseball team, 1911.

R. Lee Sharpe, editor of the *Free Press,* shown in his office about 1912.

The *Free Press* office, 1920.

Carroll County Confederate veterans, 1925. Front, left to right, James Kuglar, Charles Bloodworth, James Bryce, Howard Pitts, George Cheney, George Lyle, and John Mullinix. Rear, left to right, George Bowen, MacDonald Aldridge, and John Jackson, W. O. Perry, John Moore, Kuglar, Charles Bloodworth, James Bryce, Howard Pitts, George W. Harper, Brainard Hewey, Henry C. Reeves, Billy Spence, Thomas

Judge W. C. Adamson

Edwin R. Sharpe

L. Clifton Mandeville

William O. Perry

Above, the Appleton Mandeville House in Carrollton. *Below*, the Samuel Hart House, earliest house in the Villa Rica area, circa 1824.

were for black children. In addition there were thirty-two private schools, only one of which accommodated black children. The latter group accommodated slightly over twelve hundred pupils and ran for approximately four and a half months each year. The average monthly tuition was $1.38. The so-called public schools accommodated 3,190 children, each of whom paid a tuition of $1.15 per month, while the state contributed to each seventy-five cents. The term "public school" was therefore somewhat a misnomer, for in no single instance was the full cost of tuition paid from public funds.[4]

Rural schools throughout the county were still known locally as "settlement schools," a term which originated in the frontier era. Lena Sewell Jackson observed one of these in 1888 located eight miles from Bowdon on the old Columbus road. She described a log house 18 feet square with no windows, but having a door at each of two opposite sides. Puncheon seats were arranged in a circle around the room, which had only a dirt floor. In the center of the room was a rough pine table. A teacher's stool stood near the door. A small hand bell to call the children in from play was the only additional equipment.[5]

The private schools often were no improvement over the settlement schools, since the cost of operating them was paid entirely by the pupils. The better private schools were found only in the larger or the more progressive communities. Typical of these was the Carroll Masonic Institute, which was under the sponsorship of the local Masonic lodge. This school in 1872 was presided over by Major John M. Richardson, formerly president of Bowdon College, who had acquired the school property for five dollars.[6] Augustus C. Reese, a teacher with a master of arts degree, had come to Carrollton after the Civil War and began teaching at the Old Academy, where the depot later stood on Bradley Street. At his own expense, he erected still another school building west of Depot Street near the Square to accommodate two hundred pupils. Dedicated on November 14, 1872, as Reese's Polytechnic High School (but known locally as the New Academy) it offered bookkeeping and music in addition to modern and ancient languages, grammar, spelling, geography, orthography, and history, "including the history of our own country by impartial writers." [7] That Reese, whose wife had been a Northern-born abolitionist, should include history in his curriculum at this early date was doubtless a concession to his Southern clientele, who were highly sensitive to the manner in which the Civil War was being interpreted by national writers.

Reese's Academy, as it came to be called, soon became the local school for girls, while the Masonic Institute became a male academy. These schools ran for almost a full twelve months each year, although not usually with the same component of pupils. The fall term began on the third Monday in July and ran through December. The spring term began in the third week of January and ended in July. The monthly tuition varied from $2.00 to $3.50. The Masonic Institute offered free rooms to young men who desired to board themselves.

In 1882 Thomas Bog Slade (1834–1926) came to Carrollton from Columbus with his wife, the former Almarine Cowdery. He was the son of Thomas Bog Slade (1800–1882), one of the early leaders in public education in Georgia, having taught with distinction at the Clinton Female Institute in Jones County, at Wesleyan Female College, and in Columbus.[8] An honors graduate of the University of North Carolina in 1855, the younger Slade and his family long remained an influential force in Carrollton's educational development. In 1884 Mrs. Slade was in charge of the girls' school, where she taught the standard academic subjects. Minnie Reese, daughter of the school's founder, was the music teacher. Elocution and calisthenics were taught by Kate Cowdery, a sister of Mrs. Slade.[9]

Commencements were unknown in the schools and academies of this period. A student might continue in school as long as he felt the urge to do so or as long as he could pay tuition. Instead of graduating he dropped out. Since drop-outs reduced the school's income, this was discouraged by the teacher except in rare instances where the pupil was planning to continue in a college.

The "exhibition" occupied a place on the school calendar comparable to the modern commencement. It was an annual performance staged at the end of the spring term in July. These occasions afforded the community a pleasing social evening, and they were well attended. In July, 1884, "an immense audience" assembled at Reese's Academy to witness the exhibition of Mrs. Slade's school, including performances by girls of all ages in attendance. People jammed the little auditorium and the worst kind of disorder prevailed. A local observer characterized it as an "unappreciative and boistrous house." This observation is not surprising, for the program lasted until midnight and featured recitations, dialogues, tableaus, operettas, and calisthenics. There were songs and other types of musical performances.

Taking a lesson from such experiences as these, the Masonic

Institute held its exhibition on two successive evenings, separating the young pupils' performance from that of the older pupils. The house was filled on both occasions and good order prevailed. "Music was furnished by Misses Caffie Merrill and Mollie Sims on the organ, assisted by Messers Reese, Carlton, Merrill, and Johnson with violins," according to the report. The performances by the pupils were for the most part limited to declamations and dialogues. "The dialogues with one or two exceptions, where parties did not have their parts well memorized, were gone through in good style," wrote an observer.[10]

Augustus C. Reese's proclivity for founding private schools in the county was irrepressible. In December, 1885, he announced the opening of the Plowshare Academy a few miles west of Carrollton "at reduced tuition rates of $1.25 to $2.00 per month." He stated that board could be obtained for as little as $6.00. Elsewhere in the county were schools where pupils could board in private homes near the schoolhouse. At Whitesburg Principal H. M. Newton in 1873 announced the opening of the Whitesburg Seminary with tuition ranging "from $1.00 to $4.50 per month and board at reasonable rates." Board for pupils was also advertised at Roopville and Mount Zion. In listing its tuition costs, the latter school announced "free calisthenics." [11]

Mount Zion was organized as a private school in 1880 under a joint stock plan conceived and executed by James Mitchell. Born an Episcopalian of Scotch-Irish parents, Mitchell came to America in 1837 and joined the Methodist Episcopal Church at a camp meeting in Indiana. Licensed to preach in 1840, he afterward became a violent abolitionist and served as secretary of the American Colonization Society in Indiana. After the war he became interested in education. In 1876 he attended the Georgia Conference of his church in Atlanta, which conference he now joined. He was appointed a presiding elder of the Atlanta District, which included churches in Fulton, Douglas, Carroll, Heard, Pike, Upson, Spalding, and Clayton counties. He turned his attention to establishing church-sponsored schools at Mount Zion and other strategic areas in Georgia, including one at Demorest in Habersham County, an institution which later became Piedmont College.

The joint stock plan under which his schools were organized provided that a majority of the stock be held by the conference and the remainder sold to local laymen of the community which the school was to serve. Mount Zion challenged Mitchell's special interest. On a preaching mission to the church there in 1877, he noted few Negroes in the community. He preached in a log cabin to a congregation of small farmers who were simple in their tastes but extremely hospitable. He was particularly impressed by the large number of children and young people in the congregation. He returned later and discussed with community leaders the possibilities of a nine-month school, with a boarding department. The idea met an enthusiastic response. Because the church was set upon a hill, he named the community Mount Zion.[12]

Subscriptions were secured in 1878, and shares were sold at $25 each, payable in four installments. These shares were purchased by twenty-four families including the Entrekins, Walkers, Jordans, McBurnetts, Trimbles, and sixteen others. Since the shareholder had a vote equal to the shares he held, Joseph Entrekin with ten shares became president of the board of trustees. According to the charter, the board's president had power to vote the stock held by the conference. The first meeting of the shareholders was on August 24, 1880, at Bethel campground. The school opened in 1882, and three years later a girls' boarding hall was erected to house forty students. The lumber for this structure was donated and the construction work was performed by men in the community without compensation. A public park was laid out on the east side of the Carrollton road, and a number of dwellings sprang up around the schoolhouse, now known as the Mount Zion Seminary.

The course of study laid out in 1881 envisioned the ultimate development of a college. The program included primary, high school, and college work, each organized into a separate department called Primary, Academic, and Collegiate, respectively. The last included courses in Latin, Greek, rhetoric, natural science, higher mathematics, ancient and modern history, music, and "moral obligation, and science drawn from the Bible." [13] The school maintained a distinct religious atmosphere under Mitchell, who moved to Mount Zion and for many years served as the school's president. In 1894 his nephew's widow, Mrs. Anna Mitchell, came to Mount Zion to live, bringing her two daughters. Two years later James M. Savitz and his two sons of Vandalia, Illinois, and Mrs. Emily S. Allard, all of whom were Mitchell's relatives, also settled at Mount Zion. These people brought education, charm, and graciousness to this rural community and contributed unusual leadership to its social and intellectual life. So dominant was the influence of these leaders that they are said to have succeeded in changing the speech patterns of the children. For many years it was claimed that a Mount Zion graduate could be spotted by his middle-western accent.

The support of the school was unsteady, coming largely from the church's Conference Fund for Education, the Freedman's Aid Society, and miscellaneous contributions. Endowments were small and infrequent, totaling only $5,000 by 1900. The Collegiate Department languished from the beginning and soon died. By 1890 the three departments were Primary, Normal, and College Preparatory. Under Professor Robert Henry Robb, who served the dual role of minister and principal, the seminary's three classrooms became well equipped. A new church and a boarding hall for men were built. Board in private families was $6 per month. State aid came to the rescue of the Primary and Academic departments, but at no time in the century did this pay more than four months of the teachers' salaries. In 1893 the enrollment was 185 students. As the century closed, this figure had reached 200; the dormitories were filled to capacity, and many were boarding in private homes. The students came from Carroll and adjoining counties, and a few from Alabama.[14]

Philanthropy from quite a different source played a key role in the organization of a school at Whitesburg. The early success of this school was a result of the influence of Authur Hutcheson. An ardent Methodist, he bought and deeded to the North Georgia Conference of the Methodist Episcopal Church, South, the school building at Whitesburg which became known as Hutcheson Institute. He bequeathed to this institution thirty shares of his company's stock, the income from which was to be used for the education of underprivileged children. An additional provision was made specifically for the education of the children of his employees.[15] By 1890 a rival institution was opened in Whitesburg which was called the People's Institute, advertising free tuition. However, it charged a nominal "matriculation fee" of 50 cents per month in the Primary Department and $1.25 in the Collegiate and Business departments. Board in private homes was advertised at $5 to $8 per month. W. H. Andrews was the principal and proprietor. At this time Professor J. K. Smith of Fairburn was in charge of the older school, which was now called the "Old Academy."

It is not certain how the People's Institute was financed as "a benevolent enterprise, its doors open to every child." [16] However, the growing sentiment in Georgia for public education throughout the 1890s resulted in a steady increase in the Common School Fund.

The growth of this fund already foreshadowed the doom of private schools and academies except in those rare instances where support had been assured by a substantial endowment. No institution in Carroll County possessed such an endowment. The private schools survived only for a brief period after the turn of the century. Some attempted to prolong their life by converting to institutions of college rank. Such was the procedure of the Hutcheson Institute which in June, 1898, was granted a charter as Hutcheson College "to build, equip, and maintain a college at Whitesburg which could confer and award all such honors, degrees, and licenses as are usually conferred in colleges." At Carrollton in 1893 was set up a short-lived College of Practical Business and Art, which offered courses in shorthand, business law, correspondence, and "a normal course for teachers." [17]

Public education in the county was given its first real impetus at Carrollton in 1886. In that year the legislature, under provisions of the Constitution of 1877, authorized the city of Carrollton to hold an election to permit the levy of a special local tax for school purposes, requiring a two-thirds vote for approval. Members of this first Carrollton school board were named in the authorization law and they were empowered to elect teachers, prescribe textbooks and courses, to build or rent a schoolhouse, and to administer finances. Tuition, now called "a registration fee," was limited to $3 a year, except for students living outside the city and those over eighteen years of age.[18]

The Carrollton Public School began on February 1, 1887, and ran for five months, during which term the total expenditures were $2,993.30. The fall term began in September and ended at Christmas. For the next several years the public school ran ten months each year, following the original pattern of two terms. During the first few years the principal's salary was $75 a month and the four teachers each received from $30 to $50 a month. Grammar school pupils paid a $1.00 registration fee for the first term and $2.00 for the second term. High school students paid $2.25 and $4.00 respectively for the fall and winter terms. Nonresident high school students paid $10.00 each term.

During the first three years of the school's operation, the school tax which the city levied averaged seventy-two cents on each hundred dollars of assessed property evaluation.[19] Despite these low tax rates there were many who objected to paying even a small tax for the education of children who were not their own. On the other hand, there were some who wanted to extend the system to the entire county. The former group framed a bill for the 1889 session of the legislature, which would permit the people of Carrollton to abolish its new public school system. When this effort failed, criticism of the system began to center on the selection of teachers which, it was now argued, was no longer in the hands of parents. "The public schools are frequently made the asylum of broken down teachers who have failed to sustain themselves as teachers of private schools," complained one. Again in 1891 a bill was taken to the legislature by Edwin R. Sharpe. It was endorsed by more than a hundred Carrollton voters, who wanted the local school law rescinded.[20] The bill was defeated in a legislative committee, largely by the work of George W. Merrill and Joe L. Cobb. William Charles Adamson, who in 1885 had married the daughter of Augustus C. Reese, was also prominent in the defeat of the measure. In anticipation of a return to the old system, however, Fannie Ponder opened a private school in "Liberty Hall just below the *Free Press* office," on Maple Street.[21]

When the fall term opened in 1889 the total registration at the Carrollton Public School was 167, the largest in the history of the town. Principal J. E. Witherspoon had resigned and his place was filled temporarily by William W. Roop, a Baptist minister. The high school was not at this time a coeducational enterprise. Thomas B. Slade was the teacher for the twenty-three high school boys, and his wife taught the thirty-nine high school girls. Mrs. J. H. Ward taught forty-three pupils of the first and second grades, while Roop taught thirty-five in the fifth and sixth grades. In 1890 T. E. Hollingsworth was named superintendent and one extra teacher, Henry C. Brown, was added to the faculty, apparently in an effort to upgrade the high school. Plans were begun at this time for the construction of a schoolhouse for Negro children, whose classes were being held in one of the churches. On College Street in 1898 a new brick school building was constructed which housed all the white children at all grade levels.[22]

The public school system of Carrollton apparently had weathered all opposition by 1893. However, sentiment for public education throughout the rural areas of the county was still highly conservative. At that time no schoolhouse in the county had been deeded to the county board of education and there was no way by which the board could acquire titles either to sites or to buildings. The law required only a three-month term and the State School Fund was insufficient to pay all of this cost. Many children were brought in as public school pupils and remained an extra month or two as private pupils. Since the schoolhouses often were shanties without proper heat, or drafty, high-ceiling churches, schools were held only in the summer months, with all the distractions of revival meetings, sultry heat, and after-school farm work. In 1893, after two successive recommendations by the grand jury, a countywide election was held on the question of school bonds to help improve these rural schools. The vote, 1,367 to 458, was overwhelmingly against the innovation. Only the Whitesburg district voted favorably for the measure. Carrollton's voters, apparently unwilling to impose their own system on the county, cast a three-to-two vote against the measure.[23]

One of the earliest county school commissioners was Samuel J. Brown. After the war this disabled veteran reentered Bowdon College, where he graduated in 1871. He taught school for the next four years and, in 1876, he was named school commissioner by the county board of education. He filled this office for eight years, after which he became Ordinary. Moses R. Russell then succeeded him as school commissioner. The commissioner's duty was to examine teachers, inspect the schools, and to execute contracts made by the board and to serve as general custodian of the school fund.[24] He was paid on a per diem basis, receiving one dollar per day for his services. His annual report for 1891 showed that there were ninety-seven schools in the county system, of which thirteen were for black children. There were sixty-five male and thirty-two female teachers. The average daily attendance for white pupils was 3,413, and for Negroes it was 596. The average cost of tuition was $1.12½ per month, 85 cents of which was paid by the state.[25]

At this time the county board appointed three local trustees for each school district to recommend the employment of local teachers. The county school commissioner issued teaching certificates after a special examination which he administered, the license being of only two grades, or categories. The teacher's salary was based on the average daily attendance, a figure subject to considerable manipulation by the teacher. One of these teachers, Hattie Lang, smitten by a conscience later rendered vulnerable by her work as a foreign missionary, wrote a long letter to the *Free Press* from her station at Tai Ming Fu in northern China. She confessed to having obtained fraudulently a first grade license when she should have had only a second grade license, and also to padding the attendance figures. The latter transgression gave her twenty dollars more than she was entitled to receive under the law. "I added several days to my daily roll to bring the average to 35 for one month and 25 for the other," she wrote. "Thus, I deceived many of you dear people in Carroll and Gordon. . . . I am now ready to make it right." [26] Thus it is highly probable that the precise attendance at these numerous one-teacher schools was considerably lower than statistical data would indicate.

Teachers were sorely underpaid even for their brief period of employment, which lasted only three or four months out of each year. It was impossible for anyone to support a family from the earnings of this profession, and the teacher lacked the means and often the incentive for the improvement of his own knowledge and skills. The principal auxiliary occupation of teachers was farming. The school calendar was a perfect compliment to the agricultural season. "Crops are now laid by and teaching public schools is all in order," wrote a citizen of Villa Rica in 1886. "It is marvelous the number of school teachers that are developed by the 'Public Fund.' Nearly every little empty house throughout the county contains a dozen or two children and a 'Professor' who has 'sat in to teach whar he could make some money to splice out his crop or buy a critter for next year.' " [27] The minister also found it desirable to enter teaching as an auxiliary occupation but he often found the late July and August school term in conflict with the season for revivals or "protracted meetings."

Most of the educational developments which occurred in the early part of the twentieth century were logical results of that phase of the Populist movement which reassessed the educational status of rural youth. One result was the expansion of the school curriculum to include agricultural and homemaking courses and to seek quality and efficiency through school consolidation, longer terms, and better qualified teachers.

One of the earliest attempts made in Georgia at school consolidation, combined with pupil transportation, occurred at Temple in 1903. [28] Under the leadership of Ira W. Williams and J. Phil Campbell, the school was expanded to ten grades. The student could pursue the college preparatory program or the terminal program. The former included Latin, Greek, botany, physics, and trigonometry; the latter, begun after the completion of the seventh grade, included agriculture, farm engineering, drawing, and manual training for boys; and sewing, painting, and "domestic science" for girls. In the first three elementary grades pupils were engaged in such activity as nature study, clay modeling, and paper cutting, as well as reading, writing, arithmetic, and geography.[29]

Children from outlying areas were transported to the school in mule-drawn covered wagons. Others might obtain board with local families at eight to ten dollars a month. In 1903 a total of 320 pupils were enrolled, but the school flourished for only a brief period. Although receiving gifts of money from people in Atlanta and elsewhere, the school made financial commitments it was unable to meet. Not only did the community lack the financial resources to maintain such an ambitious program, but its conservative outlook often clashed with the progressive ideas of the school's leaders. By the end of the 1907 term the school resumed a more orthodox pattern.[30]

Agricultural and homemaking education begun at Temple received statewide endorsement in 1906 with the passage of a law for establishing eleven congressional district agricultural and mechanical schools throughout the state (increased to twelve in 1919). The Fourth Congressional District at this time was comprised of ten counties of western Georgia, including Carroll on the extreme northern limits and Marion County on the south. In competition with larger cities as Columbus, LaGrange, and Newnan, Carrollton was designated as the location of the district school. The old Thomas Bonner plantation on the Bowdon road, then in possession of Bluford A. Sharp, was chosen as the site of the new school. Two brick buildings were constructed in 1907 at a cost of $25,000. The people of the county donated the land and the buildings. These donations were made by individuals and by the city and county governments.[31]

The depression of 1907 made it impossible for some subscribers to make their payments. However, the school opened in January, 1908, with a faculty of five people and with 110 pupils, nearly half of whom were boarding in the dormitory. When the students arrived doors to the dormitory rooms had not been installed. Only a frozen hydrant on the front campus promised any source of water. Buildings were without central heat and electric lights. There was neither a library nor classroom equipment. A "book shower," arranged by the wife of Principal John Holland Melson, provided the nucleus of a library when 325 volumes of nondescript books and bound volumes of magazines were donated by local people.[32] The school's operation under primitive conditions during the winter of 1908 resulted in the outbreak of sickness, which demoralized students and faculty alike. In March one-fourth of the student body was ill with measles and there were several cases of pneumonia. A number of Carrollton's young matrons came to the school to help care for the sick. One student died in the dormitory. Many went home to recuperate and never returned.

Physical conditions had improved by the opening of the fall term but the enrollment of local day students had declined. Work was required of all students to fulfill technical requirements of tuition. Books might be purchased from compensation paid for working overtime. Extra work in the form of digging stumps from newly cleared land was assigned to boys for breaches of discipline. One might attend the school for the mere cost of board, which during the first year was $6.41 per month.[33]

The experimental phase of the school came to an end in 1910, by which time the institution was guaranteed a minimum annual income from the state of $10,000. Registration gradually increased until World War I, when young men, both from the student body and the faculty, entered military service.

The period of postwar adjustment was marked by the emergence of basic changes in the state's educational pattern. In 1917 the Smith-Hughes Act provided federal funds for vocational programs, including agriculture and home economics in local high schools. In 1919 the Barrett-Rogers Act provided state funds for school consolidation. Also, there had been a phenomenal growth in the number of accredited high schools in Georgia since the inauguration of the A&M schools in the first decade of the century. These changes abruptly ended the traditional position of the district agricultural schools in the state's pattern of rural education.[34]

By 1930 considerable sentiment had developed in the legislature for the abolition of all the district agricultural schools which had not already been given college rank. In March, 1933, the newly created Board of Regents, which now had control of all state schools, announced its intention to abolish the remaining A&M schools and also to discontinue its support of Bowdon College. Later in that year it announced its decision to open an institution of college rank at Carrollton on the campus of the agricultural school. This was to become West Georgia College.[35]

Following a brief period of prosperity resulting from an influx of Confederate veterans after 1865, Bowdon College had been forced to struggle for its existence. The construction of a new building in 1900 had been a heavy drain on the little community's resources. By the fall of 1914 the price of cotton fell below seven cents, making it extremely difficult for the little farming community to maintain the institution. The college curriculum had not been revised since Reconstruction days and academic standards were lagging. The college was forced to close in 1916.[36]

In 1919 the state legislature was persuaded to grant the college a small annual appropriation and it reopened in 1922 as the Bowdon State Normal and Industrial College. In 1927 it announced the discontinuance of the preparatory department and the inauguration of a four-year degree program. As yet the college had no dormitories, although a small one was constructed in 1929. Two years later the Board of Regents withdrew state aid, which had never exceeded $27,000 annually.

Following a mass meeting held by citizens of Bowdon, determined efforts were made to keep the college open. This it did, under the old 1857 charter, but its operation as a private college almost bankrupted the town, whose population in 1930 barely exceeded one thousand persons. The institution lowered its rank to that of a junior college in 1934 and, after the 1935–1936 term, it ceased altogether.[37] The college property was deeded to the town, which had fought its battles so long and nobly against the inexorable tide of history and change. Bowdon College had served the people well.

Secondary and elementary schools in the county greatly expanded in number after 1900. The rural population reached its all-time peak between 1910 and 1920, at which period there was only a six-month public school divided into two terms.[38] No high school could be maintained out of the limited state funds available in 1910. Carrollton High School added the eleventh grade in 1911. Despite the existence of more than a hundred local schools, the county school superintendent was besieged in 1913 with requests for the creation of additional units. However, school consolidation was begun seriously after 1918. Twelve years later the number of white schools had been reduced to sixty-four, and the Negro schools to twenty-eight. At that time more than half of the children of the county attended schools served by supplementary funds from a local school tax. Outside of Carrollton, the schools at Temple, Roopville, Whitesburg, Villa Rica, Bowdon, and Mt. Zion were among the more outstanding.[39]

The Mt. Zion Seminary by 1930 had lost its traditional position in the educational pattern of Western Georgia, its old corporate structure being rendered obsolete by increased state aid and the consolidation movement. It continued to receive some funds from members of the Methodist Church in Northern states, but after the reunion of the Northern and Southern branches of this church in 1939 the school could no longer hope to secure substantial support from the church. The transfer of the school to the county system was made on September 1, 1939.[40]

By 1970 the Carrollton school system under Superintendent Holman M. Fulbright had six school units with a total registration in excess of 2,700 pupils and employing 121 teachers. All school units had full-time librarians. The county system under Superintendent Spencer Teal had been reduced to seventeen units, five of which were high schools. The universality of equal educational opportunity for all children in the county seemed an ultimate reality when these seventeen schools employed 313 teachers and enrolled approximately 7,500 pupils. No longer were expenditures for school buildings being made in terms of poor quality homes, ramshackle farms, and dilapidated church houses. Nor were teachers' salaries set on a scale of low-paid farm labor, nor academic achievements gauged by the lowest scale of bare literacy.

A single private college preparatory school near Carrollton opened in 1964, known as Oak Mountain Academy. It had fifty pupils ranging from kindergarten through the tenth grade.[41] For the first time in the county's history there were officially no "white" and no "colored" schools in the public system, although integration of the races in these facilities had only begun.

X

The Waning of Frontier Traditions

THE forty-year period ending in 1930 was characterized by agricultural expansion which reached its highest point of development about 1920. Following the depression of the 1930s there was a rapid decline of agrarian life and a phenomenal rise of urban job opportunities. This situation completely obliterated all vestiges of the frontier with which the community was identified in all of its previous history.

Farm population was at an all-time high in 1920, when more than thirty thousand rural people lived in the county. The black population also was at its highest point at this time. However, the Negro-white population ratio did not change perceptibly from the end of Reconstruction to 1965, the Negro population varying from 18.9 to 22.2 percent of the total. Also the geographic distribution of the Negroes throughout the county remained constant. Their numbers were always the highest in the central and eastern portions of the county. In 1930 Negroes composed less than 2 percent of the total population of Smithfield and Flint Corner districts, and only 7 percent of the Shiloh district. These were areas of small farms and rugged topography, somewhat characteristic of the mountain region which has its beginning at this point. On the other extreme, in the southeastern portion of the county, in the Whitesburg district, Negroes composed 37.7 percent of the total population.[1]

Racial antagonism in this period was relatively insignificant and it stemmed largely from the political influence of Thomas E. Watson. It was greatest in those communities having the lowest percentage of Negroes.[2] Although the Populist movement of which Watson was a national leader had disappeared by 1910, he carefully cultivated the remnants of his old following to enable him to dictate the course of state politics. Of the "loyal 17,000" Georgians who followed his dictates at the polls, some 600 could be found in Carroll County. In the congressional election of 1918, for example, John J. Holloway, a Watson follower living at Clem, announced as an independent candidate for Congress. In the primary which followed he received 612 votes in areas which previously had shown Populist majorities. Of the six precincts favoring Holloway, Kansas, New Mexico, and Cross Plains were carried by decisive majorities.[3] There were anti-Negro, anti-Semitic, and anti-Catholic overtones in this campaign, but the issues dealt principally with President Wilson's war-time administration, particularly the military draft, which Holloway's opponent, William C. Wright, supported.

This campaign was conducted at a time when news of war casualties was bringing anguish to many homes. Private James W. Crawford of Whitesburg, who died of pneumonia in October, 1917, was the county's first soldier to die in France during World War I.[4] It was not until May of the following year that the first Carroll soldier was killed in action. He was James Casper Holland of Hulett who, just a year earlier at the age of eighteen, had been among the first to volunteer.[5] Young Holland's letters had appeared in the local paper during several weeks preceding his death. "Guess you know that I have been transferred to the supply company," he wrote on February 28. "I am driving mules now and am better satisfied than I was. 'Tis a little more like being on the farm. . . ." As these letters continued to arrive they showed a deep premonition of the writer's impending fate. His last letter stated: "I only hope that you are satisfied [that] I am doing my bit [and] that the world will be a fit place to live in. . . . So farewell my dear mother, and may God be with you till we meet again." [6]

Letters of other soldiers reflected a nostalgic longing for the familiar scenes around their rural homes. "I would like to walk over the crop with you and talk awhile," wrote John McWhorter to his brother in July. Colonel Earl Brown described the country around Brest in terms of the more familiar countryside in western Georgia. "[It is] one to two thousand feet above sea level, broken and hilly, with more of a slope to the hills and with a light limestone soil

instead of red clay," he said.[7] William Ayers longed to be back at
Wayside teaching school. Another recalled "the singing at Macedonia on this day last year," and he expressed the hope that his
brother would make a good crop of syrup. Lieutenant William Hor-
ton, an aviator, wrote of landing a plane in a storm, miraculously
escaping injury.[8] Those who remained at home pursued somewhat
the same activities that civilians had pursued during the 1860s. The
mother of Dr. Homer L. Barker, an officer in the Medical Corps,
exemplified the spirit of the frontier, to which she was no stranger.
She clipped wool from sheep in her pasture. She washed, carded,
and spun it, and finally with loving hands she knitted it into a
sweater for her son. It was colored with homemade khaki dye.

The remains of twenty Carroll soldiers were returned from
France in the two years following the Armistice and were reinterred
in various churchyards throughout the county where appropriate
memorial services were held. These occasions bore a marked similarity to those in the period of the Civil War.[10]

Cemeteries in rural churchyards had grown considerably larger
with the passage of time, but rural churches had changed very little.
Only at Carrollton and in the towns had the twentieth century
brought new religious sects and the erection of more substantial
church buildings. On Maple Street the Presbyterians erected a brick
structure in 1902. Across Maple Street from the Presbyterian Church
was erected the Methodist Protestant Church, a building which
compared favorably to the former in size and elegance. In 1913 the
Central Baptists began the construction at Depot and Center streets
the largest church auditorium in the county. The Tabernacle Baptists, as they subsequently were called, continued to attract the
greater proportion of newcomers to the community, particularly
those from rural areas.[11]

The Primitive Baptist congregations by 1920 had begun to decrease sharply in number, as they had in many urban centers. At
this time the Carrollton group sold the structure on Tanner Street
which had been acquired from the Central Baptists. Throughout
the next decade they worshipped in the Methodist Protestant building on Maple Street. In the early 1930s this denomination ceased
to have an organization in Carrollton and the building was sold
for commercial uses. The Primitive Baptists continued to maintain organized churches in several rural areas but, failing to hold
and attract a new generation of youth, their membership steadily
declined.[12]

The decrease in the number of Primitive Baptists and Methodist Protestants in the first half of the twentieth century was more than offset by the appearance of new denominational groups. A highly evangelical group known as the Holiness Congregational Church appeared after World War I. Apparently because of the highly emotional content of their services, Bishop Henry J. Mikell denied them the use of St. Margaret's Episcopal Church in Carrollton, and they conducted their worship in a tent in the fashion of the early brush arbor meeting. Representing the conservative extreme were the Roman Catholics, who appeared in relatively large numbers after World War II. In 1953 they acquired the old Episcopal Church structure at the time that a new St. Margaret's Church was dedicated on Newnan Street.[13]

The Catholic Church was by no means new to the area. In Haralson County in 1893, during the latter phase of the Tallapoosa land boom, a group of Hungarian vinegrowers under Father Francis Janishek were persuaded to migrate from Pennsylvania to western Georgia, where they developed three agricultural villages (at Budapest, Tokay, and Bohoma) a few miles east of Tallapoosa. A group from Ohio was also attracted to the community by its wine-producing possibilities. Among the latter was a colony of Slovakians who founded the community of Nitra (Neetra). The state prohibition law of 1907 destroyed their hope of creating a flourishing wine industry and many of these settlers moved elsewhere.[14] However, a few of them remained, some becoming cotton farmers. The little Catholic mission which these settlers established at Budapest survived their economic vicissitudes. Using a converted one-room schoolhouse for a sanctuary, the church building was equipped with home-made pews and a pot-bellied stove. Yet in its heyday it served two hundred families and perhaps five hundred parishoners.

By the middle of the twentieth century several Catholic families in the West Georgia area were traveling to Budapest each Sunday for mass. Subsequently, the mission was moved to a more central location at Carrollton. In 1965 the parish was officially organized as Our Lady of Perpetual Help. Under Father Richard B. Morrow, a masonry edifice was constructed just west of the Carrollton-Temple road. The new church property joined the ranch estate of actress Susan Hayward whose husband, Eaton Chalkley, donated the original thirteen acres to the church.[15]

The number and diversity of community social activities reached an all-time high in the three decades before 1930. This was the

173

period which witnessed the appearance of the automobile, the motion picture, and the radio, followed later by television, all of which revolutionized many social aspects of community life. In the first two decades of the century, the brass band was the center of local interest and pride. The most notable of these was the Carrollton Zouaves, which appeared in the early part of the century under the directorship of George Gray. In 1915 there were bands at Roopville and other small communities. Among more than a dozen social clubs in Carrollton at this time were the Lit-Mu, Penelope, Three K, and Jokers clubs, all of which were women's organizations. A total of sixteen Masonic lodges were active throughout the county in the 1920s. During the first third of the century James D. Hamrick of Carrollton was elected to all the principal offices in the Grand Lodge of Georgia.[16]

Evidence of social exclusiveness appeared as early as 1909 when the Halcyon Club was chartered as a social and literary organization. It included forty Carrollton families.[7] More social than literary, it maintained rooms for many years on the fourth floor of the First National Bank Building, where dancing and other forms of sophisticated diversions were held. In 1917 the club merged with the Elks Club, the latter closing its rooms in the Roop Building.

In June, 1910, the first of many community chatauquas was held in Bradley's refurbished warehouse near the Presbyterian Church. Lectures were given by ex-Governor Hoke Smith and by James K. Vardaman, a Mississippi grassroots political leader. Glee club, band, and instrumental music were also featured in its programs. Later dramatic performances were added, these being held under a tent in a pasture near the City Hall. When the new City Hall auditorium opened in 1914 it became the center of all community activities in the town. During the first year it was the scene of performances by the Royal Welsh Choir, the Chicago Glee Club, and a female quartette called "The Four Bostonians." There were also illustrated lectures and debates by local groups.[18]

Motion picture shows were introduced in 1909. In opening this enterprise, Bernard Bass and A. A. Wall promised only high-class entertainment and stated that nothing would be allowed "which might offend the most refined taste." In 1911 the Vaudette Theatre opened on the east side of the Square, having a seating capacity of 350 and featuring a small orchestra. Manager Peter R. Cefalu staged one matinee and one evening performance daily and the admission was five and ten cents.[19] During World War I interest in the movie theater reached a high level when large audiences witnessed such productions as "The Beast of Berlin" and "The Birth of a Nation." At this time sound movies had their origin in a manually operated piano installed in a pit near the screen. The musician not only rendered appropriate selections throughout the main feature, but he also operated such instruments as whistles and bells. When a small paddle was applied to a leather cushion, the resulting sound was an excellent simulation of a rifle shot. The Western movie was thus made to possess unusual realism.

Much of the social life of the people in the first two decades of the new century is illustrated by the annual occasion of the Fourth District A&M Fair, held on the grounds of the agricultural school for one week each fall from 1909 through 1920. In addition to a variety of farm exhibits, the initial program included a baby show in which "town babies" and "country babies" competed in separate categories; a balloon ascension, a greased pig chase, a three-legged race, and horse races. There were speeches each day by various state officials, including Governor Joseph M. Brown. In the evenings there were performances of the Old Plantation Show, and also a snake charmer and similar attractions.[20]

An added feature in 1910 was "Automobile Day." Annie Shaffer entertained large audiences by riding a wild bull, but Bill Jones's Wild West Show was the main feature of the evening entertainment. An innovation in 1912 was the scheduling of aeroplane flights by the Douglas-Hulbert Aero Exhibition Company. The aeroplane with mechanics and equipment arrived in a special railway car, but the aviator failed to appear because of an accident. The monoplane nevertheless was placed on exhibit, attracting curious viewers, among whom was this writer who doubted that it could ever leave the ground. The aviator finally arrived more than a month late and prepared to perform according to his contract. On Friday, November 22, after a football game between the agricultural school and LaGrange, "the crowd gathered at the race track and saw the bird man take his flight." On the following day the takeoff was delayed because of strong winds, but late in the afternoon the plane again left the ground. "We can say that the aeroplane is not a fake," wrote the local editor. It was in this manner that the air age came to western Georgia.[21]

By 1918 the fair had become so commercialized and so limited in its educational features as to jeopardize its continued association with the agricultural school. The "Forty-Nine Shows," which had been featured in recent fairs, were described as consisting of three or four Negroes playing jazz music "with young men, boys, and sometimes old men on the 'ballroom' floor hugging a highly painted and scantily clad girl," and it was complained that the behavior of the showgirls "would not be permitted in a bawdy house." [22] Reorganized in 1921 under the name of the Carroll County Fair, it was moved to a new location in Carrollton, on Newnan Street. With the passage of time its agricultural features further diminished in importance and it became largely an organized carnival.

The first amateur radio transmitting station in Carrollton was installed and operated by Louie Bonner in 1927. In February of that year the *Free Press* noted that "through the courtesy of Mr. West, local battery and tire man, a fine radio receiving set will be installed to receive the address of . . . President Coolidge." [23] This event coincided with Carroll County's centennial celebration held in October of that year, when an estimated 35,000 visitors were present to witness an historical pageant and some to participate in a square dance on the public square. Thus it was that the first hundred years of the county's history came to an end at the threshold of far-reaching and dramatic changes in the life of its people.[24]

The centennial, among other things, featured the Confederate veteran, but he was rapidly passing from the scene. His political influence had begun to wane with the opening decade of the new century. By 1920 only Company K of the Thirty-fourth Georgia Regiment was able to muster a corporal's guard for the traditional annual reunion. This occasion, held at the home of Pelham Staples at Roopville, consisted principally of a sumptuous dinner followed by quiet conversation and reminiscences.[25] In that year veteran J. T. Norman was elected for the tenth consecutive term as justice of the peace for the Carrollton district. His total official life of almost a half-century was perhaps the longest political tenure in the county's history. By 1934 the number of veterans attending annual Memorial Day services had dwindled to five, although pension rolls showed a total of eighteen residing in the county, and a total of fifty widows of veterans.[26]

The first two decades of the new century were a period of rapid transition in medical practice, wrought by the revolutionary ideas of Pasteur and Lister. However, the older school died hard in Western Georgia. Until 1920, when the Carroll County Memorial Hospital was established in the Kaylor Building on Maple Street, there was no hospital in the county and even then only a few intensive-care patients could be accommodated. Children continued to be born at home, and the mid-wife was much in evidence. The physician's delivery fee in this period often was as low as three dollars.[27]

Rural physicians were the rule rather than the exception before 1920. It was customary for young doctors to begin their practice in the rural countryside before moving into town, as most of Carrollton's physicians did. However, Dr. Benjamin J. Veal, who graduated from the Medical College of Georgia in 1891, began his practice at Roopville and continued there until he died. Dr. Albert G. Wortham was perhaps somewhat typical of the better rural physicians of this period. He attended medical school briefly on savings from his job as bartender at Newnan, after which he moved to Heard County. He practiced at Centralhatchee for more than forty years, but his patients were residents of four counties. Dr. Jeptha Nutt practiced in the Tyus-Veal community for more than half a century. When he died in 1970 he was the last of the county's rural physicians. A few of Carroll's young physicians achieved successful practice in the larger cities. Among these were Roy Harris, who practiced in Atlanta where he helped to organize the State Board of Health in 1903, and Lloyd Aycock, who did notable research on polio in Boston, New York, and England.[28]

Heralding a new trend in medical organization and professional standards was the formation in 1895 of the Carroll County Medical Society. This group met at frequent intervals and heard papers by visiting physicians who were specialists on various aspects of medicine.[29] Not all physicians in the county affiliated with the new organization, nor did they greatly concern themselves with professional standards. Foremost among this group was Dr. Meda W. Hancock-Lewis. He was born in 1864 and began the practice of medicine in the western part of the county in 1909 apparently under the name of W. C. Lewis.[30]

Almost immediately Lewis came to the attention of the county medical society, whose members accused him of practicing without proper credentials. They made an effort to have him indicted by a grand jury of the superior court and warned him to leave the county. These incidents served only to arouse the ire of Lewis's rural clients who were impressed both by the winning personality of their doctor and the low fees charged for his services.

The supporters of Lewis held an indignation meeting on August 12, 1909, at the house of Jesse M. Mobley near Mt. Zion. Resolutions were adopted condemning "the medical trust" for efforts to chastise one of its profession who "will not be controlled by them." They resolved also not to employ any doctor who aided in Lewis's prosecution nor vote for any public official who favored it. It was claimed that "at least 1500 men" in that part of the county would see that Lewis remained in the community. More than a hundred men signed his bond of three hundred dollars. Among those who spoke in his behalf at this meeting were three ministers.[31]

Lewis and one or two others formed at Mt. Zion an independent county medical association for the stated purpose of getting physicians to reduce their charges. Lewis took the leading role in this movement and it won for him new friends among rural people in other parts of the county. By 1913 he had acquired an automobile, which widened his practice. On office days his yard was crowded with horses and buggies. "He has produced some cures which seem almost miraculous," claimed one of his friends. "We are certainly proud of our doctor. . . . We can't do without him. . . ." [32] In May, 1915, Lewis formed a partnership with Dr. J. Roland Hughes of Atlanta and the two opened an office in the Roop Building in Carrollton.

Lewis claimed that the controversy over his presence in the county was inspired by the Carroll County Medical Association because he charged lower fees than the association had set for its members. However, he faced several charges which were wholly unrelated to his professional practice. He was accused of being a former Alabama convict who had served two sentences in the penitentiary of that state under the name of Walter Franklin. It was claimed that one of these sentences was for embezzlement and the other for bigamy. A warrant charging him with bigamy in Georgia was also obtained. He was charged with having married and deserted one wife in Toadville, Alabama, and later married another in Birmingham before marrying his third wife in Georgia. A Birmingham attorney, Hollis P. Parrish, declared that Lewis was indeed Franklin, but Lewis denied it. Also, a woman claiming to have been married to him in Alabama identified him as Franklin, as did a former Negro convict who said that he had known him in prison.

In 1914 Lewis was charged with practicing medicine under a fraudulent license. One Meda W. Hancock was said to have received a medical diploma from Sewanee in 1908. It was claimed that Hancock died soon afterward and that Lewis married his widow, thus coming into possession of the diploma. It was alleged that this diploma had been altered so that the recipient's name was made to read

"Hancock-Lewis." Indeed, records at Sewanee show that a student registered there under the name of W. C. Lewis who later came to be a resident of Carroll County.

Such charges as these did not appear to impress the doctor's loyal supporters. When criminal charges were made against him in Atlanta, a group of friends met the train bringing him from that place and immediately posted his bond. In the following year he was arrested and held in the county jail without bond on the charge of having performed an abortion on a Negro woman who lived near Roopville. The abortion, it was alleged, resulted in the death of the patient and that of her child.[33]

On the last charge Judge R. W. Freeman granted bail of $5,000 and immediately twenty-one substantial citizens showed up to sign his bond. A jury subsequently acquitted him of the charge of practicing medicine under a fraudulent name, after which Solicitor Terrell nol-prossed the charge of bigamy. The question of identity was the principal factor in both decisions.[34]

In 1916 Lewis was convicted of larceny in the Haralson Superior Court and, as a result of this conviction, his license was revoked by the State Board of Medical Examiners. He was ably defended in the hearing in Atlanta by William C. Wright of Newnan and John O. Newell of Carrollton, while Sidney Holderness presented the charges. The decision of the state board was appealed, an injunction was granted, and Lewis continued his practice. He had now secured aid of the Boykin and Boykin legal firm and claimed that the law under which his license was revoked by the State Board of Medical Examiners was unconstitutional. This contention was later affirmed by the Supreme Court of Georgia. Once again Lewis appeared to be secure in his practice of medicine.[35]

The year 1918 marks the turning point in the stormy career of this enigmatic physician. At that time his wife was given a divorce with ample alimony. In 1921 his house on Cedar Street, used as a hospital for his patients, was completely destroyed by fire.[36] In the following year Lewis was fined $500 in Atlanta and given six months in jail for the illicit sale of narcotics.[37] He later served a similar sentence from the Carrollton City Court and a brief sentence on a federal charge. On May 20, 1924, he began a twelve-month sentence on the Carroll County chain gang, again for violation of a narcotics law.[38] During this period he worked on the roads of the county. After completing this sentence, he apparently was without funds, but loyal friends again came to his rescue. They collected a substantial sum by subscription and with it purchased an automobile and other equipment and put the doctor back in business. He had helped construct the county's roads and now it was his privilege to use them.

Lewis reopened a hospital on Cedar Street, but the mayor and council of Carrollton declared it a public nuisance and ordered it closed. He remained in the county only a short period after this development. He now outfitted his automobile with new tires, which he secured on credit, and left the county. He never returned except for one or two clandestine visits. One story claims that he went to New Mexico where he again ran afoul of the law but escaped and resumed practice in Corinth, Mississippi, and later still at Hartshorn, Oklahoma. He lived in a shabby boarding house in Birmingham in 1947. Here he became ill wtih pneumonia. He was alone and unattended until a short time before his death.

The career of M. W. Hancock-Lewis had become a legend in Carroll County by 1970. One story affirmed that he came to the county as a book salesman, walking from door to door. At a farmhouse where he spent the night a child was suffering from croup, causing his parents great alarm. By administering a concoction of hot water and mustard, a standard folk remedy, Lewis achieved relief for the child and the undying gratitude of his parents. According to this story, it was the news of this "miraculous cure" which spread rapidly throughout the community and encouraged the itinerant book agent to shift his career to that of general medical practitioner.

Another story relates how he pretended to perform an appendectomy by making a superficial incision in the side of a patient and then exhibiting a diseased appendix which he always carried in a jar of alcohol. His personal drug store was stocked largely with jars of liquids of various colors which upon analysis once were found to contain no drug of medicinal value. His verbal prescription to the Negro boy in charge of this dispensary was "a bottle of the red" or a "bottle of the blue," or some other specified color. It was said that he possessed a book which listed diseases and their symptoms in one column and the procedure for treatment in the other. After a summary examination of a patient he would invent an excuse for leaving the room in order to ascertain the treatment procedure from this well-concealed book.

Positive evidence on these matters is difficult to assemble. However, the records do show that he was indicted at one time or another for murder, abortion, larceny, bigamy, assault and battery, practicing medicine without a license, impersonating another (he was listed under three aliases), and illicit use of narcotics. There were at least four convictions in twice as many charges.[39]

It is difficult to separate truth from legend in some of these stories, but there are two irrefutable facts about Lewis's career. He was a master of human psychology and his patients had an inordinate faith in his ability to cure them. That a high percentage of his patients did recover may be due to the simple fact that man gets sick often but dies only once. Lewis apparently combined practical psychological genius with narcotics in the treatment of disease. His story is a significant aspect of the medical history of the twentieth century, for his career spanned the period between a dying frontier and that of an organized, mature society.

Dr. M. W. Hancock-Lewis was one of the last of Carroll County's folk characters. The type of physician which he exemplified had vanished by 1970. At that time Carrollton alone had thirteen physicians, nearly all of whom were highly trained specialists. In addition there were six dentists and two chiropractors. There were three physicians in Bowdon, four in Villa Rica, and one at Temple. There was a hospital in each of the three larger towns, the most important being the Tanner Memorial Hospital at Carrollton, with 127 beds. A Hillburton hospital which had been in operation since 1949, it was named in memory of Charles M. Tanner who contributed $75,000 toward its construction.[40]

Such vast changes in the social fabric of the community were wrought by forces of the Industrial Revolution that had scarcely penetrated the county before the twentieth century. The 1900 business register for Carrollton listed only sixty-five firms, of which twenty-four were general stores. Small industrial enterprises included a harness-making establishment, a tannery, a planing mill, and blacksmith shops. A sawmill was operating within the limits of the town.[41]

The town had barely made a beginning in corporate industrial enterprise. The foremost leader in this development was Joseph Amis Aycock (1852–1910), a man of varied talents, among which were remarkable engineering and technical skills. After graduating from the University of Georgia in 1871, he worked briefly as a newspaperman in Nashville, Tennessee, and in Galveston, Texas. He began the manufacture of sash doors and blinds at Whitesburg in 1880, later moving his business to Carrollton where in 1890 he built the county's first modern cotton ginnery. Eight years later he organized the Carrollton Oil Mills along with Clifton Mandeville, Charles H. Stewart, and others. At this time he proposed the building of a cooperative cotton textile mill, but this idea later was abandoned in favor of a joint stock company, organized in 1899. Aycock became vice-president and general manager of the oil mill and the textile firm, which later were merged under the name of Mandeville Mills. This firm was incorporated in 1902 with a paid-in capital stock of $200,000. Five years later the company's annual payroll reached $120,0000, the largest in the county.[42]

By 1927 the corporation had a paid-in capital stock of $500,000 and possessed two cotton mills operating 35,000 spindles, a cottonseed oil mill with sixteen linters and four presses, a fertilizer plant, and eight ginneries. The ginneries had a total capacity of 30,000 bales of cotton and could process nearly all of the lint produced in the county. The textile operation required 8,000 bales annually; the oil mill at full capacity consumed 12,000 tons of seed which were processed into hulls, meal, and oil.

Before the Great Depression of the 1930s slowed down its production, Mandeville Mills employed four hundred workers with a total weekly payroll of $350,000. The annual cost of raw materials was $1.5 million, which were converted into a product valued at $2.5 million.[43] By the end of World War II this corporation was in decline. The aging stockholders were matched by the growing obsolescence of the company's machinery and its processing methods. The corporation was liquidated in 1954.[44]

In the meantime, in the 1920s, two knitting mills were organized in Carrollton, and the old yarn mill at Banning, in operation since antebellum times, was acquired by an Akron, Ohio, group. In 1930 it was operating 6,700 spindles and employing 173 workers. Small textile and cottonseed oil mills began to appear at Bowdon, Bremen, Whitesburg, and Villa Rica during this period.[45]

In the demise of Mandeville Mills Carrollton lost its most important single industry. Destined to take its place as the county's leading industrial establishment was the Southwire Company, which opened in 1950 with twenty workers. By 1970 this company had 1,950 employees and its plant covered sixty acres. Its products consisted of wire and cable of both aluminum and copper, as well as galvanized steel strand for electrical uses. These found a market in all the states and in forty-five foreign countries. Its founder and principal owner was Roy Richards, a native of the Hulett community and an alumnus of the A&M School.[46]

There was renewed activity in various other nonagricultural aspects of the county's economy during the first three decades of the new century. The adoption of a single gold monetary standard in 1900 brought new vigor to the county's mining area. The old Pine Mountain mine whose vein was now known to run a distance of fifty miles, was leased in 1915 to T. H. Aldrich, Jr., of Birmingham, who used the newer cyanide method in processing the ore. This process was based on a chemical reaction between potassium cyanide and the gold in the ore when the two were mixed with water in a large concrete tank. Gold cyanide was filtered from the mud and the gold was captured by electroplating or by displacement with a cheaper metal such as zinc. The high cost of potassium cyanide during World War I, together with the scarcity of skilled labor, caused Aldrich to abandon operations until 1923, when the mine was reopened for two years. It opened again in 1933 as a result of New Deal gold policies but remained in operation only briefly. At this time the mine was said to be producing an estimated $1.50 per ton.[47]

New extractive industries were also developed in this period although these did not survive to the mid-century. In 1907 Lewis K. Smith, Eldred M. Bass, and others formed the Randall Clay Mining and Manufacturing Company for the purpose of mining and processing clay, iron, manganese, and other minerals. In 1910 the Wallace Mining Company was organized by a Troup County group for carrying on mining activities in Carroll County. The Reid Mountain Mining Company was organized by a group of financiers from Illinois, Oklahoma, and Kentucky with a working capital of $30,000. In 1917 a group of Carrollton, Villa Rica, and Atlanta financiers organized the Southern Pyrites Ore Company. In the following year a group of investors from the Middle West formed the Villa Rica Mining Company. Sulphur was mined in the Villa Rica area by the Carolina Chemical Company. Most of these operations came to an end during or after World War I.[48]

Changing conditions affected retail business in a variety of ways. The chain store made its appearance in the early 1920s when a Rogers Store was opened on the northwest corner of the Square. This began a trend which was to revolutionize the food retail business. Typical of the experience of those who succeeded in changing with the times was James M. Johnson. Early in the century he constructed a large brick building on Rome Street near the City Hall for a stable to accommodate his mule retail business and to house a custom grist mill. In 1916 this building was refurbished to be used exclusively as a showroom for Buick automobiles and for automobile repairs. At this time Johnson constructed on an adjoining lot a frame millhouse with a basement to accommodate a restricted mule trade.[49] The original masonry building at various times after 1925 housed a small textile mill, a bowling alley, a furniture store, and an art gallery. In 1965 it was the seat of Holmes Supply Company, dealing in electrical supplies and modern home equipment.

The financing of new enterprises with local capital was relatively difficult because the county's banks were geared to farming and commercial needs. As the century opened there were two banks in Carrollton and one at Villa Rica. The total capitalization of these three institutions was only $115,000. By 1912 two additional banks had opened in Carrollton and one in each of the towns of Temple, Roopville, Whitesburg, and Bowdon, giving the county a total of nine such institutions.[50]

These rural banks were small and they suffered from inadequate patronage. They also were highly sensitive to fluctuations in the agricultural economy of the community. As a result of the boll weevil depression of 1921 and readjustments following inflationary land prices after World War I, there were two bank failures. The Bank of Whitesburg closed at this time as did the Carrollton Bank, the latter being the second oldest in the county. Later the First National Bank (which was a reorganization of the old Merchants and Farmers Bank) took over the receipts and liabilities of the Carrollton Bank and in effect created a merger of the county's two oldest financial institutions. Then, on January 1, 1926, the Citizens Bank went into the hands of receivers, bringing consternation to its many patrons whose deposits were uninsured in that period.[51]

In the accounts of the Carrollton Bank a shortage of some $170,-000 was reported. Its cashier was indicted and tried for embezzlement but was not convicted of the charge. On February 3, 1928, the records of Judge Leon Hood, liquidating agent for the Citizens Bank, were destroyed in a fire which razed the courthouse. These circumstances created persistent rumors concerning which no proof was ever produced. There is little doubt that the principal reason for these bank failures was the over-expansion of credit and the declining value of securities, most of which consisted of land.

The depression of 1930 brought a second wave of bank failures, at which time the First National Bank closed and was taken over by the Peoples Bank.[52] Then on May 5, 1932, the latter bank found itself in the hands of state banking authorities. From this time to December 12, Carrollton was without banking services of any kind, thus reverting to its condition before 1888. Even more distressing was the fact that depositors had lost their working capital. A bank failure in this period was a catastrophe for the entire community. Depositors shared the risks of the banking business but none of its profits.

Six months after its closing, the Peoples Bank was permitted to reopen when most of its depositors signed an agreement to cancel 50 percent of their accounts. The citizens of the town, including some stockholders, contributed $30,000 in cash, and a loan of $225,000 was granted the bank by the Reconstruction Finance Corporation. The bank was completely reorganized and it proceeded to work itself out of its difficulties. On June 30, 1970, the institution possessed total assets of over $13 million and its demand deposits exceeded $8 million.[53] The expanding economy of the community after World War II brought unprecedented prosperity to all other financial institutions. The Carrollton Federal Savings and Loan Association (which began in 1930 with a capitalization of $50,000) reported assets in 1970 in excess of $44 million and its savings capital was $34,800,000.[54]

Somewhat parallel to developments in banking and industry was the expansion of public utilities during the first two decades of the twentieth century. A franchise for the operation of a telephone exchange in Carrollton was awarded to M. E. Whitehead in 1896, who set a maximum rate of two dollars for business telephones. At that time there was only a single-wire service and no calls could be placed at night or on Sundays except for four hours in the middle of the day.[55] Two years later Whitehead sold his franchise to Clifton Mandeville and James G. Cheney. Later this franchise was acquired by the Gainesboro Telephone Company, which had just been reorganized by a group of incorporators from Carrollton, Cedartown, Dallas, and Atlanta. By 1910 there were 736 city and rural subscribers and plans were under way to extend lines to three rural communities. By 1930 the Gainesboro company, with headquarters in Carrollton, held franchises in thirteen cities of western Georgia. That year its franchise was sold to the Southern Bell Telephone Company.[56]

A total of ten utility companies were on the county's tax digest in 1910. In addition to two railroads and an express company, these included four telephone and telegraph companies and three electric companies.[57] In 1909 the Carrollton Electric Company offered to sell its plant to the city for $14,000. In February, 1915, the city acquired the Drewry Foundry property on Dixie Street with the view of providing its own current. However, three years later the Georgia Railway and Power Company acquired for $40,000 the franchise and property of the Carrollton Electric Company and thus had a monopoly on the distribution of electric current in the city.[58]

A city waterworks had been in existence at Carrollton since the beginning of the century, but meters were not installed until 1909. In the previous year a hose wagon and a pair of fire horses were installed at the Mandeville Building on the Square, then being used as a city hall. There were two paid firemen but as yet the town had no automatic alarm system. Until 1912, when the gong system was wired to the courthouse clock, fire alarms were sounded by hand.[59] Bowdon obtained both electric lights and waterworks in 1913, but not before a large business section was destroyed by fire in March of that year. It was not until 1924 that Villa Rica voted bonds for a water and light system.[60]

The year 1912 was significant for several civic improvements at Carrollton. In that year voters approved $60,000 in bonds, the proceeds from which were used to construct a city hall with a large auditorium, sewerage and waterworks improvements, street and sidewalk development, and an elementary school building on Maple Street. At the same time the Holderness Building on Newnan Street and a new 42-room hotel on Maple Street were completed. Two years later central heating replaced the coal heaters at the courthouse and in a few other public buildings.[61]

Carrollton's commercial growth was reflected in its increasing postal receipts. In 1913 a post office building was constructed at a cost of approximately $42,000. City delivery of mail began in October, 1911, when post office receipts had increased to $10,000 annually, resulting partly from a campaign of merchants to buy in advance a year's supply of stamps. The rural delivery of mail was already under way and the number of rural post offices had been reduced to ten. After 1920 only three remained, whereas there were more than thirty at the beginning of the century.[62]

The consolidation of mail routes began in 1915 as a result of the increasing use of automobiles by carriers. Automotive transportation was introduced in the community as early as 1886 when a "road engine" made its appearance in Carrollton. This was a steam-propelled tractor owned by William C. Aycock of Whitesburg, who came "steaming into Carrollton from Tallapoosa" one evening just after nightfall. This novel mode of travel created great commotion, according to the local editor. "[Aycock] swung up at the Commercial Hotel and on Saturday morning proceeded on his way," he wrote. "He was seen off by a goodly number of our citizens . . . and the small boy was in all his glory as he swung on to the wood wagon as it went capering down Newnan Street." [63]

While remaining a novelty in rural communities, the automobile by 1909 had ceased to produce excitement on Carrollton's streets. In that year a city ordinance required "all automobiles, oldsmobiles or like machine" to pay a registration fee of fifty cents. It was unlawful to operate an automobile within the city at night "without having two lamps lighted on the front and one on the rear." The *Free Press* called for a uniform state law for "numbering automobiles" in order to identify "automobilists who have ridden down . . . and passed on without stopping." [64] The automobile for a long period was unpopular because it frightened horses and caused runaways.

A typical accident was one which occurred in the summer of 1911 when a car driven by Russell Smith, and occupied by Shirley Boykin and Charles Adamson, Jr., collided with a mule and buggy on Newnan Street, destroying the buggy and killing the mule. No assessment was made of the blame. There were few traffic regulations at this time and no parking ordinances. Automobiles were simply abandoned at any place or in any position on the Square. In 1914 car owners on their own initiative instituted systematic parking when they agreed to park in a straight line thirty feet from the sidewalk, leaving the open areas for wagon traffic.[65]

The automobile retail business and such cognate enterprises as gasoline marketing entered a new phase in 1912 when W. Luby Folds acquired the agency in Carrollton for the Ford Motor Company. Not only was the product of this company ideally suited to the roads of this era, but Folds was a diligent and aggressive salesman who operated the business successfully for the next two decades. In 1916 an "auto fire truck" was locally constructed for the Carrollton Fire Department by Chief J. S. Dempsey, who proudly announced the abandonment of the horse-drawn fire wagon. A year later James N. Johnson, now an undertaker, acquired the first auto hearse in Carrollton. Gasoline sales had reached such volume by 1917 that the Gulf Refining Company erected a storage plant near the Maple Street crossing. Just after World War I the Carrollton Automobile Club was organized "to log and map the main roads of the county, to mark them with signs and mile stones and to greet and direct tourists passing through." [66] By 1921 a bus line was in operation between Carrollton and Atlanta. It left Carrollton at 7:00 A.M. and departed from the Grady Monument in Atlanta at 4:00 p.m. on its three-hour return trip.

Carrollton merchants were by no means neglecting their important wagon trade, still larger than most towns in western Georgia. In 1919 the old circus grounds on the west side of Rome Street near the City Hall were acquired to provide farmers with new space for parking their wagons. Sheds were erected and sanitary troughs for feeding and watering animals were provided. The courthouse well, with its iron-bound oaken bucket from which farmers quenched their thirst, was declared unsanitary and was replaced by a fountain.[67]

The automobile provided a strong impetus for the improvement of roads and bridges, which had its logical beginning in the larger towns. In 1915 Depot Street, long criticized as Carrollton's most disreputable thoroughfare, both literally and figuratively, was ordered plowed up, the rocks removed, and then topped with a purple-blue surfacing material obtained from the pyrite mines. On this street was a Negro hotel which was sold and razed. Later removed was a laundry operated by Charley Fong, the community's only Chinese resident. Fong and a brood of children with Afro-Asian characteristics had long been associated with this street. In 1918 a $50,000 bond issue was used for paving the Square and the four streets leading into it. At the same time plans were laid for a whiteway along the paved area.[68] Additional street paving occurred in 1926.[69]

In 1919 the county gave a sixteen-to-one vote for bonds to improve rural roads, a few of which were now graded and soiled. None was paved until after 1930. At this time there were less than ten thousand automobiles in the entire state, and Carroll's share was less than five hundred. Ten years later the number increased 35-fold.[70] The daily automobile count on the Carrollton-Newnan road in 1929 was 746 vehicles, a fact used in urging the paving of this road. By 1940 all of the principal highways through the county had been paved.[71]

Ironically, the paving of rural roads came in a period of declining agricultural activity and a decrease in the rural population. This decay of rural life actually began in 1921 as a result of boll weevil infestation of cotton. The county's largest cotton crop was that of 1914 when 45,371 bales were produced. In 1921 cotton production dropped to slightly over 26,000 bales, a decline of 8,000 bales since the previous year. By 1924 the crop was slightly over 27,000 bales, yet this figure made Carroll one of the largest cotton-producing counties in the state, being second only to Burke. For each of the next two years the crop exceeded 30,000 bales and the county retained second place in the state. In 1927 the crop again exceeded 40,000 bales, the second largest in the county's history.[72] At this time boll weevil control had been well established, but a new menace to growers had appeared. This was an over-supply of the staple, resulting in falling prices, a situation later rendered more acute by the development of synthetic fibers.

Approximately 75,000 acres of the county's land annually was devoted to cotton during the 1920 decade, and 53,000 acres were planted in corn. Before the New Deal cotton control program began in 1933, Carroll's cotton acreage had been reduced to approximately 63,000 acres and the average per-acre production was 250 pounds. In 1933 her quota was set at 21,000 acres with approximately 42,000 acres to be plowed under. Approximately two thousand farmers cooperated with the federal agricultural program and signed acreage-reduction contracts.[73]

This virtually marked the end of the county's position as a cotton-producing area, although the dramatic results were not immediately noticed. The extent to which her farmers had turned to other enterprises after the passage of three decades is indicated by the agricultural statistics of 1960. These show 104 livestock and dairy farms and only a little more than 27,000 acres of all cropland being harvested annually. Of the latter, cotton accounted for a mere 3,035 acres. There were only 220 cotton farms in operation, on which were produced less than 3,000 bales. Significantly, this cotton was being produced under imaginative management and scientific care and no longer was the cotton furrow, as in previous decades, leading directly to the poorhouse. Slightly over 14,000 acres were devoted to corn, of which 304,412 bushels were harvested in 1959. The average per-acre value of farm land was $95.56, the highest in the county's history. This value was only $3 in 1850 and $24 in 1935.

Many farmers in the early 1960s had a substantial acreage in the Soil Bank, in timber, and in pasture, for the old type of farm had all but disappeared. Fewer farmers were living on the land. Timber and pulpwood were now as important as cotton once had been. Setting woods afire was a greater criminal hazard than the malicious burning of a cotton-house in picking season forty year earlier. For the most part, former cotton tenants had migrated to urban centers or were commuting to industrial jobs at Carrollton, Newnan, Marietta, and Bremen. There were only 3,155 farm operatives in 1954, a figure which six years later had declined to 1,753. During the same period farm tenancy in the county had dropped from 28.1 percent of the total to 16.5 percent. The Negro population, as in previous decennial census years, showed the highest percentage of tenancy. Nearly 60 percent of the 224 Negro farm operators were in this category. Farm tenancy, however, had practically vanished as an economic burden.

Only 380 horses and mules were recorded in the county in 1959 and most of the former were pleasure animals. Farm tractors outnumbered work animals by almost three to one and their combined horsepower exceeded 31,000.[74] This increased horsepower from gasoline and diesel engines was responsible for improved tillage and better conservation measures. Ironically, the number of work animals diminished just as a greater abundance of grain and hay was being produced. Cattle, hogs, and poultry supplanted work stock as heavy consumers of the new grain production. A significant aspect of the new cattle industry was the quality of the animals as well as their number. Profits from a single well-bred animal in 1970 might well have equalled that of an entire herd of scrub range cattle in 1890.

The 1970 census revealed a total population of 45,404 in the county, of which only 16.6 percent were blacks. However, the most noticeable changes have been the uprooting of traditional community boundaries, the closing of small schools, the desertion of some churches, and the demise of cross-roads villages. Such social displacements have in large measure erased traditional social and economic problems, but new ones have been raised to take their place, and these are largely urban in nature. To a far greater extent than anyone had anticipated at the beginning of the century, these new problems have important national and international implications. Greater changes of both a technical and a social nature have occurred since 1930 than in all the previous years of the county's existence. The ability of contemporary and future generations to meet the challenge of these changes will be the measure of the community's future welfare.

Notes

Chapter I

1. U.S., Congress, House, Select Committee; *The Georgia Indian Controversy*, 19th Cong., 2d sess., March 3, 1827, House Report No. 98 (Washington, D.C., 1827), 835. Hereafter cited as *House Reports, No. 98*.   2. John R. Swanton, *The Indians of the Southeastern United States* (Washington, 1946), 70, 439–72, 817.   3. John Pitts Corry, *Indian Affairs in Georgia, 1732–1756* (Philadelphia, 1936), 35.   4. The name Kenny Young appears in the records of Carroll County at a later period. See for example the Carroll County Tax Digest for 1832, Georgia Department of Archives and History, Atlanta. Hereafter cited as CCTD, followed by the appropriate year.   5. Rufus Anderson, *Memoir of Catherine Brown, A Christian Indian of the Cherokee Nation* (New York, 1825), 1 *et passim*; *Niles' Register*, XXXIX (Sept., 1830), 992; Jedidiah Morse, *A Report to the Secretary of War of the United States on Indian Affairs* (New Haven, 1822) 159, 162.   6. *House Reports, No. 98*, 277, 542–43, 717.   7. An inventory of the McIntosh estate can be found in the National Archives, Washington, D.C.; a copy of the inventory is in possession of the Georgia Historical Commission, Atlanta.   8. *House Reports, No. 98*, 339.   9. *Washington City Weekly Gazette*, June 8, 1816.

10. Thomas L. McKenney and James Hall, *The Indian Tribes of North America* (3 vols., Edinburgh, 1933–34), II, 18 *et passim*.   11. Grant Foreman, "John Howard Payne and the Cherokees," *American Historical Review*, XXXVII (July, 1933), 726.   12. Joseph G. B. Bullock, *A History and Geneology of the . . . With a Short Sketch of the Family of McIntosh* (Green Bay, Wis., 1898), 70; Edward Jenkins Harden, *The Life of George M. Troup* (Savannah, Ga., 1859), 8.   13. Thomas S. Woodward, *Woodward's Reminiscences of the Creek or Muscogee Indians* (reprint, Tuscaloosa, Ala., 1939), 35; Thomas Gamble, *Savannah Duels and Duellists, 1733–1877* (Savannah, 1923), 318; *House Reports, No. 98*, 813.   14. Swanton, *The Indians of the Southeastern United States*, 703; Benjamin Hawkins, *A Sketch of the Creek Country in the Years 1798 and 1799* in *Collections of the Georgia Historical Society* (Savannah, 1848), Vol. 3, Pt. I, 73.   15. *House Reports, No. 98*, 225; Benjamin Hawkins, *A Sketch of the Creek Country* (Americus, Ga., 1938), appendix, v, 1. This work is a reprint of Hawkins's work cited above, and

it also contains material not included in the earlier edition. 16. Records of Carroll County, Deed Record Book E, 90–91; *American State Papers: Military Affairs,* I, 774–78, John E. D. Shipp, *The Last Night of a Nation* (Americus, Ga., 1938), appendix, vii–xi. 17. *House Report, No. 98,* 47, 283, 336; John Bartlett Meserve, "The McIntoshes," *Chronicles of Oklahoma,* X (1932), 320–23. 18. Woodward, *Reminiscences,* 114. 19. Meserve, "The McIntoshes," 319, 324; Carolyn T. Foreman, "A Creek Pioneer," *Chronicles of Oklahoma,* XXI (Sept. 1943), 271; *House Report, No. 98,* 254–56.

20. Carolyn T. Foreman, "A Creek Pioneer," 271; Annie H. Abel, *The American Indian as Participant in the Civil War* (Cleveland, 1919), 62; Meserve, "The McIntoshes," 321. 21. Mary G. Jones and Lily Reynolds, *Coweta County Chronicles for One Hundred Years* (Atlanta, 1928), 38. 22. Meserve, "The McIntoshes," 320, 323; Carolyn T. Foreman, "A Creek Pioneer," 271; Corry, *Indian Affairs,* 35–36; Abel, *The American Indian in the Civil War,* 60 *et passim.* 23. For a more complete discussion of this factionalism, see James C. Bonner, "Tustunugee Hutkee and Creek Factionalism on the Georgia-Alabama Frontier," *The Alabama Review,* X (April, 1957), 121–25. Much of the data on William McIntosh has been taken from James C. Bonner, "William McIntosh," in Horace Montgomery, ed., *Georgians in Profile* (Athens, Ga., 1958), 114–43. 24. Robert S. Cotterill, *The Southern Indians* (Norman, Okla., 1953), 178. 25. *Carrollton Advocate,* Nov. 2, 1860. 26. Cotterill, *The Southern Indians,* 152–80. 27. U. S. Commissioner of Indian Affairs, *Treaties Between the United States of America and the Several Indian Tribes from 1778 to 1837* (Washington, 1837), 162 (hereafter cited as *Indian Treaties*); *House Reports, No. 98,* 254–55, 334–35, 825. 28. *American State Papers: Indian Affairs,* II, 563. 29. *Ibid.,* 56, 573.

30. *Ibid.,* 579–80; *House Reports, No. 98,* 440, 632. 31. *American State Papers, Indian Affairs,* II, 578; Annie H. Abel, *The History of Events Resulting in Indian Consolidation West of the Mississippi* (Washington, 1908), 339. 32. *Indian Treaties,* 32–35; Abel, *Indian Consolidation,* 340; *House Reports, No. 98,* 254–55, 334–35, 825. 33. *House Reports, No. 98,* 97, 277. 34. *American State Papers: Indian Affairs,* II, 563–64. 35. *House Reports, No. 98,* 412, 470. 36. *Ibid.,* 327. 37. *Ibid.,* 7–8, 269, 484. 38. *Ibid.,* 352, 572, 705, 717; *Georgia Journal,* May 17, 1825; *American State Papers: Indian Affairs,* II, 869. 39. *American State Papers: Indian Affairs,* II, 566–69; Jane Hawkins to Duncan C. Campbell and James Meriwether, May 3, 1825, in the Telamon Cuyler Collection, University of Georgia Library.

40. *Cherokee Advocate,* March 6, 1846. 41. *American State Papers: Indian Affairs,* II, 869. 42. *House Reports, No. 98,* 712, 759. 43. See the original land maps for Carroll County, in Georgia Department of Archives and History. 44. *House Reports, No. 98,* 85; John H. Goff, "Edward Lloyd Thomas, Surveyor," *Emory University Quarterly,* XVIII (Summer, 1962), 111–13. 45. *Ibid.,* 113. 46. See Rogers's field notes for January and February, 1826, in Georgia Department of Archives and History. The spot where Rogers was accosted by the Indians is on the Bowdon-Wedowee road (Highway 100) near where the northern line of lot 177 crosses the highway. 47. James A. Rogers to Governor Troup, Jan. 23, 1827, in Georgia Department of Archives and History. 48. Wiley Williams to Governor Troup, Jan. 22, 1827, in *American State Papers: Indian Affairs,* II, 865. 49. Harden, *The Life of George M. Troup,* 487.

50. Goff, "Edward Lloyd Thomas," 112–13. 51. *Carroll Free Press,* Dec. 3, 1908. Hereafter cited as *CFP.* 52. Goff, "Edward Lloyd Thomas," 112–15. 53. *House Reports, No. 98,* 825. 54. Goff, "Edward Lloyd Thomas," 115. 55. *Ibid.,* 112–15; William C. Dawson, *Compilation of the Laws of the State of Georgia* (Milledgeville, Ga., 1831), 253–57. *Acts of the General Assembly of the State of Georgia,* 1825 (Milledgeville, Ga., 1825), 3–16. Hereafter cited as *Georgia Laws,*

followed by the appropriate date.   56. Original Land Grants and Land Record Files Georgia Department of Archives and History. A copy of these, although containing many errors of transcription and some omissions, is found in Martha Lou Houston, *Reprint of the Official Register of the Land Lottery of Georgia, 1827* (Columbus, Ga., 1928).   57. George Sharp, "Reminiscences of Old Carroll County," in *CFP*, Aug. 6, Oct. 4, 1895; [Geo. F. Cheney], *Carroll County Souvenir-Historical Edition* [Carrollton, Ga., *ca.* 1910] is without pagination. Cited hereafter as Cheney, *Carroll County*.   58. Absalom H. Chappell, *Miscellanies of Georgia, Historical, Biographical, Descriptive, Etc.* (Atlanta, 1874), pt. 2, 22. 59. See the decennial manuscript census reports of Carroll County, for 1830 to 1860 inclusive. In 1850 and 1860 three separate schedules have been particularly useful in this study. They are Schedules I, II, and IV; that is, "Free Inhabitants," "Slave Inhabitants," and "Productions of Agriculture," respectively. These schedules for Carroll County, together with the list of free inhabitants for 1830, 1840, and 1880, have been copied from the originals in the National Archives and alphabetized. They are on file in the library of The Woman's College of Georgia. (After the final preparation of this book the name of Woman's College of Georgia was changed to Georgia College at Milledgeville.) Unless otherwise indicated, all citations to census data in this study refer to these alphabetized lists.

Chapter II

1. *Georgia Laws* (1826), 57.   2. Adiel Sherwood, *Gazeteer of the State of Georgia, 1827* (Charleston, S.C., 1827), 13.   3. Records of the Inferior Court of Carroll County, 1827–1846 (a manuscript in three volumes in the ordinary's office at Carrollton), I, 48. Hereafter cited as Inferior Court Records.   4. *Ibid.,* I, 1, 2, 109.   5. *Carroll County Times,* May 31, 1878. Hereafter cited as *CCT.* 6. Inferior Court Records, I, 51–52, 56.   7. *Georgia Laws* (1831), 84.   8. *Ibid.* (1829), 84, 201.   9. *Ibid.* (1831), 84, 130.

10. CCTD (1832).   11. Inferior Court Records, I, 66; Minutes of the Seventy-fourth Regiment, Georgia Militia, Aug. 12, 1831–Aug. 14, 1849, in private possession.   12. *Georgia Laws* (1833), 135.   13. Militia Districts of Carroll County, in Georgia Department of Archives and History.   14. Inferior Court Records, I, 17–18.   15. *Ibid.,* 67–68, 59; Cheney, *Carroll County.*   16. Inferior Court Records, I, 59–68.   17. Inferior Court Records, I, 151, 172.   18. *Ibid.,* I, 59.   19. *Ibid.,* 59, 240; Cheney, *Carroll County.*

20. Inferior Court Records, I, 92, 148; Cheney, *Carroll County.* 21 CFP, April 21, 1893; Cheney, *Carroll County.*   22. Cheney, *Carroll County*; Inferior Court Records, I, 67, 146.   23. Sherwood, *Gazeteer of the State of Georgia, 1827,* 139; Cheney, *Carroll County.*   24. Carroll County Post Offices (a photocopy made from records in the National Archives), in Georgia Department of Archives and History.   25. John H. Goff, "Some Major Indian Trading Paths Across the Georgia Piedmont," *Georgia Mineral Newsletter,* VI (Spring, 1953), 125; Peter Brannon, *Fort Okfuski* (Alexander City, Ala. [n. d.]), 1–5.   26. John H. Goff, "Some Old Road Names in Georgia," *Georgia Mineral Newsletter,* XI (Autumn, 1958), 101; Inferior Court Records, I, 54.   27. Inferior Court Records, I, 9, 10, 17, 54, 62–63.   28. Adiel Sherwood, *Gazeteer of the State of Georgia, 1827,* 60–63. 29. *Georgia Laws* (1826), 57, (1827), 69, (1828), 56, (1830), 48, (1855–1856), 110.

30. *Georgia Laws* (1828), 88, (1830), 53–54; *Journal of the Senate of the State of Georgia . . . November and December, 1827* (Milledgeville, Ga., 1828), 127.

Hereafter cited as *Senate Journal, 1827*. In Dec., 1931, this territory became part of Cherokee County. Georgia Laws (1831), 74.   31. Inferior Court Records, III, 57.   32. Isaac Wood to Governor George R. Gilmer, Nov. 15, 1830, in Georgia Department of Archives and History.   33. Jiles Boggess *et al.* to Governor George R. Gilmer, Dec. 1830, in Georgia Department of Archives and History. 34. Inferior Court Records, III, 49.   35. *Ibid.,* I, 5, 17, 64, III, 72.   36. *Georgia Laws* (1828), 89.   37. Cheney, *Carroll County;* Records of Carroll County, Will Book A, 288.   3. Cheney, *Carroll County; CCT,* Jan. 27, 1916; Presentments, Carroll County Grand Jury, Jan. 23, 1833, in private possession.   39. Inferior Court Records, I, 118.

40. *Georgia Laws* (1832), 68, (1833), 76–77, (1835), 74, (1837), Appendix, 18. 41. Stephen F. Miller, *The Bench and Bar of Georgia: Memoirs and Sketches* (2 vols., Philadelphia, 1858), I, 203–17.   42. Inferior Court Records, I, 143; *Georgia Laws* (1829), 12, 14, (1832), 18, (1835), 4, (1837), Appendix, 35; Elbert W. G. Boogher, *Secondary Education in Georgia, 1732–1858* (Philadelphia, 1933), 73, 378.   43. Boogher, *Secondary Education in Georgia,* 147, 219, 314, 365, 378; *Georgia Laws* (1831), 4, (1837), 8, (1838), 5. Union Academy's original trustees were Benjamin Barnes, Jason McKleray, B. Huckeba, Leroy Williams, and Charles B. Haughton.   44. William W. Merrill, "Autobiography" (an unpublished manuscript in private possession).   45. [George R. Gilmer], *A Sketch of Some of the First Settlers of Upper Georgia* (New York, 1855), 397–99.   46. George Sharp, "Old Times in Carroll County," in *CFP,* Oct. 4, 1895, Nov. 1, 1895.   47. Adiel Sherwood, *Gazeteer of the State of Georgia, 1827,* 77.   48. Cheney, *Carroll County;* CCTD (1847), 8–10.   49. Inferior Court Records, III, 1.

50. Carroll County Deed Book A, 538.   51. *Georgia Laws* (1834), 193; Adiel Sherwood, *Gazeteer of the State of Georgia, 1827,* 103, 317; George White, *Statistics of the State of Georgia* (Savannah, Ga., 1849), 20. Hereafter cited as White, *Statistics.*   52. Hawkins, *A Sketch of the Creek Country,* 52.   53. For the Muscogee meaning of "Chatta" and "Uchee" and other words in the Creek language, see Robert M. Loughridge and Daniel M. Hodge, *English and Muskokee Dictionary* (Philadelphia, 1914).   54. See for example, "Letters of Benjamin Hawkins" in *Collections of the Georgia Historical Society,* IX (1916), 345.   55. See "Journal of the Commissioners of Georgia Appointed to Run the Dividing Line Between the Boundaries of the State and Alabama," 1–17, in Georgia Department of Archives and History.   56. *CFP,* May 10, 1894.   57. George W. Yarbrough, *Boyhood and Other Days in Georgia* (Nashville, Tenn., 1917), 128. 58. *CFP,* Nov. 27, 1891.   59. A comprehensive list of data on all Georgia post offices and postmasters of this period has been compiled from records in the National Archives and indexed by Prof. Edward B. Dawson. The list has been collated and placed in the library of Georgia College. For data on the Springer family, see a typescript under this heading in the Georgia Department of Archives and History.

Chapter III

1. The University of Oklahoma Press at Norman has specialized in books on the Southern Indians. Among these are Grant Foreman, *Indian Removal: The Emigration of the Five Civilized Tribes* (1932), and Grace S. Woodward, *The Cherokees* (1963). A good general account of the Cherokees is Henry T. Malone, *Cherokees of the Old South: A People in Transition* (Athens, Ga., 1956).   2. Grant Foreman, *Indian Removal,* 294–312.   3. *Ibid.,* 119.   4. *Ibid.,*

141.   5. *Ibid.*, 149–50.   6. Other officers of this company were Zadok Bonner and Emanuel B. Martin, lieutenants; David White, ensign; William L. Parr, Otto Bell, Robert Long, and William W. Merrill, sergeants; and corporals John Boggs, Cornelius and Peter Johnson, and P. E. B. Hadrick. "A List of . . . Officers and Privates of a Company . . . of Georgia Militia raised at Carrollton, 21st May 1836" in Georgia Department of Archives and History. The *Carroll Free Press* for Feb. 23, 1894, gives a list of the surviving pensioners of the Creek War.   7. Carroll County Volunteer Company to Governor William Schley, June 7, 1836, in Georgia Department of Archives and History.   8. Joseph Little *et al.* to Governor William Schley, June 18, 1836, in Georgia Department of Archives and History.   9. Gilmer, *Sketches of Some of the First Settlers of Upper Georgia*, 397–99.

10. Foreman, *Indian Removal*, 154.   11. Thomas S. Woodward, *Reminiscences of the Creek, or Muscogee Indians*, 108.   12. Foreman, *Indian Removal*, 127.   13. *Ibid.*, 177, 187.   14. *Ibid.*, 128.   15. Bonner, "Tustunugee Hutkee and Creek Factionalism on the Georgia-Alabama Frontier," 111–25; Meserve, "The McIntoshes," 320, 323.   16. *Sixth Census, or Enumeration of the Inhabitants of the United States . . . in 1840* (Washington, D.C., 1841), 232 *et seq.* 17. Cheney, *Carroll County;* W. S. Yeates, *Geological Survey of Georgia, Bulletin No. 4* (Atlanta, 1896), 242.   18. Samuel W. McCallie, *Geological Survey of Georgia, Bulletin No. 19* (Atlanta, 1907), 128; *CCT*, July 28, 1878.   19. *Georgia Laws* (1842), 94.

20. *CFP*, Dec. 7, 1894.   21. Cheney, *Carroll County;* Joe Cobb, *History of Carroll County* ([Carrollton, Ga., *ca.* 1906]), 3.   22. Mary Ann Turner, Villa Rica, Ga., to Frances A. Williams, Nov. 3, 1854, in possession of the author. 23. *Id.* to *Id.*, June 26, [1855?].   24. The manuscript census records of free inhabitants, 1840, lists Mary Oglesby as an "instructress."   25. *Georgia Laws* (1849–1850), 26, (1853–1854), 132; Boogher, *Secondary Education in Georgia*, 365. 26. Cheney, *Carroll County.*   27. *CFP*, Dec. 21, 1883; Render R. Caswell, "The History of Bowdon College" (M.A. thesis, University of Georgia, 1952), 20–23. The author has relied upon this excellent work for information on Bowdon College, for which no specific citations are given.   28. *Ibid.*, 23 *et seq.*   29. James D. B. DeBow, *The Seventh Census of the United States, 1850* (Washington, D.C., 1853), 369.

30. For the charter, see *Georgia Laws* (1857), 137–38.   31. Caswell, "Bowdon College," 42 *et passim;* Boogher, *Secondary Education in Georgia*, 125.   32. *Catalogue of the Bowdon Collegiate Institution, 1858–1859* [Bowdon, Ga., 1858], 14–15.   33. *Ibid.*, 13, 16.   34. *Bowdon Bulletin*, Nov. 11, 1913; Caswell, "Bowdon College," 43.   35. *Georgia Laws* (1859), 136–38.   36. *CFP*, Dec. 21, 1883; *Statistics of the United States, 1860* (Washington, D.C., 1866), 365 *et passim.* 37. *CFP*, Dec. 21, 1883; George White, *Historical Collections of Georgia* (New York, 1854), 294; Minute Book, First Baptist Church, Carrollton, Aug. 1847–Dec., 1875, 1–3. Hereafter cited as Baptist Minute Book.   38. *CFP*, March 30, 1888; *Statistics of the United States, 1860*, 365 *et passim;* Cheney, *Carroll County.* 39. *CCT*, Aug. 17, 1922.

40. The Christian Index, *History of the Baptist Denomination in Georgia* (Atlanta, 1881), 161.   41. *Ibid.*, 213; *Georgia Laws* (1834), 55; Baptist Minute Book, 8, 18–19.   42. Baptist Minute Book, 74, 302.   43. *Ibid.*, 40, 302.   44. *Ibid.*, 9–10; *Directory and Manual of the First Baptist Church of Carrollton, Georgia* (Carrollton, Ga., 1923), 6.   45. *Directory and Manual of the First Baptist Church of Carrollton, Georgia*, 9, 15, 23, 32, 109; Franklin C. Talmadge, *The Presbytery of Atlanta* (Atlanta, 1960), 262.   46. Baptist Minute Book, 145. 47. *Ibid.*, 15–72.   48. *Ibid.*, 47, 54.   49. *Ibid.*, 14, 26.

50. *Ibid.*, 74. 103.   51. *Ibid.*, 78, 83, 110.   52. *Ibid.*, 68, 158.   53. *History*

of the Baptist Denomination in Georgia, 440–42; H. G. Hillyer, *Reminiscences of Georgia Baptists* (Atlanta, 1902), 136.   54. H. G. Hillyer, *Reminiscences of Georgia Baptists*, 32; Christian Index, *History of the Baptist Denomination in Georgia*, 204.

Chapter IV

1. *Georgia Laws* (1859), 57.   2. *Ibid.* (1831), 72.   **3**. *Ibid.* (1834), 73, (1847), 68, (1855–1856), 129, (1860), 46.   4. *Ibid.* (1860), 139; (1873), 232. For other changes in the line between Carroll and its adjoining counties see *ibid.* (1849–1850), 132, (1855–1856), 110, (1860), 139, (1864), 28, (1865–1866), 50, (1869), 168, 177, (1870), 13, (1871–1872), 266, (1877), 273, and (1874), 371.   5. *Ibid.* (1878–1879), 42.   6. CCTD (1842); Frances A. Walker, *A Compendium of the Ninth Census, 1870* (Washington, D.C., 1872), 34.   7. "Militia Districts of Carroll County," Georgia Department of Archives and History; *Georgia Laws* (1855–1856), 110, (1870), 13.   8. *Georgia Laws* (1853–1854), 64.   9. *Ibid.* (1859), 57.

10. *Carrollton Advocate*, Aug. 3, Sept. 7, Oct. 26, 1860.   11. *Georgia Laws* (1851–1852), 408, (1857), 33, 330; *Carrollton Advocate*, Nov. 16, 1860; White, *Statistics*, 20–21.   12. *Georgia Laws* (1851–1852), 448. Original stockholders were Appleton Mandeville, John T. Meador, John W. Wood, Sheppard K. Williams, Joseph C. Benson, Franklin Diamond, William W. Merrill, Thomas Chandler, Frederick Palmer, D. M. Bloodworth, Thomas and Zadok Bonner.   13. *Carrollton Advocate*, Aug. 3, Oct. 26, 1860.   14. *Georgia Laws* (1847), 285.   15. Inferior Court Records, II (no pagination), Jan., 1852.   16. *Georgia Laws* (1853–1854), 224, 251; *Carrollton Advocate*, Oct. 26, 1860.   17. The town's commissioners were William B. Conyers, John W. Wood, Charles Rodahan, William H. Acklin, and Henry Asbury. *Georgia Laws* (1855–1856), 390–93.   18. *Ibid.* (1858), 139.   19. Adiel Sherwood, *Gazeteer of Georgia, 1860* (Macon, 1860), 39.

20. *Carrollton Advocate*, Aug. 3, Nov. 16, 1860.   21. *CFP*, Aug. 31, 1911, Dec. 18, 1913; Sallie Robinson, "Just Some Memories of Carrollton as a Village Long Ago," *CFP*, Oct. 2, 1930. For further identification of residents see "Schedule of Free Inhabitants of Carroll County, 1860." Since the census enumerator listed residents in the order in which they were visited, it is possible to determine the approximate location of each house.   22. Archibald T. Burke to Eugenia Du-Bignon, Jekyll Island, Jan. 30, 1853, in private possession.   23. James D. B. De-Bow, *A Statistical View of the United States . . . A Compendium of the Seventh Census* (Washington, D.C., 1854), 206, 210, 345; DeBow, *The Seventh Census of the United States*, 354 *et passim;* George White, *Statistics*, 147.   24. *Carrollton Advocate*, Oct. 26, 1860.   25. See Schedule I, "Free Inhabitants of Carroll County, 1860" and Schedule IV, "Productions of Agriculture in Carroll County, 1860" (an alphabetized listing in the library of Georgia College, Milledgeville).   26. CCTD (1832, 1847).   27. See Schedule I, "Free Inhabitants," and Schedule IV, "Productions of Agriculture for Carroll County, 1860."   28. *Carrollton Advocate*, Nov. 16, 1860, March 1, 1861; Joseph C. G. Kennedy, *Population of the United States in 1860* (Washington, D.C., 1864), 63, 74.   29. CCTD (1842); Schedule II, "Slave Inhabitants of Carroll County, 1860."

30. *Carrollton Advocate*, Nov. 16, Dec. 14, 1860.   31. *Ibid.*, Dec. 14, 1860; John B. Beall, *In Barrack and Field* (Nashville, Tenn., 1906), 352.   32. *Carrollton Advocate*, Dec. 14, 1860; *Journal of the . . . Proceedings of the Convention of the People of Georgia . . .* (Milledgeville, Ga., 1861), 34–35.   33. *Carrollton Advocate*, Dec. 7, 1860.

Chapter V

1. *Carrollton Advocate,* March 1, 1861.   2. Wiley C. Howard, *Sketch of Cobb's Legion Cavalry and Some Incidents and Scenes Remembered* (Atlanta, 1901), 1 *et passim.*   3. Caswell, "The History of Bowdon College," 102 *et passim; CFP,* Dec. 21, 1883. See also Lillian Henderson, *Roster of the Confederate Soldiers of Georgia, 1861–1865* (5 vols., Hapeville, Ga., 1955–1960).   4. Beall, *In Barrack and Field,* 129, 287, 297, 367; *CFP,* Jan. 13, 1961.   5. *CFP,* April 18, 1884; Beall, *In Barrack and Field,* 319. Walter Prescott Webb, ed., *The Handbook of Texas* (2 vols., Austin, Texas, 1952), II, 99, 508.   6. Webb, *The Handbook of Texas,* II, 352.   7. *Ibid.,* 294; *CFP,* June 1, 1888.   8. Beall, *In Barrack and Field,* 307, 321.   9. *Ibid.,* 401.

10. *Ibid.,* 404.   11. *CFP,* Oct. 1, 1886.   12. Cheney, *Carroll County;* Baptist Minute Book, 131; Henderson, *Roster of the Confederate Soldiers of Georgia,* II, 734.   13. Baptist Minute Book, 109.   14. Henderson, *Roster of the Confederate Soldiers of Georgia,* II, 734.   15. *CFP,* Aug. 27, 1908, June 5, 1913.   16. *Georgia Laws* (1861), 117; Beall, *In Barrack and Field,* 294.   17. *Henderson* (Texas) *Daily News,* Oct. 7, 1964. The Carroll County Tax Digest for 1842 shows that Jiles S. Boggess at that time owned in excess of 6,000 acres of land in various parts of Georgia. By 1844 this acreage had been reduced to 4,800. By 1847 his name had disappeared from the county tax list.   18. Beall, *In Barrack and Field,* 408; Victor M. Ross, *Ross' Texas Brigade* (Louisville, Ky., 1881), 106 *et passim; The War of the Rebellion: A Compilation of the Official Records of the Union and Confederate Armies,* (129 vols. and index; Washington, D.C., 1880–1901), Ser. I, Vol. XXVIII, Pt. I, 79, 162. Hereafter cited as *Official Records.*   19. *Ibid.,* 706.

20. *CFP,* Sept. 16, 1887.   21. *Official Records,* Ser. I, Vol. XLIX, Pt. I, 418–30.   22. *Memoirs of Georgia, Historical and Biographical* (2 vols.; Atlanta, 1895), I, 448–49.   23. Cheney, *Carroll County.*   24. Beall, *In Barrack and Field,* 395.   25. *Ibid.,* 397–400.   26. *CCT,* March 29, 1872, March 30, 1922.   27. Beall, *In Barrack and Field,* 397–400.   28. *CCT,* Aug. 31, 1911; *CFP,* March 29, 1872; Records of the Bureau of Freedmen, Refugees and Abandoned Lands (Georgia), Box 187, in the National Archives, Washington, D.C. Hereafter cited as Records of the Freedman's Bureau.   29. Records of the Freedman's Bureau, R.G. No. 105, Box 186.

30. *Ibid.*   31. *CCT,* May 26, 1872. Representing the county at the Republican Convention in Macon that year were W. B. Bracewell, Benjamin Long, William W. Merrill, Robert McCurdy, A. H. Harrison, John Costin, S. T. Sims, James R. Thomason, and George West.   32. *CCT,* June 7, 1872.   33. *Ibid.,* June 14, Oct. 18, Nov. 8, 1872.   34. *Ibid.,* Oct. 18, Nov. 8, 1872.   35. *Ibid.,* Oct. 25, 1872; *Georgia Laws* (1872), 175, (1875), 158, 332, 338; Cheney, *Carroll County.* 36. *Georgia Laws* (1866), 22, (1875), 45; Melvin Clyde Hughes, *County Government in Georgia* (Athens, Ga., 1944), 13–17.   37. *Georgia Laws* (1871), 100; *CCT,* March 1, April 12, 1872, Oct. 17, 1873.   38. *CCT,* April 19, Dec. 20, 1872.   39. *Ibid.,* Jan. 5, 19, Feb. 2, 9, April 5, 1872, Aug. 1, 1873.

40. *Ibid.,* March 1, 1872, June 6, 1873; *Georgia Laws* (1875), 338.   41. *CCT,* July 19, 1878, April 8, 1881.   42. *Ibid.,* Jan. 12, March 1, 22, 1872; Walker *Compendium of the Ninth Census,* 139, 723, 816; Kennedy, *Population of the United States in 1860,* 22–24, 73–74; Robert P. Porter, *Compendium of the Eleventh Census, 1890* (Washington, D.C., 1892), 12.   43. *Manufactures of the United States in 1860* (Washington, D.C., 1865), 63 *et passim;* Walker, *Compendium of the Ninth Census,* 139, 723.   44. Frances A. Walker, *Statistics of the Wealth and Industry of the United States . . . Ninth Census* (Washington, D.C., 1872), 123, 128; Joseph C. G. Kennedy, *Agriculture of the United States in 1860* (Washington, D.C., 1864), 24–25.

Chapter VI

1. *Georgia Laws* (1853–1854), 457–60.   2. *Carrollton Advocate*, Aug. 3, 1860.   3. *CCT*, June 14, 1878; Carroll County Deed Record Book JJ, 135; M, 124; N, 109, 183, 287–88, 290, 394; O, 111, 758; Q, 190.   4. *Carrollton Advocate*, Aug. 3, Sept. 7, 1860.   5. *CFP*, Aug. 11, 1910; *CCT*, Jan. 19, 26, 1872.   6. *CCT*, Dec. 20, 1872, March 14, 21, 1873.   7. *Ibid.*, April 11, June 13, 1873.   8. *Ibid.*, May 2, 23, 1873.   9. *Georgia Laws* (1874), 170.

10. *CFP*, July 31, 1885, June 15, July 6, 1888.   11. *Ibid.*, June 15, 1888. 12. *Ibid.*, March 1, 14, 1884, Sept. 17, 1885.   13. *Ibid.*, May 18, 1894.   14. *Ibid.*, Sept. 5, 1890; The Central of Georgia Railroad Company, *The Right Way*, XLVIII (Dec., 1958).   15. *CCT*, June 13, 1873.   16. Cheney, *Carroll County*.   17. *CCT*, Sept. 8, Dec. 15, 1876, Jan. 5, 1877, March 8, Sept. 13, 1878, Feb. 14, March 14, 1879.   18. *CFP*, Oct. 17, 1890; Register of Charters, Carroll County, Book I, 23, 25, 179.   19. *CFP*, March 21, 1884, April 17, 1885, Aug. 27, 1886, Aug. 17, Sept. 14, 1888, Oct. 25, 1889; *CCT*, Aug. 23, 1878.

20. *CFP*, April 29, 1887, Sept. 21, 1888, Sept. 20, 27, 1889, Aug. 29, 1890.   21. *Ibid.*, Nov. 13, 1885, May 17, 24, Nov. 15, 1889.   22. *Ibid.*, May 11, Aug. 31, Sept. 21, 1888.   23. *Ibid.*, Sept. 14, 1888, Feb. 7, May 30, Aug. 29, Dec. 19, 1890, March 6, 1891.   24. *Ibid.*, April 25, 1890, Oct. 28, 1892.   25. *Ibid.*, Aug. 13, 1890; *CCT*, Sept. 8, 1876, April 22, 1881.   6. *CFP*, Jan. 29, 1892.   27. *Ibid.*, Nov. 15, 1889, April 6, 1893.   28. *Ibid.*, Feb. 24, May 12, Sept. 23, 1893, Jan. 26, 1894.   29. White, *Statistics*, 146–47; *Georgia Laws* (1850), 253.

30. *CFP*, Sept. 16, 1887, June 7, 1889; *Georgia Laws* (1865–1866), 134; Deed Record Book O, 736.   31. Deed Record Book I, 30; *CCT*, June 3, 1881; *CFP*, April 5, 1895, March 12, 1914, Aug. 15, 1929; *Memoirs of Georgia*, I, 425–26; Mrs. Benjamin L. Camp, "Whitesburg and Her People," *CFP*, Feb. 9, 1928.   32. *CFP*, June 23, 1893.   33. *Ibid.*, April 18, 1890, June 26, 1891, June 9, 1893.   34. *Ibid.*, March 21, 1890, Jan. 27, 1893, June 1, 1910.   35. *CCT*, July 4, 1876, April 19, 1878; Cheney, *Carroll County;* Yeates, *Geological Survey of Georgia*, 288.   36. *CFP*, Dec. 21, 1883, Nov. 21, 1884, Aug. 8, 1890, Sept. 1, 1893, Dec. 7, 1894, March 1, April 26, 1895, July 3, 1933.   37. *Ibid.*, Sept. 17, 1886, May 17, Dec. 13, 1889. Early prominent citizens of that town included William Sheets, John Velvin, J. H. Dobson, Thomas Tolbert, William P. Stone, George Waddy, Francis Fielder, William Malone, and William B. Candler.   38. Charles Howard Candler, *Asa Griggs Candler* (Atlanta, 1953), 26–28 *et passim; Memoirs of Georgia*, II, 415.   39. *Memoirs of Georgia*, I, 438–39; *CFP*, April 8, 1884, Nov. 17, 1893.

40. *CFP*, May 8, 1889, March 6, 1891, Nov. 12, 1894.   41. *Ibid.*, Nov. 22, 1889, Feb. 5, 1892.   42. James C. Bonner, *A Short History of Heard County* (Milledgeville, Ga., 1962), 1 *et passim.*   43. *CFP*, Oct. 23, 1885; *CCT*, Jan. 3, 1873.   44. *CFP*, July 2, 1886, May 29, 1892.   45. *Ibid.*, Feb. 1, Sept. 6, 1895. 46. *CCT*, May 11, 1878, April 11, 1879; *Memoirs of Georgia*, I, 44.   47. *CCT*, Dec. 20, 1878; Walker, *Compendium of the Ninth Census*, 1870, 816.   48. *CCT*, March 12, 1880; Caswell, "The History of Bowdon College," 72–73, 90.   49. *CFP*, Feb. 18, 1887, April 8, 1892; Caswell, "The History of Bowdon College," 90; Sanford H. Cohen, *Compendium of Georgia: Legal and Commercial Guide for 1901* (Augusta, Ga., 1901), 151.

50. Georgia-Alabama Investment and Development Co., *Prospectus of the City of Tallapoosa* (Boston, 1891), 1–4.   51. *Ibid.*, 64; Lee S. Trimble, "A Connecticut Yankee in Tallapoosa," *Georgia Review*, VI (Fall, 1952), 353–57.   52. *Prospectus of the City of Tallapoosa*, 4, 12, 30, 66.   53. *Atlanta Constitution*, June 9, 1891. 54. *CFP*, Dec. 1, 1893.   55. *CCT*, July 22, 1891; *CFP*, July 19, 1895.   56. *Ibid.*, Nov. 23, 1883, May 2, 1884, July 19, 1889.   57. Norman H. Winfrey, *A History of*

Rusk County, Texas (Waco, Texas, 1961), 128–29; Mrs. C. F. Potts, Dallas, Texas, to James C. Bonner, Feb. 22, 1965; *CCT*, Jan. 9, 1880, Oct. 28, 1881.   58. *CCT*, Oct. 28, 1881, June 14, 1884; *CFP*, Nov. 23, 1883, Feb. 8, 1884.   59. *CFP*, Dec. 21, 1883.

Chapter VII

1. Quoted in *CFP*, May 24, 1889.   2. *Ibid.*, Nov. 25, 1887; *CCT*, Aug. 31, 1877.   3. Register of Charters, Carroll County, Book I, 7; *CFP*, April 6, 1889. 4. *CFP*, April 20, 1894, Oct. 13, 1927, July 18, 1929.   5. *CCT*, Jan. 17, 1879.   6. *CFP*, Aug. 17, 1888, March 1, 1889.   7. *CCT*, Feb. 23, 1877.   8. *CCT*, Feb. 14, 1873, Jan. 4, 1878.   9. *Ibid.*, June 6, 1873, Feb. 23, 1877, Feb. 18, 1887; *CFP*, April 4, 1890.

10. *Ibid.*, Jan. 12, 1890, April 14, 1893, Feb. 23, 1894.   11. *CCT*, March 23, 1877:   12. *CFP*, Dec. 31, 1886.   13. *CCT*, Jan. 2, 1880.   14. *Ibid.*, Jan. 5, 1877.   15. *CFP*, Nov. 15, 1889, Jan. 3, 1893.   16. *CCT*, Jan. 5, 1872, Sept. 8, 1876.   17. *CFP*, March 1, 1889.   18. *CCT*, May 7, 1880.   19. *CFP*, Jan. 6, 1888.

20. *Ibid.*, Nov. 8, 1889.   21. *CCT*, March 3, 1876.   22. *CFP*, March 28, 1890, Nov. 20, 1891.   23. *CCT*, Aug. 9, 1872.   24. *CFP*, Feb. 20, Oct. 23, 1891. 25. *Ibid.*, April 8, May 16, 1884.   26. *Ibid.*, Nov. 8, 1889, April 24, 1891.   27. *Ibid.*, July 16, 1886, Sept. 6, 1889.   28. *Ibid.*, June 28, 1889.   29. *Ibid.*, July 12, 1888.

30. *Ibid.*, July 26, 1889.   31. *Ibid.*, April 26, 1889.   32. *CCT*, May 11, 1877. 33. *CFP*, July 25, 1884.   34. *Ibid.*, Sept. 5, 1884.   35. *Ibid.*, Aug. 22, 1890.   36. *CCT*, Jan. 5, 1877.   37. *CFP*, Jan. 9, 1885.   38. *Ibid.*, Jan. 4, 1884.   39. *Ibid.*, Jan. 9, 1885.

40. *Ibid.*, Jan. 23, Dec. 18, 1885.   41. *Ibid.*, March 27, 1885, June 17, 1887. 42. *Ibid.*, June 24, 1887.   43. *Ibid.*, Dec. 1, 1893, May 11, 1894.   44. *Georgia Laws* (1876), 181.   45. *CCT*, March 3, 10, 1876.   46. *Ibid.*, April 14, Sept. 8, 1876.   47. *Georgia Laws* (1876), 359, 596, 634, 640, 716.   48. *CFP*, Sept. 10, 1876, Jan. 6, 1894.   49. *Ibid.*, Aug. 2, 1909.

50. *Ibid.*, Feb. 13, 1891.   51. John Boykin McGehee, *Autobiography of Rev. J. B. McGehee, D. D. of the South Georgia Conference* ([Buena Vista, Ga.], n.d.), 136, 139; *CCT*, Dec. 19, 1873.   52. *CCT*, Oct. 26, 1878.   53. *Ibid.*, Feb. 11, June 23, 1876.   54. *Ibid.*, March 11, Aug. 12, 1881.   55. Irby Henderson, "Carroll Methodism from 1828 to 1927" in *CFP*, Oct. 13, 1927; *ibid.*, Oct. 31, 1918; *CCT*, April 4, 1879.   56. *Who Was Who in America 1797–1942*, Vol. I (Chicago, 1962); *CCT*, Dec. 10, 13, 1880.   57. *CFP*, Sept. 4, 1885; Register of Charters, Carroll County, I, 78.   58. *CFP*, Oct. 31, 1918; Baptist Minute Book, 131, 140. 59. *Minutes of the Third Annual Session of the Carrollton Baptist Association* (Atlanta, 1876), 1 *et passim; Minutes of the Fourth Annual Session of the Carrollton Baptist Association* (Atlanta, 1877), 1 *et passim.*

60. *Minutes of the Seventeenth Annual Session of the Carrollton Baptist Association 1890* (Atlanta, 1890), 1 *et passim.*   61. Register of Charters, Carroll County, Book I, 35; Irby Henderson, "Carroll Methodism" in *CFP*, Oct. 13, 1927; Baptist Church Minutes, Jan. 3, 1874.   62. *Directory and Manual of the First Baptist Church of Carrollton, Georgia*, 6.   63. Minutes, Tabernacle Baptist Church, Dec. 15, 1899; Baptist Tabernacle Enrollment Book (n.d.).   64. Presbyterian Church Records, Book II, 8, 63; *Manual and Directory of the Presbyterian*

Church of Carrollton, Georgia, 1841–1845 (Carrollton, Ga., *ca.* 1845), 7–9. 65. Talmadge, *The Presbytery of Atlanta*, 220 *et passim*. 66. *Ibid.*, 6, 26, 62, 100. 67. Baptist Minute Book, 54. 68. Presbyterian Church Records, Aug. 25, 1871, Aug. 17, 1879, Feb. 27, 1880. 69. *Ibid.*, Book I, 56–57, 61; *CCT*, Jan. 30, 1880.

70. *CCT*, March 26, 1880; *CFP*, Aug. 7, 1919; Talmadge, *The Presbytery of Atlanta*, 92, 100, 226. 71. *CFP*, Aug. 7, 1919. 72. *CCT*, March 26, 1880. 73. Record Book, St. Margaret's Parish, Jan. 20, 1894, *et passim;* Henry T. Malone, *The Episcopal Church in Georgia* (Atlanta, [1960]), 150, 214, 226, 263, 276, 288–91. 74. *CFP*, Sept. 4, 1885, July 2, 1886, Jan. 1, 1917; Dermon A. Sox to James C. Bonner, July 28, 1965. 75. *CCT*, Nov. 27, 1876. 76. Schedule I, Free Inhabitants of Carroll County, 1880; Porter, *Compendium of the Eleventh Census, 1890*, Pt. 1, 480, 517. 77. Porter, *Compendium of the Eleventh Census, 1890*, Pt. II, 265. 78. Register of Medical Practitioners, Carroll County, 1881–1961, 1–5. 79. Harvey Young, *The Toadstool Millionaires* (Princeton, N.J., 1961), 158.

80. *CFP*, April 18, 1890, Feb. 24, 1893. 81. *Ibid.*, April 4, 1884, Nov. 25, 1892. 82. *Ibid.*, Jan. 10, 1891, July 7, 1893; *CCT*, May 24, 1872. 83. Young, *The Toadstool Millionaires*, 68–69, 221–22, 226, 227, 240, 244, 247. 84. *CFP*, Jan. 20, 1888, Jan. 8, 1888. 85. Register of Charters, Carroll County, Book I, 88 *et passim*. 86. *CFP*, Sept. 25, 1885. 87. Porter, *Compendium of the Eleventh Census, 1890*, Pt. II, 34–37. 88. *CFP*, Sept. 25, 1885, July 16, 1886. 89. *CCT*, Dec. 21, 1877.

90. *CFP*, Nov. 30, 1894. 91. *Ibid.*, Sept. 25, 1891, Feb. 19, 1892.

Chapter VIII

1. *CCT*, Aug. 17, 1877, June 6, 1879, Jan. 16, 1880. 2. *Ibid.*, Jan. 10, 1873, May 3, 1878. 3. *CFP*, Feb. 22, 1884, Sept. 10, 1886. 4. *CCT*, July 15, 1881. 5. *Ibid.*, March 2, 1877; *CFP*, March 9, 1886, May 3, 1889. 6. *Georgia Laws* (1872), 34–36; David Irwin, *The Code of the State of Georgia* (Atlanta, 1882), 300–301. 7. *CFP*, Sept. 18, 1885. 8. *Ibid.*, Feb. 22, 1884, April 1, 15, May 20, July 8, Sept. 16, Dec. 16, 1887. 9. *Ibid.*, Feb. 1, Aug. 9, 1889; *CCT*, Dec. 16, 1881; *Georgia Laws* (1884–1885), 29.

10. *CFP*, Aug. 30, 1889, May 16, 19, 1890. 11. *Ibid.*, May 15, 1885, July 16, 1886, March 27, 1891. 12. *CCT*, July 24, 1876. 13. *Ibid.*, March 17, Aug. 18, 1876, Jan. 26, 1877, March 21, 1879. 14. *CFP*, Sept. 2, Oct. 28, 1887. 15. *Ibid.*, Jan. 27, July 20, 1888, Jan. 24, Feb. 28, 1890. 16. *Ibid.*, March 8, May 10, July 26, 1889. William O. Perry was secretary and John W. Brooks was president of the board of directors. W. W. Goodman and Jesse Travis were assistants. 17. *Ibid.*, Feb. 21, 1890, Aug. 6, 1895. 18. Arthur S. Link, *American Epoch* (New York, 1956), 8. 19. *CCT*, Jan. 5, 1877.

20. *Ibid.*, Aug. 18, 1876, Aug. 9, 1878. 21. *CFP*, Aug. 31, 1888; James C. Bonner, "Legislative Apportionment and the County Unit System in Georgia," *Georgia Historical Quarterly*, XLVII (Dec., 1963), 351–74. 22. *CFP*, Aug. 1, 13, Nov. 14, 1890. 23. *Ibid.*, May 18, 1888, May 23, June 6, 1890, June 6, 1891, Nov. 15, 1928. 24. *Ibid.*, April 15, 1892. 25. *Ibid.*, Sept. 5, 1890, Nov. 4, 11, 1892, Jan. 6, 1893. 26. Educational History of Carroll County, 1871–1928 (Scrapbook in the office of the Carroll County Superintendent of Schools, Carrollton, Ga.). 27. *CFP*, April 28, Nov. 17, 1893; U.S. Congress, *Testimony . . . To Inquire Into The Conditions of Affairs in the Late Insurrectionary States* (13 vols.; Washing-

ton, D.C., 1872), VI, 549–55. 28. *CFP,* Dec. 22, 1893, April 24, 1894; *CCT,* March 3, 1876. 29. *CFP,* April 20, Dec. 7, 1894.

30. *Ibid.,* May 21, June 29, 1894. 31. *Ibid.,* June 1, Sept. 14, 1894. 32. *Ibid.,* Oct. 5, 1894; Olive Hall Shadgett, *The Republican Party in Georgia* (Athens, Ga., 1964), 114. 33. *CFP,* Oct. 5, 1894. 34. *Ibid.,* Oct. 19, Nov. 9, 1894, Jan. 4, 1895. 35. *Ibid.,* Dec. 14, 1894. 36. *Ibid.,* Feb. 1, March 8, 15, 1895. 37. *Ibid.,* Feb. 14, 1896. 38. *CCT,* Aug. 18, 1876. 39. *CFP,* March 25, 1892, Feb. 14, 1896; *Georgia Laws* (1890–1891), 471–74.

40. *CFP,* Nov. 20, 1891, April 8, 1892, Aug. 4, 1932; Register of Charters, Carroll County, I, 179. 41. *CFP,* March 18, 1892, June 9, 1893; *CCT,* June 3, 1873. 42. *Ibid.,* Feb. 7, 1873, March 3, 1876; *CFP,* Oct. 24, 1912. 43. *Georgia Laws* (1877), 52–53; Educational History of Carroll County (scrapbook). 44. *Georgia Laws* (1884–1885), 427, 429; *CFP,* Sept. 18, 1889, April 21, 1893, Nov. 7, 1918. 45. *CFP,* Aug. 1, 1890; *Biographical Directory of the American Congress, 1774–1961* (Washington, D.C., 1961), 1366, 1853. 46. *CFP,* Jan. 10, 1929; *Official Congressional Directory* (Washington, D.C., 1900), 15.

Chapter IX

1. Educational History of Carroll County. 2. *CCT,* May 10, 1872. 3. *Ibid.,* April 13, 1877. 4. *Ibid.,* April 15, 1881. 5. *CFP,* March 1, 1928. 6. *Ibid.,* Oct. 13, 1927; *CCT,* Jan. 5, 1872. 7. *CCT,* Oct. 25, 1872; Sallie Robinson, "A Sketch of My Life" in *CFP,* Sept. 18, 1930. 8. Dorothy Orr, *A History of Education in Georgia* (Chapel Hill, N.C., 1950), 110, 113, 117–18, 119, 122, 124, 152, 165–68; 413; *CFP,* Jan. 7, 1926. 9. *CFP,* Jan. 11, March 7, 1884.

10. *Ibid.,* July 4, 1884. 11. *Ibid.,* Dec. 25, 1885; *CCT,* Jan. 31, 1873. 12. Mary Edward Mitchell, *Memoirs of James Mitchell* (n.p., n.d.), 15 *et passim.* 13. *Ibid.,* 18 *et passim;* Minutes of the Mount Zion Seminary Association of Carroll County, Georgia, 1778–December, 1895, 1 *et passim.* There is another minute book dated 1878–May 12, 1916, the earlier entries of which appear to be copies made from the first minute book. 14. *Ibid.,* 24 *et passim; CFP,* Jan. 3, 1890, Aug. 11, 1893; *Mount Zion Methodist Church Centennial, 1865–1965* ([Carrollton, Ga., 1965]). 15. *CFP,* April 12, 1895; *Memoirs of Georgia,* I, 425–26. 16. *CFP,* Jan. 16, 1891. 17. Register of Charters, Carroll County, Book I. 18. Orr, *Education in Georgia,* 225; *Georgia Laws* (1886), 306. 19. *CFP,* Aug. 19, Sept. 23, 1887, Sept. 7, 1888, Sept. 13, 1889.

20. *Ibid.,* Sept. 20, 1889, Feb. 19, 1892. 21. *Ibid.,* July 31, 1891, July 7, 1893; William J. Northen, *Men of Mark in Georgia* (7 vols.; Atlanta, 1907–1912), IV, 1; Caswell, "The History of Bowdon College," 200. 22. *CFP,* Sept., 13, 1889, May 9, Sept. 5, 1890, June 24, 1898. 23. *Ibid.,* July 21, 1893, June 24, 1898; Orr, *Education in Georgia,* 216–18. 24. *CFP,* April 14, 1893; *Memoirs of Georgia,* I, 413. 25. *CFP,* April 22, 1892. 26. *Ibid.,* Nov. 4, 1909; Orr, *Education in Georgia,* 218. 27. *CFP,* Feb. 2, 1933. 28. *The Model School* ([Temple, Ga., *ca.* 1904]), 6. 29. *Ibid.,* 5, 17, 27.

30. Paul Cobb, Temple, Ga., to James C. Bonner, Aug. 20, 1965. 31. *CFP,* Jan. 9, 18, Feb. 20, 1908; Dec. 6, 1934; *The First Annual Commencement of the Agricultural and Mechanical School of the Fourth Congressional District of Georgia* (Carrollton, Ga., July 25, 1907); Minutes, Board of Trustees, A&M School, 1907–1914, 8. 32. *CFP,* Jan. 20, 13, March 20, April 9, 1908. 33. *Ibid.,* April 16,

June 16, 1908; Irvine S. Ingram, "Development and Significance of the District Agricultural and Mechanical Arts Schools in Georgia," in James C. Bonner and Lucien E. Roberts, eds., *Studies in Georgia History and Government* (Athens, Ga., 1940), 172–90.   34. John T. Wheeler, *Two Hundred Years of Agricultural Education in Georgia* (Danville, Ill., 1948), 67, 222, 225, 250.   35. *CFP*, March 30, April 20, 27, 1933; *Carroll County Georgian*, Aug. 19, 1965.   36. *Carroll County Georgian*, Aug. 25, 1921, Sept. 8, 1927; Caswell, "The History of Bowdon College," 104–105.   37. Caswell, "The History of Bowdon College," 110; *Abstract of the Fifteenth Census of the United States, 1930* (Washington, D.C., 1933).   38. *CFP*, May 18, 1911, April 10, 1913, May 16, 1918, Aug. 21, 1919.   39. *Ibid.*, Oct. 28, 1908; Nov. 4, 1919; Carrollton *Times-Free Press,* Dec. 13, 1955; Lee S. Trimble, "Personal Memoirs," in private possession; Mitchell, *Memoirs of James Mitchell,* 24 *et passim.*

40. *CFP*, Jan. 21, 1932, July 27, 1965; Carrollton *Times-Free Press,* Aug. 24, 1965; *Carroll County Georgian*, Sept. 2, 1965; *Georgia Educational Directory 1963–64* (Atlanta, 1964), 75–76, 179.   41. Carrollton *Times-Free Press,* Aug. 31, 1965; *Carroll County Georgian*, Sept. 9, 1965.

Chapter X

1. *CFP*, Aug. 23, 1923; *Thirteenth Census of the United States . . . 1910* (Washington, D.C., 1913).   2. *CFP*, Jan. 28, 1909.   3. *Ibid.*, Aug. 23, 1917, Jan. 3, 1918.   4. *Ibid.*, Nov. 1, 1917.   5. *Ibid.*, May 30, 1918.   6. Quoted in *ibid.*, June 20, 1918.   7. *Ibid.*   8. *Ibid.*, May 9, 1918.   9. *Ibid.*, Dec. 21, 1918.

10. *Ibid.*, April 17, May 8, 1919.   11. *Manual and Directory of the Presbyterian Church of Carrollton, Georgia, 1841–1954* ([Carrollton, Ga., 1954]), 9 *et passim*; Presbyterian Church Records; Register of Charters, Carroll County, 79; *CFP*, May 1, 1913, Nov. 25, 1915; Minutes, Tabernacle Baptist Church, Oct. 12, 1912, Feb. 5, 1913, June 8, 1914.   12. *CFP*, Dec. 11, 1913, Dec. 21, 1921.   13. St. Margaret's Parish Handbook, 1963; Record Book, St. Margaret's Parish, Aug. 1, 1921.   14. Lee S. Trimble, "A Connecticut Yankee in Tallapoosa," 353–55.   15. Richard B. Morrow, *The Story of Our Lady of Perpetual Help* (Carrollton, Ga., 1965), 1–11; *Carroll County Georgian*, Jan. 13, 1966.   16. *CFP*, Oct. 21, 1915, July 17, 1924, Oct. 13, 31, Nov. 17, 1927, March 1, 1929; James D. Hamrick, "The Masonic Institute in Carroll County," in *ibid.*, Oct. 13, 1927.   17. Register of Charters, Carroll County, 128.   18. *CFP*, April 3, 1913, May 8, 1914.   19. *Ibid.*, July 13, 1911, Jan. 4, 1912.

20. *Ibid.*, Oct. 7, 1909, Aug. 25, 1910.   21. *Ibid.*, Nov. 21, 1912.   22. *Ibid.*, Sept. 25, 1919.   23. *Ibid.*, Feb. 17, Oct. 13, 1927.   24. *Ibid.*, Oct. 27, 1927.   25. *Ibid.*, July 26, 1917, July 20, 1920, July 6, 1922.   26. *Ibid.*, Nov. 2, 1933, May 3, 1934.   27. *Ibid.*, Sept. 14, 1920.   28. *Ibid.*, June 10, 1891, June 20, 1909; *Boston Transcript*, Oct. 1, 1927; Rebecca Paschal, "The Romance of a Doctor's Life," a typescript in private possession.   29. Arthur D. Little, "A Leaf Out of Medical History," *The Journal of the Medical Association of Georgia*, XXXII (1942); 5–7; *CFP*, May 29, 1924.

30. Carroll County Marriage Licenses, Book K, 29.   31. *CFP*, Aug. 19, 1909.   32. *Ibid.*, July 11, 1912, May 15, 1913, April 16, 1914.   33. *Ibid.*, Nov. 3, 1913, June 24, 1915; University of the South, Alumni Records, Class of 1908, Sewanee, Tenn.   34. *CFP*, June 24, 1915.   35. *Ibid.*, June 15, 1916, May 1, 1919; State Board of Medical Examiners v. Lewis, 149 Ga. 716–24.   36. *CFP*, Jan. 13, 1921.

37. *Ibid.*, March 20, 1922.   38. *Ibid.*, May 22, 1924.   39. *Reports, Georgia Court of Appeals*, XXXI, 177; Minutes Haralson Superior Court, Jan., 1916, 3; Bench Docket No. 2, Records of the Superior Court of Haralson County, p. 12.

40. M. Virginia Dwyer, ed., *American Medical Director, 1958* (Chicago, 1958); Dr. David S. Reese to James C. Bonner, Dec. 20, 1965.   41. Cheney, *Carroll County; CFP*, Aug. 24, 1911, Aug. 15, 1929; Cohen, *Compendium of Georgia*, 99, 151.   42. Register of Charters, Carroll County, 54, 72–74; *CFP*, Feb. 21, 1896, Aug. 11, 1910; L. C. Mandeville, "Annual Report, 1914" in *CFP*, July 23, 1927.   43. *CFP*, Aug. 11, 1927.   44. John R. Newell to James C. Bonner, Sept. 15, 1965.   45. *CFP*, Nov. 1, 1923, Sept. 22, 1927; Register of Charters, Carroll County, 267, 247.   46. *Southwire* [a report for 1970] (Carrolton, 1970).   47. Russell O. Cleghorn, "Villa Rica Mines" in *CFP*, July 6, 1933; T. H. Aldrich, Jr., Assay Log Book, Jan., 1915–Dec., 1917, in private possession.   48. Register of Charters, Carroll County, Book I, 98, 146, 155–58, 232, 242–45.   49. *CFP*, Nov. 30, 1916.

50. *Ibid.*, Feb. 4, Aug. 26, 1909, Oct. 7, 24, 1912, Feb. 12, 1925; Cohen, *Compendium of Georgia, 1901*, 105; Minutes, Bank of Villa Rica, Feb. 14, 1899.   51. *CFP*, Jan. 4, April 12, Oct. 13, 1921, March 8, 1923, March 25, 1926, Jan. 6, 1927.   52. *Ibid.*, Feb. 2, 1928, Nov. 2, 1930.   53. *Ibid.*, Nov. 3, Dec. 1, 1932; Financial Statement, Peoples Bank, June 30, 1970.   54. Financial Statement, Carrollton Federal Savings and Loan Association, Dec. 1, 1970.   55. *CFP*, April 28, 1910.   56. Register of Charters, Carroll County, Book I, 66; *CFP*. Feb. 4, 1909, April 21, Sept. 29, 1910, March 27, 1930.   57. *CFP*, April 22, 1909.   58. *Ibid.*, Jan. 28, 1909; Deed Record Book KK, 469.   59. *CFP*, Aug. 20, 1908, Aug. 5, 1909.

60. *Ibid.*, Feb. 13, March 13, 1913.   61. *Ibid.*, Sept. 11, 1911, April 4, 1912, July 20, 1913, Nov. 18, 1915.   62. *Ibid.*, Aug. 20, 1908, June 10, 1909, Aug. 24, 1911, Aug. 22, 1912, Oct. 21, 1915; Cohen, *Compendium of Georgia, 1901*, 65–90.   63. *CFP*, Feb. 23, 1933.   64. *Ibid.*, April 14, 1910.   65. *Ibid.*, Dec. 9, 1909, May 19, 1910.   66. *Ibid.*, Aug. 10, 1916, Jan. 18, June 7, 1917, Oct. 25, 1921, May 18, 1922, April 19, 1928.   67. *Ibid.*, June 26, Sept. 8, Oct. 22, 23, 1919, Oct. 7, 1920.   68. *Ibid.*, Nov. 25, 1915, March 28, 1918, July 3, Aug. 14, 1919.   69. *Ibid.*, Feb. 4, April 8, 1926.

70. *Ibid.*, Oct. 17, 1920, Nov. 17, 1927, July 23, 1925.   71. *Ibid.*, Oct. 17, 1920, Nov. 17, 1927, June 18, 1931; William C. Roop to Mrs. H. M. Byrd, Jan. 14, 1965, in private possession.   72. *CFP*, Jan. 28, 1915, March 30, 1916, Feb. 3, 1921, May 11, 1922, Nov. 26, 1925, Feb. 3, 9, Dec. 13, 1928; U.S. Department of Agriculture, *Soil Survey of Carroll County, Georgia* (Washington, 1924), 1–5.   73. *CFP*, July 20, 1933.   74. *United States Census of Agriculture, 1959, Georgia*, Vol. I, pt. 28 (Washington, 1961), 182.

Appendix I

A List of Slaveholders in Carroll County in 1860

This data was compiled from the manuscript census returns for 1860, namely, Schedule II, "Slave Inhabitants" and Schedule IV, "Productions of Agriculture."

The names of slaveholders who do not also appear on the agricultural schedule are indicated by an asterisk. The figure given for livestock represents the combined total of horses, mules, cattle, hogs, and sheep. No changes have been made in the spelling used by enumerators.

NAME	SLAVES	IMPROVED ACRES	UNIMPROVED ACRES	BALES OF COTTON	TOTAL LIVESTOCK
Acklin, W. H.*	1				
Adams, Alsa	4	85	130	1	80
Adams, B. T.	1	35	70	1	5
Aderhold, Wm. N.	4	30	70	1	20
Allan, S. W.	2	60	90	2	22
Allen, A. H.	5	80	80	17	54
Allman, Estah*	12				
Arnold, A. C.	2	60	140	2	35
Avery, Mary	11	100	200	2	62
Avery, Richard	5	30	170	2	24
Awtry, W. H.	9	115	185	–	86
Awtry, Geo. W.*	1				
Ayres, A. G.	4	100	40	17	40
Ayres, John	1	60	110	2	20
Ayes, J.*	2				
Backus, Jas.	1	75	725	3	63
Barnes, J. H.	2	65	137	5	52

Slaveholders in Carroll County in 1860

NAME	SLAVES	IMPROVED ACRES	UNIMPROVED ACRES	BALES OF COTTON	TOTAL LIVESTOCK
Barrow, John*	1				
Barrow, Wm.*	1				
Baskin, C. W.	2	75	95	1	24
Baskin, Jas.	9	125	525	15	76
Baskin, Jas. L.	3	23	15	4	20
Baxter, Ruben	6	100	300	4	77
Beall, L. T. Z.*	6				
Beall, Nancy*	2				
Bell, Wm. L.	10	75	325	4	150
Benson, E.*	8				
Benson, Edi*	22				
Benson, Eli	6	200	75	7	100
Benson, J. W.	3	75	380	3	50
Benson, John W.	1	70	385	–	45
Bird, Willy*	1				
Blackburn, E. P.	6	100	107	8	18
Blackinson, A. G.	7	200	600	21	96
Blackwell, Jas. M.*	3				
Blanchard, B. L.	2	62	40	6	21
Bledsoe, W. H.*	1				
Bloodworth, D. M.	18	200	400	15	74
Bloodworth, W. L.	1	33	17	4	25
Bomwell, J. T.*	2				
Bonner, John	8	80	320	26	81
Bonner, Smith	13	250	256	20	95
Bonner, Thos.	24	350	350	10	205
Bonner, W. F.	14	90	162	9	116
Bonner, Zadock	32	500	800	47	232
Bonson, Jas. C.*	7				
Boon, Nancy	14	200	375	21	91
Boon, Wm. R.	6	150	750	19	103
Boyd, H. H.	1	125	75	–	18
Bridges, Ensel*	8				
Bridges, Jas. M.	5	150	450	3	44
Brodme, Jas. H.*	1				
Brooks, Robert*	5				
Broom, Gray	9	150	150	16	69
Broome, S.*	14				
Brown, David*	8				
Brown, T. T.	11	55	185	2	21
Browning, H. B.	6	125	275	10	56
Bruds, Lucy*	1				
Bryan, Ann	1	60	250	3	26
Bryan, U. W.*	4				

NAME	SLAVES	IMPROVED ACRES	UNIMPROVED ACRES	BALES OF COTTON	TOTAL LIVESTOCK
Bryce, Jas.	2	100	255	5	42
'Burke, T.	5	100	300	4	76
Burns, Samuel	4	80	122	6	60
Buckum, Finz*	1				
Burks, A. G.*	17				
Burrow, Teresa	2	75	75	8	47
Byron, W. W.	4	200	400	20	72
Campbell, F. C.	9	175	600	8	64
Candler, S. C.	18	230	140	33	136
Cardin, Thos.	3	50	109	–	15
Carnes, Thos.	7	152	552	3	47
Carson, Jas. W.	1	–	–	–	5
Carter, J. M.	3	–	–	3	3
Chambers, J. T.	10	100	475	1	103
Chance, W.	1	40	60	4	33
Chandler, Thos.	11	80	400	2	60
Chapman, S. B.	19	200	170	7	67
Cheves, Jas. M.	7	–	–	13	31
Cobb, J. M.	1	75	85	5	42
Cobb, J. N.	2	50	50	7	20
Cobb, Mary	5	25	380	1	43
Cobb, W. W.	4	90	180	5	45
Cockrell, J.	1	50	50	2	28
Cohen, Abram*	1				
Colclough, C. H.*	4				
Colcough, Alex	14	160	470	4	70
Cole, E. F.	4	25	75	2	44
Colquitt, W. L.	5	30	50	–	40
Connell, Geo. G.*	9				
Cook, Sarah*	1				
Cook, Sherm	3	40	150	9	44
Cooper, J. P.*	5				
Cooper, Wm. B.	6	35	465	2	46
Copeland, David*	4				
Copeland, Wm.	2	45	155	12	39
Crider, Martin	3	70	80	1	70
Crow, David	3	100	102	11	33
Curtis, Nancy*	4				
Daniel, W. H.	21	40	540	–	96
Davis, Ethan	3	37	112	5	31
Davis, John	7	15	10	2	26
Dickson, S. C.*	6				
Dobbs, Elijah*	45				
Dobbs, J. D.	1	40	100	–	40

NAME	SLAVES	IMPROVED ACRES	UNIMPROVED ACRES	BALES OF COTTON	TOTAL LIVESTOCK
Dobbs, Linny*	1				
Dorrough, J. M.	2	25	175	3	29
Driver, G. W.	5	200	400	17	95
Duke, Ed	8	70	132	2	37
Duke, Jas. H.	7	225	275	11	61
Duke, Thos.*	1				
Duncan, Elias	6	25	35	3	10
Dyer, John	1	55	245	4	68
Echols, Jno. C.	17	175	125	5	136
Echols, Winston	13	175	175	9	115
Edge, Jas.	2	60	142	17	29
Elam, John	4	75	200	1	62
Embry, A. O.	3	90	112	1	67
Espy, Eliz.*	8				
Eston, Jas. B.*	1				
Evans, F. P.	19	200	135	40	99
Fidder, T. M.*	5				
Fiddler, F. M.	7	130	270	6	46
Fletcher, Eliz.	4	20	120	–	11
Gamaney, Wm. L.*	5				
Gamble, J. B.	14	125	175	–	71
Garrison, B. J.	1	90	120	1	54
Garrison, P. S.	2	25	70	2	14
Gary, B. M.*	13				
Gary, John*	7				
Gates, W. W.*	3				
Gibson, John	1	40	60	3	24
Gillespy, P. H.	3	60	140	4	57
Gray, E.	1	40	100	5	29
Gray, Jas.	2	100	305	4	65
Green, A. P.	1	67	105	–	56
Gregory, O.	2	75	72	3	47
Gresham, Ed	16	160	75	31	90
Grey, Jesse	1	140	120	14	68
Griffin, Jas. M.	1	127	73	3	13
Gunner, Wm. G.*	11				
Hamick, Jas. W.*	5				
Hammick, R. W.*	1				
Hammock, G. B.	4	70	230	2	84
Handly, Jas. M.	1	225	1100	1	75
Hanson, Margaret*	4				
Harden, Thos.	7	75	127	5	37
Harmick, Harrison*	3				
Hargrave, B. W.	17	100	50	8	23

NAME	SLAVES	IMPROVED ACRES	UNIMPROVED ACRES	BALES OF COTTON	TOTAL LIVESTOCK
Harrison, A. H.*	4				
Hart, Jas. L.*	1				
Hart. J. T.*	2				
Hart, Sam	24	340	100	16	180
Harvey, Lucy*	3				
Hay, D. R.*	7				
Hay, Howell	2	80	20	1	21
Hesterly, F. P.*	1				
Hildebrand, J. H.	5	75	125	5	28
Hill, J. B.	4	67	67	5	44
Hilton, Amon*	2				
Hilton, S. L.	2	30	70	–	17
Hixon, W. E.*	2				
Hogan, H.	1	55	150	6	19
Holland, Jas.	1	150	350	–	32
Holman, C.*	2				
Holton, John*	2				
Housworth, John	8	60	440	25	83
Hudson, E. H.	2	50	150	2	38
Ingram, Thos.	1	100	125	9	49
Irvin, I. M.	1	40	60	5	35
Jackson, Jas.	1	40	210	4	56
Jean, Hardy H.*	5				
Johnson, Aaron	10	75	100	22	56
Johnson, W. A.	10	400	600	46	124
Johnson, Wm. F.	3	150	550	1	55
Jones, Elizabeth*	8				
Jones, Jas.	2	50	50	5	21
Jordan, James*	9				
Kimboro, J. B.	3	22	178	–	26
King, W.*	1				
Kingsbury, Sanford	3	100	235	4	40
Kizer, George W.	2	40	100	1	41
Lambert, J.	1	100	200	5	30
Lasiter, Wm.	1	100	400	18	66
Lassiter, J. H.	3	175	431	17	49
Latimer, J. W.	5	33	65	4	36
Lester, Olliver*	4				
Lester, Wm.*	5				
Lilly, Wm. B.*	11				
Little, S. B.	7	80	140	15	38
Long, Thos.	6	60	140	5	37
Lovelace, Thos.	5	45	290	2	23
Lyles, Kirby	1	30	50	3	51

Slaveholders in Carroll County in 1860

NAME	SLAVES	IMPROVED ACRES	UNIMPROVED ACRES	BALES OF COTTON	TOTAL LIVESTOCK
Lyles, Wm.	2	30	70	2	48
McAllister, A.	2	35	65	0	28
McBarnett, Nancy*	1				
McBurnett, Nick	2	100	102	6	69
McClure, Jas.	20	300	170	6	109
McCollister, Eliza	2	150	600	2	43
McDaniel, Char. A.	2	120	330	–	41
McDaniel, J. B.	5	200	385	11	40
McDaniel, S. A.*	2				
McDaniel, W. A.*	1				
McGarity, John	3	125	375	10	92
McKee, R. W.	1	40	60	1	48
McKinta, S.*	1				
McKissack, Arch*	8				
McKissack, Mary*	1				
McLean, A. W.	4	35	65	–	25
McLean, W. B.	14	200	250	16	58
McLondon, I. N.*	1				
McMallian, A. M.*	2				
McMullin, Jame	3	90	112	4	79
Mabry, B. M.	17	150	750	16	97
Mandeville, A.*	7				
Manndle, W. J.*	1				
Martin, E. B.	7	150	850	9	100
Martin, Joab	2	50	50	3	56
Meeks, J. G.*	9				
Merrill, H. F.*	5				
Merrill, W. W.*	7				
Michael, Peter	1	15	10	3	32
Miles, Wm.	1	–	–	1	–
Moon, A. R.*	3				
Moon, H. W.	5	180	420	10	63
Moon, Jas. D.*	10				
Moon, W. W.*	2				
Moore, Elias F.	2	150	250	20	17
Morgan, E. S.	1	–	–	7	40
Morris, B. A.	1	85	117	11	71
Morris, Bluford	4	50	130	2	43
Morris, J. L.	1	15	85	2	25
Morris, John T.	3	150	250	10	89
Morris, Thos. J.	9	100	80	5	82
Mudder, Wm.*	2				
Newton, Jas. W.*	3				
Nichols, J. W.	4	50	100	2	41

NAME	SLAVES	IMPROVED ACRES	UNIMPROVED ACRES	BALES OF COTTON	TOTAL LIVESTOCK
Nunn, W. P.*	11				
Orr, Robt.	2	35	65	3	31
Pang, Pink*	1				
Parker, W.	4	75	160	3	6
Payne, L.*	2				
Pettigrew, Thos. R.*	2				
Philips, Thos. A.	1	50	150	5	60
Polson, Jonathan	12	100	100	7	59
Pope, H.	2	150	200	3	70
Powell, W. F. S.	11	200	790	11	121
Price, Lang*	6				
Reese, John W.*	6				
Reynolds, Jas. W.	3	75	75	3	18
Richards, F. M.*	1				
Richardson, J. M.*	2				
Roberts, James	1	35	35	2	18
Roberts, Jesse*	23				
Roberts, John*	1	250	300	20	62
Roberts, Newton*	5				
Roberts, Thos. H.	3	40	60	2	37
Robinson, Jesse*	3				
Robinson, W. O.	9	20	30	3	13
Rogers, Jas. H.	4	100	305	—	21
Roop, Martin	3	50	350	3	56
Rowe, Allan	7	140	300	10	68
Russell, R. N.*	1				
Russer, J. A.*	5				
Samson, Jas. T.*	1				
Scales, Jacob*	9				
Shackelford, J. C.	5	75	126	5	56
Shepard, O. P.*	3				
Sharpe, Hiram	2	100	300	—	24
Sharpe, Hiram, Jr.	2	45	105	10	33
Sharpe, W.*	1				
Shullnutt, A. J.	1	50	254	1	18
Slaughter, John G.*	1				
Sloan, N. F.*	2				
Smith, F. W.*	3				
Smith, Frederick*	6				
Smith, Matt	4	50	300	3	28
Smith, W. G.*	1				
Spencer, John	2	75	127	1	23
Springer, R. H.	17	400	1260	91	97
Stamps, John*	2				

Slaveholders in Carroll County in 1860

NAME	SLAVES	IMPROVED ACRES	UNIMPROVED ACRES	BALES OF COTTON	TOTAL LIVESTOCK
Steed, Thomas*	1				
Steel, A. M.*	6				
Stevenson, Elvina*	3				
Steward, J. W.*	5				
Stidham, Jas. H.	5	57	100	1	48
Stogun, John*	1				
Stovall, France	1	25	70	6	34
Stovey, Mary*	8				
Strickland, E.*	11				
Strickland, Jas.	12	150	665	15	50
Stripling, James	2	110	390	13	65
Summerlin, H.	13	250	750	47	165
Summerlin, J. J.	2	45	157	7	47
Summerlin, Mary*	2				
Tanner, A. J.	4	50	150	1	22
Taylor, Beng.	10	85	117	4	32
Taylor, Mary*	1				
Taylor, Rhoela	10	100	120	23	24
Taylor, W. H.	4	80	125	4	59
Thommeson, Jas. R.*	6				
Thompson, B. D.	6	75	68	–	30
Thorne, J. W.*	1				
Thornton, B. F.	1	75	127	9	17
Thurman, J. M.	1	15	45	4	23
Thurmond, J. C.	1	50	137	1	34
Tidwell, Ben.*	3				
Tumblin, W. W.*	8				
Tyson, Josiah	7	80	195	5	83
Tyson, M.*	1				
Veal, John*	17				
Waddell, Simean*	1				
Wandel, Jas. B.*	3				
Watkins, Rhen.*	5				
Wick, J. B.	7	200	700	1	17
Wilderman, E.*	1				
Williams, Ben.	2	8	40	–	13
Williams, E.*	8				
Williams, John*	2				
Williams, Robt.*	1				
Williams, S. R.	3	70	280	–	118
Williams, W. W.	6	90	250	20	64
Williams, Wm. M.	12	100	305	10	49
Williamson, Thos.	6	40	162	10	13
Wills, Thos. F.*	5				

NAME	SLAVES	IMPROVED ACRES	UNIMPROVED ACRES	BALES OF COTTON	TOTAL LIVESTOCK
Wilson, Wm.	1	97	223	2	35
Womble, E. G.*	1				
Woods, J. B.	5	40	10	3	22
Woody, Jas. B.*	4				
Wooten, H. P.	40	120	228	9	90
Wooten, Jas. G.*	3				
Wootten, Jas. C.*	2				
Wright, A. S.	14	100	117	8	83
Wright, B. H.*	10				
Wright, W. D.	5	75	120	5	60
Wipte, John J.	14	120	283	5	96
Wynn, Sherman	14	12	3	2½	17

Appendix II

Post Offices in Carroll County, 1827–1965

DATE ESTABLISHED	NAME	APPROXIMATE LOCATION	FIRST POSTMASTER	DISCONTINUED
1. March 31, 1827	McIntosh Old Place	S. E. of Whitesburg	William O. Wagnon	1829
2. Sept. 10, 1827	Carroll Court House	N. of Carrollton	William O. Wagnon	1829
3. Feb. 27, 1829	Rotherwood	S. E. of Whitesburg	Wm. G. Springer	1868
4. March 16, 1829	Carrollton	Carrollton	Isaac Wood	
5. Jan. 6, 1831	Villa Rica	Villa Rica	James L. Adair	
6. July 19, 1832	Tallapoosa*	Tallapoosa	John Robinson	1878
7. July 31, 1833	Laurel Hill	W. of Roopville	H. P. Mabry	1901
8. Oct. 20, 1837	Hickory Level	N. of Carrollton	James Baskin	1848
9. Sept. 16, 1847	Cerro Gordo	Bowdon	Edward G. Womble	1859
10. Sept. 16, 1847	Burnt Stand*	near Tallapoosa	Robert A. Reid	
11. July 11, 1848	Bowdon	Bowdon	Edward G. Womble	
12. Feb. 15, 1849	Bowenville	N. of Whitesburg	William Bowen	1883
13. Feb. 18, 1854	Trickum	Lowell	John Haisten	1857
14. Aug. 9, 1854	Flint Hill	S. of Villa Rica	Wm. H. Autrey	1861
15. Oct. 28, 1854	Tall Pine	Near Clem	Calvin Simmons	1856

* In Haralson County after 1856.

DATE ESTABLISHED	NAME	APPROXIMATE LOCATION	FIRST POSTMASTER	DISCONTINUED
16. Nov. 11, 1854	Copper Hill	near Villa Rica	Thomas Farmer	1857
17. March 18, 1856	Central Point	?	James T. Reaves	1861
18. April 15, 1856	Buffalo	S. W. of Carrollton	John B. Gamble	1866
19. Aug. 7, 1856	Wimberly	S. of Bowdon	John Fouse	1866
20. Sept. 16, 1856	Buck Horn	W. of Villa Rica	Joseph L. Hart	1857
21. July 16, 1857	Chanceville	S. W. of Villa Rica	Henry Chance	1866
22. Nov. 4, 1857	Mistletoe Bower	?	James H. Rogers	1860
23. Oct. 24, 1860	Tompkinsville	N. E. of Whitesburg	John Tompkins	1866
24. Jan. 11, 1870	Loyal	W. of Carrollton	Wiles G. Robinson	1873
25. Dec. 13, 1870	Allen's Mills	S. of Villa Rica	Wm. T. Richards	1903
26. Sept. 19, 1872	Whitesburg	Whitesburg	Jeremiah McMillan	
27. March 12, 1873	Victory	S. of Bowdon	Henry W. McDaniel	1913
28. July 6, 1875	Shady Grove	N. E. of Carrollton	James B. Lawing	1901
29. May 11, 1876	Turkey Creek Mills	S. of Mount Zion	John Entrekin	1878
30. July 20, 1876	Simsville	near Temple	George W. Autry	1883
31. Oct. 14, 1876	Kansas	near Bowdon	Jefferson McBurnett	1884
32. Dec. 4, 1876	Holland's Mills	N. of Whitesburg	Lindsey Holland	1905
33. March 4, 1878	Lowell	W. of Whitesburg	Joseph M. Walker	1903
34. May 21, 1878	Mount Zion	N. W. of Carrollton	Joseph Entrekin	1918
35. May 23, 1878	Lairdsborough	W. of Roopville	Andrew J. Laird	1888
36. Nov. 29, 1878	Sackville	W. of Carrollton	Preston Hesterly	1882
37. Dec. 29, 1879	County Line	N. E. of Whitesburg	Henry M. Head	1903
38. March 16, 1880	Plowshare	N. W. of Carrollton	David J. Moore	1904
39. April 12, 1881	Curtis	near Carrollton	Amos J. Fitts	1889
40. May 19, 1881	Rett	near Whitesburg	Lucy Russell	1905
41. April 24, 1882	Temple	Temple	James H. Allen	

DATE ESTABLISHED	NAME	APPROXIMATE LOCATION	FIRST POSTMASTER	DISCONTINUED
42. Nov. 1, 1882	Roopville	Roopville	Thomas M. Roop	1892
43. Nov. 1, 1882	Fitts	near Carrollton	William N. Chandler	1883
44. Dec. 26, 1882	Cheeves	near Villa Rica	Zachary Allen	1915
45. Jan. 2, 1883	Emily	N. E. of Clem	Emily McClendon	1931
46. March 12, 1883	Banning	near Whitesburg	James H. Barron	1896
47. Dec. 6, 1883	Rilla	near Bowdon	Albert J. Simpson	1896
48. Dec. 26, 1883	Burwell	Burwell	Joseph A. Roberson	1926
49. Nov. 24, 1884	Mabry	S. W. of Roopville	James G. Adamson	1905
50. June 29, 1885	Joel	S. of Bowdon	Joel P. Yates	1904
51. Dec. 27, 1885	Clem	Clem	John H. Jones	1888
52. Jan. 14, 1886	Gold Village	Old Villa Rica	William P. Statnaker	1896
53. June 1, 1887	Lang	near Hulett	Benjamin F. Lang	1904
54. Jan. 24, 1888	Plug	S. of Whitesburg	Charles J. Levans	1915
55. Oct. 16, 1888	Mandeville	N. W. of Carrollton	William C. Shelnutt	1902
56. June 6, 1889	Cross Plains	N. E. of Clem	C. J. Hallum	1891
57. May 19, 1891	Catie	near Whitesburg	James T. Nolan	1903
58. July 11, 1891	Siver	S. W. of Carrollton	James M. Lee	1897
59. Jan. 7, 1892	Ratherwood	S. of Whitesburg	Mattie Springer	1900
60. March 25, 1892	Bennie	W. of Clem	Jesse A. Murrah	1894
61. April 2, 1892	Sprewell	E. of Bowdon	Caleb M. Sprewell	1905
62. April 8, 1892	Tyus	S. E. of Bowdon	Andrew J. Hallum	1902
63. Sept. 1, 1892	Horace	N. E. of Bowdon	Charles W. Bonner	1898
64. Sept. 16, 1892	Labor	near Waco	Americus Maudin	1902
65. Sept. 29, 1892	Ithica	S. of Villa Rica	Robert Boyd	1898
66. March 3, 1893	Veal	S. of Bowdon	James W. Simpkins	1893
67. March 25, 1893	Moses	near Carrollton	Charles B. Williams	

DATE ESTABLISHED	NAME	APPROXIMATE LOCATION	FIRST POSTMASTER	DISCONTINUED
68. July 7, 1893	Gulledge	?	Andrew J. Gulledge	1894
69. Oct. 30, 1893	Bonner	N. W. of Roopville	George A. Bonner	1894
70. Nov. 25, 1893	Billow	W. of Carrollton	Benjamin F. Wilder	1894
71. Feb. 1, 1894	Harman	S. E. of Bowdon	William T. Harman	1903
72. June 6, 1894	Abilene	N. of Carrollton	James M. McCalman	1901
73. Aug. 7, 1894	Barge	near Bowdon	Hiram M. Ring	1906
74. Sept. 19, 1894	Stogner	N. of Bowdon	James J. Stogner	1905
75. Feb. 9, 1895	Dot	S. of Bowdon	Susan V. Wilder	1916
76. April 24, 1895	Ditto	?	Richard E. Harper	1895
77. Feb. 14, 1896	Hulett	E. of Carrollton	Isaac H. Smith	1903
78. Nov. 25, 1896	Henley	S. W. of Whitesburg	Susan Dickson	1904
79. Jan. 28, 1897	Birtha	near Temple	June Waddell	1898
80. Nov. 16, 1897	Elon	near Whitesburg	Eli Kilgore	1903
81. Feb. 16, 1898	Berlene	N. of Temple	James K. Haney	1898
82. July 16, 1898	Corbett	W. of Bowdon	William E. Lovvorn	1901
83. Oct. 29, 1898	Sine	?	W. E. Smith	1899
84. Nov. 16, 1898	Jake	near Waco	Benjamin F. Robertson	1912
85. June 23, 1899	Coraxi	N. of Temple	John C. Hicks	1900
86. April 18, 1900	Lilac	S. of Temple	Elijah M. Yates	1902
87. Aug., 1900	Buckingham	N. of Carrollton	James Levans	1902
88. Dec. 19, 1900	Sackville	W. of Carrollton	Olive M. Bonner	1903
89. April 19, 1901	Hodge	N. of Whitesburg	Charles B. Williams	1904
90. March 17, 1903	Jet	W. of Mt. Zion	Mattie D. Stogner	1905
91. April 8, 1903	Katharine	W. of Mt. Zion	James T. Patterson	1904
92. April 15, 1903	Reavesville	S. of Bowdon	Herman J. Reaves	1904
93. Sept. 8, 1903	Still	near Carrollton	John M. Fletcher	1905

DATE ESTABLISHED	NAME	APPROXIMATE LOCATION	FIRST POSTMASTER	DISCONTINUED
94. April 29, 1911	Bowdon Junction	N. W. of Carrollton	George S. McElroy	1920
95. Oct. 22, 1915	Genola	W. of Carrollton	J. Holland Nelson	1933

Bibliography

I. Articles

Bonner, James C. "Legislative Apportionment and the County Unit System in Georgia." *Georgia Historical Quarterly,* XLVII (Dec., 1963).
————. "Tustunugee Hutkee and Creek Factionalism on the Georgia-Alabama Frontier." *The Alabama Review,* X (April, 1957).
Camp, Mrs. Benjamin L. "Whitesburg and Her People." *Carroll Free Press,* Feb. 9, 1928.
Cleghorn, Russell O. "Villa Rica Mines." *Carroll Free Press,* July 6, 1933.
Foreman, Carolyn T. "A Creek Pioneer." *Chronicles of Oklahoma,* XXI (Sept., 1943).
Foreman, Grant. "John Howard Payne and the Cherokees." *American Historical Review,* XXXVII (July, 1933).
Goff, John H. "Edward Lloyd Thomas, Surveyor." *Emory University Quarterly,* XVIII (Summer, 1962).
————. "Some Major Indian Trading Paths Across the Georgia Piedmont." *Georgia Mineral Newsletter,* VI (Spring, 1953).
————. "Some Old Road Names in Georgia." *Georgia Mineral Newsletter,* XI (Autumn, 1958).
Hamrick, James D. "The Masonic Institute in Carroll County." *Carroll Free Press,* Oct. 13, 1927.
Henderson, Irby. "Carroll Methodism from 1828 to 1927." *Carroll Free Press,* Oct. 13, 1927.
Little, Arthur D. "A Leaf Out of Medical History." *The Journal of the Medical Association of Georgia,* XXXII (1942).
Mandeville, L. C. "Annual Report, 1914." *Carroll Free Press,* July 23, 1914.
Meserve, John Bartlett. "The McIntoshes." *Chronicles of Oklahoma,* X (1932).
Robinson, Sallie. "Just Some Memories of Carrollton as a Village Long Ago." *Carroll Free Press,* Oct. 2, 1930.

————. "A Sketch of My Life." *Carroll Free Press*, Sept. 18, 1930.

Sharp, George. "Old Times in Carroll County." *Carroll Free Press*, Oct. 4, 18, Nov. 1, 1895.

————. "Reminiscences of Old Carroll County." *Carroll Free Press*, Aug. 6, Oct. 4, 1895.

Trimble, Lee S. "A Connecticut Yankee in Tallapoosa." *Georgia Review*, VI (Fall, 1952).

II. Books

Abel, Annie H. *The American Indian as Participant in the Civil War.* Cleveland: Arthur H. Clark Co., 1919.

————. *The History of Events Resulting in Indian Consolidation West of the Mississippi* (in American Historical Association, Annual Report . . . for the Year, 1906). Washington, D.C. 1908.

Anderson, Rufus. *Memoir of Catherine Brown, A Christian Indian of the Cherokee Nation.* New York: J. P. Haven, 1825.

Beall, John B. *In Barrack and Field; Poems and Sketches of Army Life.* Nashville: Smith and Lamar, 1906.

Bonner, James C., and Roberts, Lucien E., eds. *Studies in Georgia History and Government.* Athens: University of Georgia Press, 1940.

Boogher, Elbert W. G. *Secondary Education in Georgia, 1732–1858.* Philadelphia: privately printed, 1933.

Bullock, Joseph G. B. *A History and Geneology of the Family of Baillie of Dunain . . . With a Short Sketch of the Family of McIntosh. . . .* Green Bay, Wis.: The Gazette Printers, 1898.

Candler, Charles Howard. *Asa Griggs Candler; Coca Cola and Emory College, 1888.* Atlanta: The Library, Emory University, 1953.

Chappell, Absalom H. *Miscellanies of Georgia, Historical, Biographical, Descriptive, Etc.* Atlanta: Meegan, 1874.

[Cheney, George F.] *Carroll County Souvenir-Historical Edition.* [Carrollton, Ga.: privately printed, *ca.* 1910.]

Christian Index, The. *History of the Baptist Denomination in Georgia.* Atlanta: George W. Harrison, 1881.

Cobb, Joe. *History of Carroll County.* [Carrollton, Ga., *ca.* 1906.]

Cohen, Sanford H. *Compendium of Georgia: Legal and Commercial Guide for 1901.* Augusta: privately printed, 1901.

Corry, John Pitts. *Indian Affairs in Georgia, 1732–1756.* Philadelphia: privately printed, 1936.

Cotterill, Robert S. *The Southern Indians.* Norman: University of Oklahoma Press, 1953.

Dwyer, M. Virginia, ed. *American Medical Directory, 1958.* Chicago: American Medical Association, 1958.

Foreman, Grant. *Indian Removal: The Emigration of the Five Civilized Tribes.* Norman: University of Oklahoma Press, 1932.

Gamble, Thomas. *Savannah Duels and Duellists, 1733–1877.* Savannah, Ga.: Review Publishing and Printing Company, 1923.

Georgia Educational Directory, 1963–64. Atlanta: Georgia Department of Education, 1964.

[Gilmer, George R.] *Sketches of Some of the First Settlers of Upper Georgia of the Cherokees, and of the Author.* New York: D. Appleton and Company, 1855.

Harden, Edward Jenkins, *The Life of George M. Troup.* Savannah, Ga.: Purse, 1859.

Hawkins, Benjamin. "Letters of Benjamin Hawkins 1796–1806 . . . " in *Collections of the Georgia Historical Society* (Savannah), IX (1916).

————. *A Sketch of the Creek Country in the Years 1798 and 1799* in *Collections of the Georgia Historical Society,* III, Pt. 11. New York: Bartlett and Walford, 1848. This work was reprinted at Americus in 1938 under the title *Creek Indian History.*

Henderson, Lillian. *Roster of the Confederate Soldiers of Georgia, 1861–1865.* 5 vols. Hapeville: Longino and Porter, 1955–1960.

Hillyer, S. G. *Reminiscences of Georgia Baptists.* Atlanta: Foote and Davies Company, 1902.

Houston, Martha Lou. *Reprint of the Official Register of the Land Lottery of Georgia, 1827.* Columbus: Walton Co., 1928.

Howard, Wiley C. *Sketch of Cobb's Legion Cavalry and Some Incidents and Scenes Remembered.* [Atlanta, 1901.]

Hughes, Melvin Clyde. *County Government in Georgia.* Athens: University of Georgia Press, 1944.

Johnson, Charles S., *et al. Statistical Atlas of Southern Counties.* Chapel Hill: University of North Carolina Press, 1941.

Jones, Mary G., and Reynolds, Lily. *Coweta County Chronicles for One Hundred Years.* Atlanta: Stein Printing Co., 1928.

Link, Arthur S. *American Epoch, A History of the United States Since the 1890's.* New York: Knopf, 1956.

Loughridge, Robert M., and Hodge, David M. *English and Muskokee Dictionary.* Philadelphia: Westminister Press, 1914.

Malone, Henry T. *Cherokees of the Old South: A People in Transition.* Athens, Ga.: University of Georgia Press, 1956.

————. *The Episcopal Church in Georgia.* Atlanta: Protestant Episcopal Church in the Diocese of Atlanta. [1960].

McGehee, John Boykin. *Autobiography of Rev. J. B. McGehee, D. D. of the South Georgia Conference.* [Buena Vista, Ga., n.d.].

McKenney, Thomas L., and Hall, James. *The Indian Tribes of North America.* 3 vols. Edinburgh: J. Grant, 1933–1934.

Melson, Nep S. *Reminiscences of the Fourth District Agricultural and*

Mechanical School, Carrollton, Georgia. Hogansville, Ga.: privately printed, 1941.

Memoirs of Georgia, Historical and Biographical. 2 vols. Atlanta: Southern Historical Association, 1895.

Miller, Stephen F. *The Bench and Bar of Georgia: Memoirs and Sketches.* 2 vols. Philadelphia: J. B. Lippincott and Co., 1858.

Mitchell, Mary Edward. *Memoirs of James Mitchell.* N.p.: privately printed, n.d.

Montgomery, Horace, ed. *Georgians in Profile.* Athens: University of Georgia Press, 1958.

Morse, Jedidiah. *A Report to the Secretary of War of the United States on Indian Affairs.* . . . New Haven: S. Converse, 1822.

Northen, William J. *Men of Mark in Georgia.* 7 vols. Atlanta: A. B. Caldwell, 1907–1912.

Orr, Dorothy. *A History of Education in Georgia.* Chapel Hill: University of North Carolina Press, 1950.

Ross, Victor M. *Ross' Texas Brigade.* Louisville, Ky.: privately printed, 1881.

Shadgett, Olive Hall. *The Republican Party in Georgia.* Athens: University of Georgia Press, 1964.

Sherwood, Adiel. *A Gazeteer of the State of Georgia, 1827.* Charleston: W. Riley, 1827.

————. *A Gazeteer of the State of Georgia, 1829.* Philadelphia: Martin and Boden, 1829.

————. *A Gazeteer of the State of Georgia, 1860.* Washington, D.C.: Peter Force, 1860.

Shipp, John E. D. *The Last Night of a Nation.* Americus, Ga.: Southern Printers, 1938.

Swanton, John R. *The Indians of the Southeastern United States.* Smithsonian Institution, Bureau of American Ethnology. Bulletin 137. Washington: Government Printing Office, 1946.

Talmadge, Franklin C. *The Presbytery of Atlanta.* Atlanta: privately printed, 1960.

Webb, Walter Prescott, ed. *The Handbook of Texas.* 2 vols. Austin: Texas Historical Association, 1952.

Wheeler, John T. *Two Hundred Years of Agricultural Education in Georgia.* Danville, Ill.: Interstate, 1948.

White, George. *Historical Collections of Georgia: Containing the Most Interesting Facts, Traditions, Biographical Sketches, Anecdotes, Etc.* . . . New York: Pudney and Russell, 1854.

————. *Statistics of the State of Georgia: Including an Account of Its Natural, Civil, and Ecclesiastical History, together with a Particular Description of Each County.* . . . Savannah: W. Thorne Williams, 1849.

Who Was Who in America 1797–1942 (Vol. I, 1897–1942). Chicago: A. N. Marquis Co., 1962.

Winfrey, Norman H. *A History of Rusk County, Texas.* Waco, Texas: Texian Press, 1961.

Woodward, Grace S. *The Cherokees.* Norman: University of Oklahoma Press, 1963.

Woodward, Thomas S. *Woodward's Reminiscences of the Creek or Muscogee Indians.* . . . Montgomery, Ala.: Barrett and Wimbish, 1859. (Reprinted at Tuscaloosa by the Alabama Book Store, 1939.)

Yarbrough, George W. *Boyhood and Other Days in Georgia.* Nashville: Publishing House of the M. E. Church, South, 1917.

Young, Harvey. *The Toadstool Millionaires.* Princeton: Princeton University Press, 1961.

III. *Manuscripts, Official and Unofficial*

A. IN GEORGIA DEPARTMENT OF ARCHIVES AND HISTORY, ATLANTA

A List of . . . Officers and Privates of a Company . . . of Georgia Militia raised at Carrollton, 21st May 1836.

Boggess, Jiles, to Governor George R. Gilmer, December, 1830.

Carroll County Post Offices (a photocopy made from records in the National Archives).

Carroll County Tax Digest, 1832–1848.

Carroll County Volunteer Company to Governor William Schley, June 7, 1836.

Journal of the Commissioners of Georgia Appointed to Run the Dividing Line Between the Boundaries of the State and Alabama.

Land Grants and Land Record Files.

Little, Joseph, to Governor William Schley, June 18, 1836.

Militia Districts of Carroll County.

Rogers, James A., to Governor Troup, Jan. 23, 1827.

Rogers, James A., Surveyor of District Eleven, Field notes for January and February, 1826.

St. Margaret's [Episcopal] Parish Handbook and Parish Records, 1891–1970.

"The Springer Family," a typescript.

Wood, Isaac, to Governor George R. Gilmer, Nov. 15, 1830.

B. IN COUNTY ARCHIVES OF GEORGIA

Bench Docket No. 2. Records of the Superior Court of Haralson County, 1915. Office of the Clerk of Court, Buchanan.

Carroll County Deed Books A, E, I, M, N, O, Q, JJ, KK. Office of the Clerk of Court, Carrollton.

Carroll County Marriage Licenses, Book K. Office of the Ordinary, Carrollton.

Carroll County Will Book, A, B, and C. Office of the Ordinary, Carrollton.

Minutes. Haralson Superior Court, January, 1916. Office of the Clerk of Court, Buchanan.

Records of the Inferior Court of Carroll County, 1827–1846. Office of the Ordinary, Carrollton.

Records, Superior Court of Carroll County, October term, 1907. Office of Clerk of Court, Carrollton.

Register of Charters, Carroll County, Book I. Office of the Clerk of Court, Carrollton.

Register of Medical Practitioners, Carroll County, 1881–1961. Office of the Clerk of Court, Carrollton.

C. IN LIBRARIES AND IN PRIVATE POSSESSION

Aldrich, T. H., Jr. Assay Log Book, Jan. 1915–Dec. 1917. In possession of A. H. Stockmar, Villa Rica, Georgia.

Baptist Tabernacle Enrollment Book (n.d).

Burke, Archibald T., to Eugenia DuBignon, Jekyll Island, Jan. 30, 1853. In private possession.

Caswell, Render R. "The History of Bowdon College." M.A. thesis, University of Georgia, 1952.

Educational History of Carroll County, 1871–1928. Scrapbook in the office of the Carroll County Superintendent of Schools.

Financial statement, Carrollton Federal Savings and Loan Association, June 30, 1932.

Georgia Post Offices and Postmasters. (A comprehensive listing compiled by Edward B. Dawson from records in the National Archives), in private possession.

Hawkins, Jane, to Duncan C. Campbell and James Meriwether, May 3, 1825. In the Telamon Cuyler Collection, University of Georgia Library, Athens, Georgia.

Merrill, William W. "Autobiography." In private possession.

Minutes. Bank of Villa Rica, Feb. 14, 1899.

Minutes. Board of Trustees, Agricultural and Mechanical School, Carrollton, Ga., 1907–1931. In the library of West Georgia College, Carrollton, Georgia.

Mary Ann Turner, Villa Rica, Georgia, to Frances A. Williams, Nov. 3, 1854, in possession of the author.

Mary Ann Turner, Villa Rica, Georgia, to Frances A. Williams, June 26 [1855?] in possession of the author.

Minute Book. First Baptist Church, Carrollton, Ga., August 1847–December, 1875.

Minutes of the Mount Zion Seminary Association of Carroll County, Georgia, 1778–December, 1895. In private possession.

Minutes. Tabernacle Baptist Church, Carrollton, Ga., Dec. 15, 1899.

Minutes of the Seventy-Fourth Regiment, Georgia Militia, August 12, 1831–August 14, 1849. In private possession.

Paschal, Rebecca. "The Romance of a Doctor's Life." Typescript in private possession.

Presbyterian Church Records, Carrollton, Ga.

Presentments. Carroll County Grand Jury, Jan. 23, 1833. In private possession.

Principal's Report. Agricultural and Mechanical School, Carrollton, Georgia, May 10, 1923. In the library of West Georgia College.

Record Book. St. Margaret's Parish, Jan. 20, 1894–Aug. 1, 1921.

Record of Donors, Mount Zion Seminary, in possession of C. C. Perkins, Carrollton, Georgia.

Records of the Peoples Bank. Carrollton, Georgia.

Treasurer's Report, Minutes. A. & M. Trustees, May 1, 1931. In the library of West Georgia College.

Trimble, Lee S. "Personal Memoirs." In private possession.

University of the South, Alumni Records, Class of 1908. Sewanee, Tennessee.

D. IN THE NATIONAL ARCHIVES, WASHINGTON, D. C.

Carroll County, Census of 1880. (On microfilm in the library of The Woman's College of Georgia. The list of inhabitants has been transcribed and alphabetized.)

Inventory of the Estate of William McIntosh, 1825. (A copy is in possession of the Georgia Historical Commission, Atlanta.)

Records of the Bureau of Freedmen, Refugees and Abandoned Lands (Georgia).

Schedule I, Free Inhabitants of Carroll County, 1860. (An alphabetized listing is in the library of The Woman's College of Georgia, Milledgeville.)

Schedule II, Slave Inhabitants of Carroll County, 1860. (An alphabetized listing is in the library of The Woman's College of Georgia, Milledgeville.)

Schedule IV, Productions of Agriculture in Carroll County, 1860. (An alphabetized listing is in the library of The Woman's College of Georgia, Milledgeville.)

IV. Newspapers and News Magazines

The Aggies [Carrollton, Ga.], 1928, 1930, 1931.

Atlanta Constitution, 1885, 1891, 1915.
Atlanta Journal, 1915.
Boston Transcript, 1927.
Bowdon Bulletin, 1913.
Carroll County Georgian, 1945–1965.
Carroll County Times, 1872–1956.
Carroll Free Press, 1883–1956.
Carrollton Advocate, 1860–1861.
Carrollton *Times-Free Press,* 1956–1965.
Central of Georgia Railroad Company. *The Right Way,* XLVIII (Dec., 1958).
Cherokee Advocate, 1846.
The Christian Standard, Cincinnati, O., 1948.
Haralson County Tribune, 1897.
Henderson [Texas] *Daily News,* 1964.
Milledgeville *Georgia Journal,* 1825.
Newnan Herald, 1890.
Niles' Register, XXXIX (Sept., 1830).
Washington City Weekly Gazette, 1816.

V. Pamphlets

Announcement of the Agricultural and Mechanical School . . . 1916–17. [Carrollton, Ga., 1916].
Bonner, James C. *A Short History of Heard County.* Milledgeville, Ga.; privately printed, 1962.
Brannon, Peter. *Fort Okfuski.* Alexander City, Ala., n.d.
Catalogue of Bowden College. [Bowdon, Ga., 1910].
Catalogue of the Bowdon Collegiate Institution, 1858–1859. [Bowdon, Ga., 1858].
Catalogue of Bowdon College, 1908–09. [Bowdon, Ga., 1908].
Directory and Manual of the First Baptist Church of Carrollton, Georgia. Carrollton, Ga., 1923.
First Annual Commencement of the Agricultural and Mechanical School of the Fourth Congressional District of Georgia. Carrollton, Ga., July 25, 1907.
Fourth District A. & M. School Catalogue, 1912–13. [Carrollton, Ga., 1912].
Georgia-Alabama Investment and Development Co. *Prospectus of the City of Tallapoosa.* Boston: L. Barta and Co., 1891.
Hamrick, Radford. *The Peoples Bank and Carroll County.* Carrollton, Ga.: privately printed, n.d.
Hawkins, Benjamin. *A Sketch of the Creek Country.* Americus: Americus Book Company, 1938.
Journal of the Fifty-Seventh Annual Convention of the Protestant Episcopal

Church in the Diocese of Georgia. Macon: J. W. Burke and Company, 1879.

Manual and Directory of the Presbyterian Church of Carrollton, Georgia 1841–1845. [Carrollton, Ga., *ca.* 1845].

Manual and Directory of the Presbyterian Church of Carrollton, Georgia, 1841–1954. [Carrollton, Ga., 1954].

Minutes of the Baptist Convention of the State of Georgia, 1859. Macon: Telegraph Stream Printing House, 1859.

Minutes . . . Carrollton Baptist Association (1964). Carrollton, Ga.: Carrollton Baptist Association, 1964.

Minutes of the Fourth Annual Session of the Carrollton Baptist Association. Atlanta: privately printed, 1877.

Minutes of the Ninety-Second Anniversary of the Baptist Convention of the State of Georgia. Atlanta: privately printed.

Minutes of the Seventeenth Annual Session of the Carrollton Baptist Association, 1890. Atlanta: privately printed, 1890.

Minutes of the Third Annual Session of the Carrollton Baptist Association. Atlanta: privately printed, 1876.

Minutes of the Twenty-Seventh Anniversary of the Georgia Baptist Convention . . . 1848. Penfield: The Index, 1848.

Model School, The. [Temple, Ga., *ca.* 1904].

Morrow, Richard B. *The Story of Our Lady of Perpetual Help*. Carrollton: privately printed, 1965.

Mount Zion Methodist Church Centennial, 1865–1965. [Carrollton, Ga., 1965].

St. Margaret's Parish Handbook, 1963. [Carrollton, Ga., 1963].

VI. Printed Public Documents

Abstract of the Fifteenth Census of the United States, 1930. Washington, D.C.: Government Printing Office, 1933.

Acts of the General Assembly of the State of Georgia, 1825–1834, 1836, 1839, 1847, 1849–1861, 1865–1866, 1869, 1870–1879, 1884–1885, 1890–1891. Prior to 1868 these items were published at Milledgeville. After that date they were published in Atlanta. Publishers and dates vary.

American State Papers, Documents, Legislative and Executive, of the Congress of the United States. 38 vols. (Vol. I. *Military Affairs*, Vol. II. *Indian Affairs*). Washington: Gales and Seaton, 1832–1861.

Biographical Directory of the American Congress, 1774–1961. Washington: Government Printing Office, 1961.

Brittain, Marion L. *Fifteenth Annual Report of the Department of Education . . . December 31, 1921*. Atlanta: Foote and Davies, State Printers, 1922.

Dawson, William C. *Compilation of the Laws of the State of Georgia.* . . . Milledgeville, Ga.: Grantland and Orme, 1831.

DeBow, James D. B. *The Seventh Census of the United States, 1850.* Washington: Government Printing Office, 1853.

————. *Statistical View of the United States . . . A Compendium of the Seventh Census.* Washington: A. O. P. Nicholson, 1854.

Irwin, David. *The Code of the State of Georgia.* Atlanta: James P. Harrison Company, 1882.

Journal of the Public and Secret Proceedings of the Convention of the People of Georgia Held in Milledgeville and Savannah in 1861. Milledgeville: Boughton, Misbet and Barnes, 1861.

Journal of the Senate of the State of Georgia . . . November and December, 1827. Milledgeville, 1828.

Kennedy, Joseph C. G. *Agriculture of the United States in 1860.* Washington: Government Printing Office, 1864.

————. *Population of the United States in 1860.* Washington: Government Printing Office, 1864.

Manufactures of the United States in 1860. Washington: Government Printing Office, 1865.

Merritt, William B. *Annual Report from the Department of Education, State of Georgia, 1903.* Atlanta: The Franklin Printing and Publishing Company, 1904.

McCallie, Samuel W. *Geological Survey of Georgia. Bulletin No. 19.* Atlanta: George W. Harrison, 1907.

Official Congressional Directory. Washington: Government Printing Office, 1900.

Porter, Robert P. *Compendium of the Eleventh Census, 1890.* Washington: Government Printing Office, 1892.

Sixth Census, or Enumeration of the Inhabitants of the United States . . . in 1840. Washington, D.C.: Blair and Rives, 1841.

Statistics of the United States, 1860. Washington, D.C.: Government Printing Office, 1866.

Stevens, O. B. *Georgia Historical and Industrial.* Atlanta: George B. Harrison, State Printer, 1907.

Thirteenth Census of the United States . . . 1910. (Supplement for Georgia). Washington: Government Printing Office, 1913.

United States Census of Agriculture, 1959, Georgia (Vol. 1). Washington: Government Printing Office, 1961.

United States Census of Agriculture, 1959. Georgia, Vol. I, Pt. 28. Washington: Government Printing Office, 1961.

United States Commissioner of Indian Affairs. *Treaties Between the United States of America and the Several Indian Tribes from 1778 to 1837.* . . . Washington: Longtree, 1837.

United States Congress. *Testimony Taken By The Joint Select Committee To Inquire Into The Condition Of Affairs In The Late Insurrectionary*

States. 13 vols. (Vols. VI and VII. Georgia). Washington: Government Printing Office, 1872.

U.S., Congress, House, Select Committee. *The Georgia Indian Controversy.* 19th Cong., 2nd sess. March 3, 1827. House Report No. 98. Washington: Gales and Seaton, 1827.

United States Department of Agriculture. *Soil Survey of Carroll County, Georgia.* Washington: Government Printing Office, 1924.

Walker, Frances A. *A Compendium of the Ninth Census, 1870.* Washington: Government Printing Office, 1872.

————. *Statistics of the Wealth and Industry of the United States . . . Ninth Census.* Washington: Government Printing Office, 1872.

The War of the Rebellion: A Compilation of the Official Records of the Union and Confederate Armies. 129 vols. and index. Washington: Government Printing Office, 1880–1901.

Yeates, William S. *Geological Survey of Georgia. Bulletin No. 4.* Atlanta: G. W. Harrison, 1896.

Index